JEB BUSH

Aggressive Conservatism in Florida

Robert E. Crew, Jr.

University Press of America,® Inc.
Lanham · Boulder · New York · Toronto · Plymouth, UK

Copyright © 2010 by
University Press of America,® Inc.
4501 Forbes Boulevard
Suite 200
Lanham, Maryland 20706
UPA Acquisitions Department (301) 459-3366

Estover Road
Plymouth PL6 7PY
United Kingdom

All rights reserved
Printed in the United States of America
British Library Cataloging in Publication Information Available

Library of Congress Control Number: 2009938784
ISBN: 978-0-7618-4982-7 (clothbound : alk. paper)
ISBN: 978-0-7618-4983-4 (paperback : alk. paper)
eISBN: 978-0-7618-4984-1

Cover image: Thomas Fluharty, Drawing of Jeb Bush;
The *Weekly Standard*, June 12, 2006.

♾™ The paper used in this publication meets the minimum
requirements of American National Standard for Information
Sciences—Permanence of Paper for Printed Library Materials,
ANSI Z39.48-1992

For Elizabeth Wideman Crew, a kindred spirit

Table of Contents

Acknowledgments

Anyone who reads this book will see the debt that I owe to the Florida press corps, to scholars of Florida government and politics, and to the outstanding research and audit organizations that the state of Florida has created to provide its citizens analysis and oversight of the actions of Florida state government. It is these people and these organizations that follow the day-to-day activities of major public officials, who inquire into the implementation of public policy by state departments, and who provide citizens a picture of the way in which public policy in the state is created and carried out. In their absence this book could not have been written and, more important, without them the citizens of Florida would be deprived of one of the essential elements in a democracy, information about the actions of their elected officials and of the impact of the policies these officials adopt.

The Florida press corps is recognized widely as one of the premier such entities in the nation. It is a large, diverse, intelligent, and active group of journalists who provide the state's citizens a balanced view of the actions of Florida's politicians and their government. In the preparation of this book, I was unable to obtain an interview with Governor Bush and therefore I was particularly reliant on journalistic accounts of his policy initiatives and of reactions to them.

I have also drawn heavily on a wide range of excellent research reports provided by the State Office of the Auditor General, the Office of Program Policy and Governmental Accountability, the inspectors general of several agencies of state government, and the Council of Education Policy. Each of these organizations is highly regarded for their independence from political pressure and for the high quality of their research.

Finally, I have made use of the work of a variety of academic scholars who have conducted research about public policy in Florida and about the social and economic forces that framed state politics over the past half century.

I have met only a few of the individuals whose work I have relied upon to write the book, but I want to thank them all, individually. They include Sherri Ackerman, Jim Ash, Cynthia Barnett, Alan Barton, Jo Becker, Kevin Begos, Maya Bell, Brad Bennett, Bill Berlow, Noah Bierman, Valerie Boey, Steve Bosquet, Tyler Bridges, Marilyn Brown, Billy Bruce, Marc Caputo, Alfonso Chardy, Deborah Circelli, Lesley Clark, Richard Conley, Deirdre Conner, Bill Cotterell, Jeremy Cox, S. V. Date, Chris Davis, Ellen Debenport, Jim Defede, Aaron Deslatte, Dan DeWitt, David Dill, Matthew Doig, Martin Dyckman, Gary Fineout, Kent Fischer, Joe Follick, Sydney Freedberg, Philip Gailey, Breanne Gilpatrick, Alex Gomez, Howard Goodman, Shana Gruskin, Stephen Hegarty, Diane Hirth, Mark Hollis, April Hunt, Jerry Jackson, Joni James, Carrie Johnson, Doug Jones, Jamil Jreisat, Alan Judd, Bill Kaczor, Chris Kahn, Dara Kam, John Kennedy, Mary Ellen Klas, Linda Kleindienst, David Koenig, Nancy

Cook Lauer, Alex Leary, Jennifer Liberto, Tamara Lytle, William March, Ron Matus, Vicki McClure, Jim McGee, Jason Grotto, Carol Marbin Miller, Kent Miller, Kimberly Miller, Lucy Morgan, Jefferson Morley, Gary Mormino, Bill Moss, Tim Nickens, Robert Nolin, Maria Padilla, Matthew Pinzur, Victor Manuel Ramos, Dottie Reder, Beth Reinhard, Bruce Ritchie, Manuel Roig-Franzia, Sean Rowe, David Royse, J. Taylor Rushing, Jim Saunders, Richard Scher, Rocky Scott, Mary Shankin, Debra Sharp, Elaine Silverstrini, Jeff Simmons, Barbara Simons, Niel Skene, Adam Smith, Brian Sokoloff, David Sommer, Paige St. John, Mitch Stacy, Jerome Stockfish, Alecia Swasy, Robert Trigaux, Chris Tisch, Scott Travis, Howard Troxler, Aelisa Ulferts, Michael Van Sickler, Kim McCoy Vann, Andres Viglucci, Kenneth Wald, Brittany Waldman, Nicki Waller, Peter Wallsten, Clyde Wilcox, Don Winchester, Alvin Wolfe, and William Yardley. These people are, of course, absolved of responsibility for any interpretation that I put on their work.

I am also indebted to several people who read the manuscript in its entirety, gave me their comments, and invariably improved the book. These include Burton Atkins, Doug Bailey, Ken Bode, Aaron Deslatte, Elizabeth B. Fugazzi, Lawrence G. Malley, Ed Montenaro, Richard Nathan, Troy Kinsey, Neil Skene, Paige St. John, Rick Watson, Carol Weissert, and William Weissert. These people are also absolved of any responsibility for limitations in the final product.

The book is dedicated to my eldest daughter, Elizabeth, a political science student and political activist whose questions about Governor Bush's early political proposals and about his leadership style prompted me to pay close attention to his behavior and subsequently to write the book.

Prologue

The night of November 6, 1999, saw the realization of a dream shared by Florida Republicans since the end of Reconstruction in 1877: ascendancy of their party to a position of complete control over the institutions of Florida state government. On that night, John Ellis (Jeb) Bush, the second son of former president George H. W. Bush, was elected governor of the state, providing a focal point for recently established Republican majorities in both the state house of representatives and the state senate and an instrument with which to launch a conservative revolution in Florida state government. The victory represented both a personal victory for Mr. Bush and the culmination of decades of change in both American and Florida politics.

For Governor Bush, the victory came after a substantial five-year effort to attain the office. His odyssey began with a contested Republican primary in 1993, suffered through a close loss to Florida political icon Lawton Chiles in 1994, created a toll on his personal life that prompted him to convert to Catholicism, continued as his brother George become governor of Texas and subsequently president of the United States when many thought that Jeb was smarter and a better campaigner, and saw him make a substantial change in campaign tactics and style. The victory came just as the Republican Party became the preeminent political party in Florida and provided the governor and his supporters an opportunity to put into place elements of a governmental and political theory that had been gaining momentum in the United States for three decades and to make sweeping changes in state public policy. The governor and his allies claimed that the implementation of this theory in Florida would transform conditions in the state.

The seeds of Jeb's and the Republican's rise to a position of preeminence in Florida state politics were planted as early as 1964 and 1965 when the national Democratic Party under the leadership of Lyndon Johnson passed the Civil Rights Act and the Voting Rights Act and succeeding Democratically controlled congresses enacted legislation guaranteeing equal protection of the law to a variety of underrepresented groups throughout the country. As shown by Thomas and Mary Edsall, these actions provided a political opening for Republicans to appeal to lower income, racially conservative white populists in Florida and other parts of the South and to European ethnic voters in the North (Edsal and Edsal 1991). Adopting its infamous "Southern strategy," the GOP "saw an opportunity to renew itself by opening its arms to white voters who could never forgive the Democratic Party for its support of civil rights and voting rights for blacks" (Herbert, October 6, 2005, A35).

Huge demographic changes in Florida aided the GOP. A stupendous population surge in the state during this same time period provided the

Republicans new bases of support. This surge was fueled by in-migration from other parts of the United States and from other countries. The population of the state nearly tripled from 1960 to 1995, and many of the new residents brought political connections from Republican communities in the suburbs of northeastern states and in the Midwest. The percentage of the white population grew steadily; the percentage of the African American population, who are typically Democrats, declined; and the percentage of the Hispanic population—many of whom were Cubans fleeing Castro's takeover—nearly doubled. All of these developments were beneficial to Republican fortunes (Beck 1997). In addition, the age of Florida's population increased more rapidly than that of any other state, and by 1998 Florida ranked first in the nation in the number of residents who were sixty-five and older.

The population surge contained other elements that were to become important constituencies for the Republicans, in particular the evangelical Christians who began to emerge in the new suburbs being developed throughout Florida. This group naturally gravitated to the Republican Party and took over local party organizations relatively quickly, since "many GOP county organizations were weak and underdeveloped, allowing a determined minority of Christian Right activists to obtain control" (Wald and Scher 2003). Upscale malls, suburban neighborhoods, and prosperous megachurches became the bases for this new religiosity and its Republican adherents. By the early 1990s, exit poll data indicated that Christian conservatives constituted about one-third of the core Republican vote in Florida primary elections.

The evangelicals allied themselves with other social conservatives who railed against crime, abortion, affirmative action, attacks on school prayer, and other issues that they believed were evidence of the nation's moral decline and combined to change the ground rules of political engagement in the state. As described in Dan T. Carter's book on the origins of the new conservatism in American politics, this group abandoned the give and take of American politics for an effort to turn the process into a battle between godly Republicans and secular antireligious Democrats (Carter 1995).

In addition to the potent "social issues" raised by new conservatives, the focus of the attack launched by the Republicans both in Florida and throughout the nation was the governing philosophy that had guided the Democrats since the 1930s. Initiated as an anti-Washington diatribe by George Wallace and Barry Goldwater, the attack on government grew to focus on discrediting government in general as a mechanism to promote social progress. Relying on a growing cadre of conservative scholars ensconced in newly created "think-tanks" and articulated most eloquently by Ronald Reagan, Republicans began to promote "the market" as the prime mechanism for social arbitration and resource allocation (Micklethwait and Wooldridge 2004; Rich 2004). Adopting theories emanating from the Heritage Foundation, the Cato Institute, the Bradley Foundation, the Hudson Institute, the Manhattan Institute and other similar

advocacy organizations, conservative politicians throughout the nation sought to defenestrate the American social state that had been in place since the days of FDR and "pushed aggressively to privatize Social Security and Medicare, loosen the laws governing workplace safety and the rights of workers to organize, roll back environmental and consumer safety regulations, privatize systems of public education, and pare back the scope, size and cost of government in numerous other arenas" (Callahan 1999). This emergent philosophical framework, labeled "movement conservatism" or "neoconservatism," and the specific ideas involved became the foundation for governmental action by Jeb Bush and the Republican Party in Florida.

These demographic and philosophical changes, the demands they placed on government, and positions taken by the national political parties on the issues of "race, rights and taxes," had a revolutionary effect on partisanship in Florida (Edsal and Edsal 1991). In 1980 two-thirds (65.8 percent) of those registered to vote in Florida were Democrats. By 1996 fewer than one-half (46.8 percent) were Democrats. Over the time period 1980 to 1996 increasing numbers of people registered as either Republican or Independent. By 1994, the combined percentage of Republicans and Independents was larger than the total percentage of Democrats. Not surprising, given these data, psychological attachment to the two parties in the state also changed. In 1964 over 70 percent of Floridians identified with the Democratic Party and only 28 percent with Republicans and Independents. By 1999, party ID was split almost evenly between Democrats at 44 percent and Republicans at 41 percent, with Independents at 15 percent (Florida State University, *Florida Annual Policy Survey* 1999).

Republicans in Florida made a concerted effort to capitalize on these changes. Heeding the adage that good candidates make good campaigns, they worked hard to recruit and support people for elective office at all levels of government in Florida, but in particular to the state legislature. Their efforts found initial success in 1994 when they took control in the state senate for the first time and in 1996 in the state house and became the first southern state Republican Party since the 1800s to simultaneously hold majorities in both houses of a state legislature. And finally, in 1995, they thought that they had found the candidate to take them over the top in Florida politics.

Concurrently with the rise of the new conservatism in Florida, Jeb Bush moved from Venezuela to Miami and established himself in south Florida's business community. Employing a strategy utilized by his family for generations, Jeb allied himself with wealthy and conservative elements in Florida politics, amassed a comfortable fortune, and used the rise of movement conservatism as an opportunity to finally make a foray into public life, an undertaking that friends and political observers had long anticipated. Foregoing the time-honored strategy of working his way up through lower-level political positions, he went straight for the top.

In many ways Jeb Bush seemed the ideal candidate to exploit the revolution being promoted by new conservatives in Florida and throughout the nation. First, his connections to the Bush dynasty, his name recognition and his access to family money sources gave him the instant visibility and credibility needed for a statewide race in a party that had held few top-of-the-ticket positions in Florida. Indeed, his announcement as a candidate was treated by Republicans with the attention usually reserved for star athletes or entertainment celebrities.

Second, unlike many of the conservative politicians who had first voiced antipathy toward a liberal government that paid too much attention to certain "groups" and "special interests," Jeb was not too crude or too southern. Instead, he was intellectual and policy oriented, asserting that he was idea-driven rather than process-driven (Broder 1994). At the same time he was a "true-believer" in the neoconservative orthodoxy, willing to campaign with the fervor of the religious convert that he was soon to become and exhibiting a visceral antipathy toward taxes and ideas such as affirmative action, support for public welfare, and rehabilitation of criminals that had come to symbolize, for conservatives at least, the failures of liberalism.

Despite these assets, Jeb's first campaign got caught up in the rhetoric of the new conservatism in Florida and overestimated its appeal. Staking out a position well to the right of two strong middle-of-the-road candidates in the Republican primary, Bush chose a Christian Right hero as his running mate and embraced both the message and the emotion of movement conservatism in his campaign. Campaigning as a zealot, he was successful in the primary, but his perceived extremism there led to a narrow loss in the 1994 general election, even though the year was one of Republican Party renaissance elsewhere in the nation. His moderate Democrat opponent was able to blunt Jeb's ideological campaign and hold on to traditional Democrats in rural areas who had been voting for conservative Republican presidential candidates.

Although this defeat was a setback, Republicans kept the faith that the tide of conservatism running in the nation and in the state was on their side and that Jeb was the person to bring it to its zenith in Florida. Thus in 1998 they renominated a chastened Bush. Facing no opposition in the Republican primary, Jeb moved his image to the center. He softened his rhetoric and took great pains to avoid appearing rigidly ideological. These changes and the presence on the Democratic ticket of a lackluster candidate who could not duplicate the turnout of his predecessor led to Jeb's victory and to the realization of Republican dreams, complete control of Florida state government.

After his election, Governor Bush reverted to his original political stance and adopted a theoretically based conservative agenda that sought to reverse or overturn policies that had found support from generations of Florida elected officials. In pursuit of his policy agenda he consciously focused his actions to appeal to a narrow coalition of conservative constituencies. Their enthusiastic support gave him the foundation to overwhelm a legislature weakened by term limits and bound to him by both partisan and ideological ties. His hand was strengthened by a booming economy and a series of fortuitous constitutional amendments that empowered the Office of the Governor in Florida. Bush's own initiatives regarding the budgetary process, judicial appointments and control of state agency heads helped consolidate more formal authority in his hands than had ever been the case for a Florida governor. Displaying a willingness to sidestep public opinion on issues to which he was committed and stubbornness in pursuit of his objectives, he utilized this power to dominate Florida politics and to put into place many, if not all, of the most cherished policies of the conservative movement that had spawned his candidacy. This policy success led both the governor and his supporters to claim that he had brought about a revolution in Florida politics and government.

In this book I describe the rise of Jeb Bush to political power in Florida, the conservative theory that guided his behavior when elected, and the aggressive manner in which he used the office of governor to pursue his goals. I also offer insight into his motivations and competencies, provide an analysis of the extent to which his "revolution" achieved its goals, and ask what the revolution meant to Florida. My own views naturally shape the analysis provided, but I offer these views as part of the analysis and invite readers to examine my argument and to propose alternative explanations for the governor's actions and the policy outcomes of his administration.

Part I
Rise to Power

Chapter 1

Becoming Governor

Introduction

In large measure the motivations and values of elected officials are formed and first displayed in what Richard Fenno refers to as their "pre-political careers" (Fenno 1996). Jeb Bush's adult prepolitical career was spent in Texas, in Venezuela, and in south Florida where most of those who followed his career say that he employed a political and business strategy long familiar to historians of the political dynasty whose name he carries (Unger 2004, 36, ch. 3; Phillips 2004, 10; Schweizer and Schweizer 2004, xvi). The strategy was to exploit the Bush family name and to draw on a huge universe of family relationships, friendships, family money, and elite contacts in order to propel himself into successful careers in both business and politics. Use of this strategy in the past is said to have permitted "the Bush family to perpetuate the myth that their successes are the product of their own talents and hard work" (Bode 2004).

The strategy was described in a variety of ways by those who followed the Bush careers. Some defined it as a conscious, formalized practice. For example, Robert Trigaux saw it as a two-step procedure: "1) leverage the Bush family name and a small personal investment into really big money, always provided by others; and 2) if any deal goes sour, exit early with personal fortune intact, or rely on a bailout from one of Dad's fairy godfathers" (Trigaux 2000).

Others viewed it more simply: "Jeb combined constant cultivation of his father's formidable political network with hard work and shrewd maneuvering in local circles," (Yardley, 2002). And still others said that his father did what any father would do, "help his kid get into the family business."

Not unexpectedly, Jeb took umbrage at the implication that he was not a self-made man and told television talk-show host Larry King that the Bush family name was really a detriment to his ambitions and that it limited his career choices, (Gladwell, 2008: 18). Nevertheless, in the twenty years that he lived in Florida prior to his inauguration as governor of Florida on January 6, 1999 and continuing after his term was over, the future governor employed his name and its connections to gain employment, to promote his business ventures, to raise money for his campaigns for governor, and to soften his re-entry to "civilian" life after his administration came to a close. Jeb's older brother George had always conceded the value of his family name, saying "it's obviously a political advantage," (Lyman and Navarro, 1998) and ultimately Jeb himself was forced to accede. In a somewhat grudging admission contained in a letter to the *Miami Herald* in 1998, he said, "Is favorable name recognition helpful … perhaps." (Conason, 2003).

Bush the Businessman

Jeb Bush graduated from college in 1974, and followed what is said to be the admonition to all in the Bush family who have political ambitions: make enough money to care for your family and then run for office. He got a degree in Latin American studies at the University of Texas and earned a reputation as something of an intellectual by graduating in three years and earning a Phi Beta Kappa key. Through his family connections he was then given a job with Texas Commerce Bank, which had been founded by the family of James A. Baker III, former secretary of the treasury and later of state in Jeb's father's presidential administration. After three years as a loan officer in Houston, Texas, Commerce promoted Jeb to vice president of the bank's Venezuelan operation and transferred him to Caracas.

Two years later, Bush realized that he did not like being a banker and left Venezuela in 1979 to return to the United States and to Miami. He said that he moved to Florida in order for his Mexican-born wife to be near her mother, to raise his children in a multicultural environment, and to "get out from under my Dad's shadow" (Lester 1994). Despite his stated interest in being on his own, Jeb's first activity in the United States was working on his father's presidential campaign, and in Miami he was introduced to Armando Codina. Codina, a friend of Jeb's father from his CIA days, was a successful Cuban-born entrepreneur who had made a fortune in an automated billing systems business and with the proceeds from this business had begun a Miami real estate company.

In the late 1970s and early 1980s "Miami was in decline as a winter resort but was re-emerging as the de-facto capital of Latin America, both culturally and economically—a boomtown" (Finnegan 2004). The city's once small-scale skyline began to change dramatically. "Loaded with drug money and oil money, the jefes descended on the area's real estate market and bought with more whim than reason—bang, bang, shoot'em up days of wild shopping" (Sherrill 1987). By 1987, Dade County politics was dominated by Cuban émigrés who shared a "distinct political perspective" (Portes and Stepick 1993; Bardach 2002). Jeb Bush began his professional life in Florida as a participant in this culture, and it was this perspective that blended with his own ideology to structure his political thinking and behavior.

The Cuban experience in Miami created a "hegemony of right-wing politics" (Portes and Stepick 1993, 142). Extremely vocal in their anticommunism, Cubans also saw themselves "as more militant in defense of American values…than the laid back natives" (Portes and Stepick 1993, 139). Liberalism in all of its manifestations had to be resolutely opposed and liberal discourse simply disappeared from view (Forment 1989, 18, 47–81). The Cubans who shared this view of the world became Jeb's principal allies in business and in politics, and it is said that he even began to develop a Cuban accent (Schweizer and Schweizer, 2004: 310). Speaking twenty years later Raul Masvidal, then president of Biscayne Bank, explained how Bush was able to insinuate himself into this culture. "Here comes a guy who is good looking; he comes from a wealthy and powerful family in Texas; he has political views that Cubans love; he speaks Spanish; he has a Mexican wife. You need any more?" (Yardley, 2002). Alex Courtelis, a Cuban businessman who had helped finance his father's presidential campaign, served as his mentor during these early days (Schweizer and Schweizer 2004, 319) and "from early on, he carefully learned the elaborate, sorrowing, furious culture of el exilio" (Finnegan, 4).

At this point in his career, Jeb had no real estate experience and, it is alleged, was so broke that he used his American Express card to pay his bill to Master Card. Nevertheless, Armando Codina offered the young Jeb a job in the real estate business. And a pretty good one. In exchange for the use of Jeb's last name on the company masthead, Codina gave the future governor 40 percent of the firm's profits plus chances to invest in other ventures. This was a classic use of the "insider" strategy for which the Bush family was famous. Bush got a job with little or no risk or personal investment that was to bring him the wealth he wanted, and Codina got the clout that came with having his name publicly associated with the son of the vice president of the United States. (Details about Jeb's business career are based substantially on reporting by Alecia Swasy, Robert Trigaux, and Adam Smith of the *St. Petersburg Times* and William Yardley, Andres Viglucci, and Alfonso Chardy of the *Miami Herald*.)

By all accounts, Bush worked hard at this job. He had a high energy level, was intense about his work, and had "a level of impatience" about doing well and making money. He certainly adopted without reservation the mores of unbridled capitalism that were then and are now widespread in the Cuban business community and has been quoted as saying "too few people have confidence in capitalism." He got a real estate license and invested a lot of time in the recruitment of clients and in negotiating leases.

At the same time, he was offered investment opportunities that almost never come to a young real estate agent without a famous name. One of these was a downtown Miami office building that was on the real estate version of the wrong side of the tracks. Armando Codina, however, saw potential in the site and invited Jeb to be an investor in the purchase. For a $1,000 investment, Bush was given a 20 percent share. He later sold this share for $346,000.

Another similar opportunity was a spot as one of five people on the board of directors of a private financial institution in Miami owned by Bank Openheim Pierson of Switzerland. For a fee, this institution managed the money of wealthy Latino investors. It, too, was the kind of opportunity that comes with being the son of a vice president. Combining hard work with opportunities like these, Bush was able to increase his net worth to $2.26 million by 1993 and when he sold his portion of Codina-Bush back to Codina before challenging Lawton Chiles for governor, Codina paid him $795,652.

While Jeb's business career in Miami was clearly successful, it was plagued by news reports describing a sense of unease about his gullibility and occasionally about his ethics. Indeed, his running mate in 1994, Tom Feeney, said that "he did business with people who later turned out to be deadbeats and crooks" (Viglucci and Chardy, 2002), and an experienced drug and organized crime law enforcement officer who had worked in Miami concurrently with Jeb's rise in the business community said, "When I see the kind of people who Jeb Bush hangs out with, I can't decide if he is very naive or very cynical" (Morley 1991). Asked later about his business associates, Bush admitted to gullibility and added, "I'm 45 years old and I have to have better radar" (Swasy and Trigaux, 1998; see also Portes and Stepick, 1993, 123–126; Schweizer and Schwiezer, 2004; 320–321; Viglucci and Chardy, 2002; Smith, 2002).

Bush in the Government

Jeb Bush interrupted his business career in 1987 for a short excursion into public service. For nearly two years in 1987 and 1988, he served as Florida's secretary of commerce in the administration of Republican governor Bob Martinez. This was not a highly visible office and the future governor made a modest impact in the position. A search of news reports of the time turned up three accounts of his service in Florida state government. The first was a memo he wrote to Governor Martinez in which he argued that changing the civil service into an "employment at will" system would improve governmental performance in the state. The ideas in this memo were subsequently implemented when he became governor.

Several reports also discussed charges that the future governor used his association with Governor Martinez to further the business interest of one of his Cuban friends, Manny Diaz. Diaz, owner of a commercial nursery, convinced Bush to arrange a private meeting with the governor. Soon after the meeting, Diaz Farms was awarded a multi-million-dollar state highway landscaping contract, despite minimal highway-landscaping experience (Pizzo 1992).

Finally, Bush took a position as secretary of commerce on an issue that subsequently became the centerpiece of his campaigns and of his own administration. And the position he took while secretary was different from that which he adopted later. The issue was his antagonism for state taxes in any form. Over the course of his administration, Jeb Bush promoted more tax cuts than any governor in the state's history and routinely excoriated any discussion about the necessity of generating greater tax revenues. Nevertheless, as a member of the Martinez administration, Bush was supportive of the tax on services that the Martinez administration had proposed in an effort to reform the state's tax system (Dyckman 1998, 15A).

Some observers of Florida politics suggest that Bush used his short-lived position in state government purely to cement ties with wealthy Republicans and with businessmen throughout Florida who were to add to his personal wealth and who would provide support in subsequent political campaigns (Swazy and Trigaux, 1998). One of the contacts he made included Richard Lawless, former CIA agent and business entrepreneur who brought Bush more than $500,000 in fees from commercial real estate deals between 1989 and 1993 (ibid.). Other people included Tom Petway, a Jacksonville insurance executive and part owner of the Jacksonville Jaguars; Peter Rummell, chairman and chief executive of St. Joe Company, the state's largest private landowner; Jim Blosser, lawyer and lobbyist; and John Ramil head of Tampa Electric Company. In subsequent years, these men were to appear often in Jeb's professional and political life, making contributions to his own political campaigns and to the Republican Party of Florida, involving him in business deals, and recommending him for positions that generated personal income.

The First Campaign: Bush v. Chiles

In late 1988, Bush returned to Bush/Codina from Tallahassee and to increasing his net worth. By the middle of 1993, he concluded that he had created an economic environment for his family that would permit him to pursue his ambition to run for public office. His federal income tax returns showed that his earnings had grown from $43,998 in 1981 to $1.2 million in 1992 (Judd 1994) and by 1993 his net worth had climbed to $2.26 million (Swasy and Trigaux, 1998). Thus he turned his attention to a suitable political position.

The Republican Party had made steady gains in Florida in the late 1980s and by 1992 had taken control of the state senate for the first time in modern history and was bearing down on control of the house of representatives. By 1993, the newly energized legislative party was engaged in political warfare with the first term Democratic governor who was showing signs of vulnerability. It was a prime opportunity for Republicans to capture this office and seven people, including Jeb, a former state senate president, and two men who had sought the GOP gubernatorial nomination in previous years, filed to run in the party's primary.

The Republican Primary

From the outset of his attempt to become governor of Florida, Bush made clear that he was not going to run as a "compassionate conservative." Nor was he to run as a political pragmatist. Saying, "I won't bend on my principles" (Broder 1994), he adopted the rigidly right-wing philosophy of "movement" conservatism and of his adopted Cuban political allies and targeted the extremes of his party. He developed a messianic style (Judd 1994) and referred to his young campaign assistants as "gladiators" in a war of ideologies (Defede, 1998).

In an effort to appeal to the substantial influence of the organized religious Right in the Florida Republican Party, Bush chose as his running mate a state legislator, Tom Fenney, who in 1993 had been named the Christian Coalition's legislator of the year and who had been given a 100 percent rating by the Florida Conservative Union. In defending this choice, Bush said that he was not seeking to balance his candidacy on such factors as age, gender, or ideology. "In the end," he said, "I decided not to hedge, not to take out an insurance policy against my own philosophy" (Judd, 1994).

Bush's campaign was described as one of fervently held ideas. "His appearances became revival meetings…and as he went from country club to country club telling stories about [welfare fraud] to his all-white audiences they would shake their heads along with him, conjuring up their own image of what the lazy welfare mother looked like, and the color of her skin" (Defede, 1998). During his campaign Bush openly espoused a conservative "constrain the beast" philosophy toward government. He proposed to dismantle the State Department of Education and to refuse federal money for welfare, He would have forced mothers and children off welfare after two years with no provision for job training or child care beyond the small amount available at the time. He spoke often of the need for lighter regulation of business and stronger private-property rights. He argued that voters as opposed to elected officials should approve tax increases. He was impatient with troubled families and saw early intervention with children as a dubious and expensive experiment. He thought the juvenile justice system "coddles these kids now," and said that "we should have punishment being the overriding philosophy in how we deal with children" (ibid.). He opposed legalized abortion, considered homosexuality a sin, and supported a ballot measure that would deny homosexuals specific protections under state civil rights laws (Debenport, 1994; Associated Press News Service 1993; Rosenbaum 1994).

In 1994, most of these ideas were at least tacitly endorsed by the conservative wing of the Republican Party and even his more moderate opponents did not try to challenge them directly. Instead they sought to exploit Bush's governmental inexperience and lack of qualifications, to scorn his reliance on his parents' celebrity and their money-raising machine, and to accuse him of enriching himself through business deals with questionable associates. Thus a former Republican governor was quoted as saying that Bush reminded him of Prince Charles: "Neither one of them had to do anything to get where they are, other than come out of the womb" (Moss 1994). And two of his opponents in the primary joined together to pay for a highly unusual joint television ad saying that Mr. Bush "made a fortune with a partner who is now an international felon, borrowing millions of dollars from a failed savings and loan company" (Berke, 1994).

Bush responded by claiming that he was a self-made man with his own ideas rather than part of a political dynasty, and he tried to deflect his ties to his family by using a line that his brother George picked up and used in his run for governor of Texas; "I'm not running because I'm George and Barbara Bush's son. I'm running because I'm George P. and Noelle and Jeb's father" (Associated Press News Service, 1993). He did not, however, refuse to take advantage of George and Barbara's visibility. Employing the well-known Bush strategy of reliance on "select" connections, he brought both of his parents to Florida frequently, and each time they toured with him they raised a million dollars for his campaign (Lester, 1994). In 1993 and 1994, George W. Bush held nine fundraisers for Jeb in Florida and others in Houston. "More than half of the $7 million Jeb would raise for his campaign came from fund-raisers in Florida featuring his parents and fund-raisers out of the state sponsored by friends of his family" (Schweitzer and Schweitzer, 2004: 416–417).

In the end, this elite version of Florida's "friends and family" strategy (Key ,1945) prevailed. While the other candidates were able to rely on special interest money from companies and organizations with whom they had worked over the years, "all of this was child's play in comparison to the Bush family money machine" (Schweizer and Schweizer, 2004: 415). Jeb's star quality and the access to money afforded him by his family combined with his hard work and substantial talents as a campaigner to produce a victory in which he won 45.7 percent of the primary vote, quite remarkable in a seven-candidate field. Although this total was not enough to avoid a runoff, his closest rival, former Democratic secretary of state and Republican gubernatorial candidate Jim Smith, realized that his chances of winning a runoff were poor, and withdrew from the race, leaving Bush as his party's choice against Florida political legend Lawton Chiles.

The General Election

Buoyed by his success in the Republican primary, Bush made no attempt to moderate his hard-line conservative positions in the general election. He referred to himself as a "head-banging conservative" (*National Review* 1998) and for a time at least candidly accepted his opponent's charge that he was a radical. He based his campaign heavily on strong anticrime and antigovernment messages. He tried to brand Chiles as a liberal who was "soft on crime," while he himself promised more executions and more prisons. He also vowed to go to Tallahassee and "club this government into submission" (Broder, 1994).

Initially, Bush's conservative message appeared to work. Further, he raised so much money that he inadvertently helped Chiles by triggering matching dollars for the governor from the state's public campaign law. By mid-October, he was ten percent-age points ahead of Chiles, a notoriously slow starter.

Chiles began the campaign by talking about infant mortality, education, and crime prevention. He tried to paint Bush as a right-wing extremist and sought the important north Florida swing vote using statements such as "the he-Coon walks just before the light of day" to appeal to the traditional "redneck Riviera" voters in the rural north-west part of the state.

As the campaign wore on, Bush made crime his central theme. He proposed building space for thousands more prisoners, removing "comforts" such as television and exercise rooms from prisons and executing more convicts who had committed serious crimes. He argued that Chiles could not be trusted on the issue and, in particular, that he had not done all that was possible to ensure that persons who had been given a death sentence were actually put to death (Rosenbaum 1994). Very quickly "crime [became] the Scud missile of this campaign and truth the casualty" (Gailey, 1994). Riding this message, Bush began to pull away and in October led by between 5 and 10 percent. Using the public funds generated by Bush's success in raising money for his own campaign, Chiles resorted to negative ads that questioned Jeb's associations with the "deadbeats and crooks" mentioned by Jeb's own running mate and attacked his integrity in an aggressive fashion (*New York Times*, 1994). Bush responded in kind and the "campaign homestretch became one of the nastiest in Florida political history" (Williams, 1994, M4).

Many political observers in Florida say that a particularly offensive Bush television ad on the death penalty was the turning point of the campaign. The ad featured a mother whose ten-year-old daughter had been murdered in 1980, fourteen years prior to the campaign. The killer had been sentenced to death but never executed, because of appeals. At the time the case was still in court. The victim's mother, both in television ads and in a mailing by the Bush campaign, said that her daughter's killer "is still on death row and we're still waiting for justice." She then said, "We won't get it from Lawton Chiles because he's too liberal on crime."

The ad, personally approved by Jeb, proved to be a disaster for his campaign. Chiles immediately pointed out that he could not speed the execution because the case was still in the courts. He went on to compare the ad to the infamous "Willie Horton" commercial used by Jeb's father in his presidential race against Michael Dukakis and, in a widely watched television debate on November 1, 1994, attacked Jeb directly for it.

According to those who saw the debate Chiles seemed barely able to control himself when given an opportunity to speak on the ad in question. He said, "All my political life I have supported the death penalty; as governor I have executed eight men. I hold the phone as they walk into the death chamber. I give the last command before they pull the switch." He wagged his finger at Jeb and said: "You knew [the ad] was false. You admitted it was false. And I am ashamed that you would use the loss of a mother in an ad like this" (Carver and Fielder, 1999: 355). Bush "seemed flustered by the force of Chiles's words and responded weakly that the symbol of crime needs a human face on it" (Cockburn, 1994: 10).

In the aftermath of the debate, the number of voters who said they disapproved of Bush went up by 10 percent and Chiles edged ahead by 48 to 45 percent. He maintained his slight lead until the end, managing to eke out the closest gubernatorial victory in Florida history. With 41 percent of voters saying in exit polls that crime was the issue that mattered most to them (Sharp, 1994), many observers claim that the misleading ad and Bush's failure to adequately answer some of the accusations made by Chiles about his personal integrity probably cost him the election (Morgan, 1994: 3D).[1]

The Interregnum

Jeb Bush's defeat came amid a national sweep for Republicans, including his brother George's victory over Ann Richards for governor of Texas. Thus the loss was particularly painful, since many pundits had considered Jeb a better politician than George (Philips, 2004: 79). Nevertheless, Jeb was gracious in defeat. According to one eyewitness account, "there were no tears, no recriminations, just sadness" (Morgan, 1994). After he called Chiles to concede, he talked to his father in Houston, who was celebrating George's victory. Then, as described somewhat melodramatically by Bill Minutaglio, "he stayed awake deep into the morning hours, sipping on scotch, thinking about his political future" (Minutaglio, 1999: 294).

Business as Usual

In the immediate aftermath of defeat, Jeb returned to Miami and went back into business with Armando Codina, although with the stipulation that he would have more activities outside of real estate. For the next three years Bush practiced business and politics from this position, readying himself for what many political observers knew would be another run for governor.

On the business side Bush used his new statewide name recognition to improve his economic circumstances and to consolidate his ties to influential Republicans who could help him in future political endeavors. His enhanced visibility made him very attractive to companies who wanted to add a "star" to their board of directors and appointments to such boards earned him $108,000 in fees in 1995 alone (Viglucci and Chardy, 2002).

But Bush did not let his business interests nor his defeat by Chiles stop his efforts to gain public office. Within weeks of his loss, Jeb created an organization that would keep him involved in public issues and keep him visible during the time period until the subsequent gubernatorial election. The organization was the Foundation for Florida's Future. The foundation, created in Palm Beach, was a "non-profit public policy center" funded by donations from admirers of Mr. Bush. It published a quarterly magazine, a regular newsletter, and a series of position papers on issues facing the state. It was also to provide direct support for programs that illustrated Bush's conception of the proper role of government.

Although Bush disputed the interpretation placed on it by critics and political observers (Troxler, 1995; Nickens, 1998; Van Osdol, 1998; Ericson, 1999) the foundation did have many of the attributes of a campaign organization—one that was unconstrained by the donation limits or reporting requirements of ordinary political campaigns. The foundation's staff came from his 1994 campaign, it paid his pollster, and the ideas discussed in its publications were those articulated in that campaign. Further, it was not designed to provide objective analysis of important issues facing the state. Rather, like other so-called think tanks at the national level such as the Manhattan Institute, the American Enterprise Institute, and the Cato Institute, it promoted specific positions on public issues and posed conservative alternatives to what Bush called the "indefensible philosophy" of liberalism (Troxler, 1995). Virtually all the positions taken by the FFF were those espoused by these organizations and by conservative "thinkers" such as William Bennett, who is reported to have been the person whose ideas were closest to those of Bush.

The Foundation for Florida's Future did keep Bush in the public eye, but at some cost. Almost immediately upon creation, it generated controversy for Bush on two issues. First, the foundation was attacked for failure to identify those who had made financial contributions, suggesting that they were simply disguised campaign contributions. Secondly, it was criticized for the proportion of its funds it devoted to programmatic concerns.

The FFF raised more than $1.7 million in 1995 and 1996, primarily in $5,000 amounts. While the foundation released the names of its donors, it did so only in general categories related to the size of their donation. Thus in 1995 FFF released the names of 131 donors of $5,000 or more, but would not connect names to specific amounts. When asked to link contributors to contributions, Bush would not, leaving reporters to ask, "Who gave $50,000 to the son of a former president who still wants to be governor, a sum that is 100 times greater than the $500 limit that could be given to the Bush re-election campaign?" (Nickens, 2001). Later, tax returns revealed inadvertently by the state showed that Odebrecht Contractors of Florida had made the single largest contribution, $70,000 (Smith, 2005).

Jeb's foundation was also criticized for devoting far less of its resources to programmatic concerns than to administration. At the time, national standards for nonprofit organizations required that 85 percent of expenses be devoted to activities related to the purpose of the organization and 15 percent to administration of the organization itself. In 1995 and 1996 the FFF had total expenses of $1.3 million. Only $350,000, 27 percent of the total, went to programs. The highest profile project was a charter school in Miami which received $33,000, 2 percent of the money raised. When asked about this apparent violation of the law, Bush said the foundation was "not a philanthropy. It was involved with advocating ideas. You should compare us with organizations such as the Heritage Foundation, the James Madison Institute" (Van Osdol, 1998). Such comparisons showed that the Tallahassee-based James Madison Institute spent 79 percent of its funds on programs and the Heritage Foundation spent 84 percent. These data left the foundation without defense to the charge that it was, indeed, simply a part of the Bush reelection machine.

Despite these criticisms of the FFF, it was a political asset to Jeb Bush. It permitted him to keep his name in public view and to acquaint himself with people throughout the state who were concerned about a variety of public issues. It gave him an opportunity to develop a preliminary legislative package for his first term and it obviously permitted him to maintain his network of financial backers. When his second campaign for governor began, these and other assets gave Bush an immediate advantage over his Democratic rivals. The foundation was subsequently merged into the James Madison Institute in Tallahassee, a conservative "think tank," and continued the promotion of Jeb's own and other conservative ideas throughout the Bush administration. In 2005, the foundation was reconstituted as a separate entity and made a primary instrument in Jeb's efforts to sustain his legacy after leaving office, a subject discussed later in the book.

The Second Campaign: Bush v. Mackay

After three years in political exile, Bush made public what everyone who knew him or had observed his political activity knew was coming. He announced that he would again seek the office of governor of Florida. The announcement came on November 12, 1997, one full year prior to the election. "Bush admitted his early timing was unusual, but saw no reason to wait once he'd made his decision" (CNN, ALLPolitics, 1997). After making his announcement, he left immediately on a campaign swing. He continued to work for Bush/Codina and although he worked only part-time for half of 1998, he grossed $755,136 in salary (Florida Ethics Commission, 1998).

Jeb's second campaign for governor was markedly different from his first. He went from a right-wing zealot pushing movement conservative ideology to a political pragmatist focused on winning the election. This difference was immediately evident in his choice for lieutenant governor which was announced at the time he made his declaration of candidacy.

Bush's first running mate, Tom Feeney, was chosen expressly because he shared the entire Bush political philosophy. His second, Secretary of State Sandra Mortham, was chosen because she did not. In particular, Mortham was pro-choice and Bush's strong antiabortion stance in his first race had hurt him among women in Florida.

Explaining his choice of Mortham, Bush said almost the exact opposite of what he had said when identifying Feeney as his first running mate. Then he had said, "I didn't want to take out an insurance policy against my own philosophy" (Judd, 1994). In choosing Morthan he said, "I wasn't looking for a clone" (CNN ALLPolitics, 1998).[2] The decision reflected a political calculation based upon the results of Bush's analysis of his 1994 race against Lawton Chiles.

Bush and his supporters claimed to have learned a valuable lesson from the Chiles race. The lesson was that you don't need to have an opinion on every subject that emerges during a political campaign. Bush said, "In '94 if someone asked me a question, I'd think about it and give a pretty provocative answer. Half the people would be incredibly pleased with it. The other half would say, 'Well now, something is wrong with this boy.' And Governor Chiles would be asked the same question and he would say, 'The he-coon came out before the light of day.' And that was it" (Defede, 1998).

The 1994 run for governor had been a campaign of ideas that Bush believed in passionately and his running mate, Tom Feeney, says that "he was recruited by Jeb's saying that this was a mission to sell ideas." Reporters who covered the race said that Bush came across as "callous and mean spirited" (BBC News, 1998). The "new" Bush dropped the angry speeches that had characterized his first race (Schweizer and Schweizer, 2004: 454). "His rhetoric was softer, fuzzier, less specific...and he talked generally about the things we have in common" (Defede, 1998). He was packaged as a likable and trustworthy person whom you might not always agree with but whose integrity and intentions could not be questioned. The campaign was more about Bush and less about ideas.

The Bush–Brogan campaign also made a determined effort to broaden its constituency base by appealing to African American, Jewish (Rowe, 1998), and Hispanic voters (Padilla, 1998). In his 1994 race, Bush had created a serious problem for both himself and the Republican Party in the African American community—always a weak point for Republicans. In response to a question about what he would do for African American voters if he won the election he responded "probably nothing." The result was that Bush got about 8 percent of the black vote when these voters constituted about 12 percent of the state's population. Thus in 1998, he campaigned hard in black churches, poor neighborhoods, and public schools and was rewarded with a much larger percentage of the African American vote.

Bolstered by the visibility generated through the Foundation for Florida's Future, by the absence of primary opposition, and by a huge campaign war chest secured in substantial part through his father's friends in Washington (Connley, Dewar, and Baker, 1997) and his brother's supporters in Texas (Schweizer and Schweizer, 2004: 455), the Bush campaign jumped out to an immediate lead over Democratic hopefuls.

In choosing an opponent for Bush, the Democrats were faced with a dilemma that continues to plague the party—finding a fresh face to run against the "new" Republican Party candidates. The early leader on the Democratic side was Buddy Mackay, the lieutenant governor for Lawton Chiles. A twenty-eight-year veteran of Florida politics, Mackay had served in the state legislature, had been a member of Congress, and had lost an extremely narrow race for the U.S. Senate in 1988. Widely respected as an intelligent, decent, and honorable man, Mackay suffered from the perception that he was a part of the past, that his campaign was slow to act, and that he couldn't raise enough money nor generate enough enthusiasm to beat Bush.

In the midst of these concerns, two former state representatives, Rick Dantzler and Keith Arnold came forward to challenge Mackay in the primary. While both met some of the objections raised against Mackay, neither had the name recognition nor the money to be serious candidates and Mackay dispatched them easily. He chose Dantzler as his running mate and set off to overcome Bush's early lead.

He was hit almost immediately by the fall-out from a disastrous action taken earlier in the year by Democrats in the Florida House of Representatives. In January, white legislators, concerned about the fundraising ability of African American representative Willie Logan, dumped him from the position as speaker-designate and installed a white woman in his place. In retaliation, Logan, U.S. congressman Alcee Hastings, and other leading black Democrats created a political action committee to oppose Democratic candidates and to urge African Americans to shun the Democratic ticket. The split was so severe that Vice President Al Gore came to the state in a vain attempt to salve African American feelings and to salvage his own political fortunes. The Mackay–Dantzler ticket never recovered from the wounds inflicted by their house colleagues and in November Bush picked up 14 percent of the black vote, up from 8 percent in 1994.

As the campaign began in earnest, Mackay criticized Bush on his lack of government experience and his past business dealings. Bush attacked Mackay on taxes and crime. Both candidates courted older voters with Bush once again trading on the appeal of his family, in this case his mother, Barbara Bush— saying, "I'm the apple of my mom's eye"—and both vowing to hold the line on taxes, protect the rights of the elderly, and control untimely placements in nursing homes (CNN.com, 2005).

Bush and Mackay both made education their top priority but they differed in how they sought to improve the system. It was this difference that became the media focal point in the campaign. Bush drew upon the conservative thinking emanating from Washington-based "think tanks" such as the Heritage Foundation to develop a reform platform based upon school choice, vouchers, and "high-stakes" testing. His "A+" plan called for testing on English, math, and writing and for assigning an A–F grade to each school based upon these tests. Students in schools that received a grade of "F" in two out of four years would be eligible for vouchers to attend any public or nonsectarian private school of their choice. The vouchers would be paid for out of the state's contribution to the "F" school. Mackay vigorously opposed the use of vouchers that would take money away from public schools. Instead he proposed to improve education by using lottery proceeds to raise the share of the state budget devoted to education from 35 to 40 percent.

Although the debate over vouchers got most of the media attention during the campaign, exit polls revealed that voters did not consider them to be a key factor in the race (Sandham, 1998). Running, as he put it, against a "mere mortal" instead of a "legend" (Schweizer and Schweizer, 2004, 455), Bush superiority in message and money proved decisive and he went on to win easily, by 10 percent of the vote.

Conclusion

The victory of Jeb Bush in 1998 was the culmination of twenty years of active business and politics on the part of George Bush's second son. It was also the beginning of a new era in Florida politics. The capture of the governor's office and the election of substantial and unified Republican majorities in both the state house of representatives and the state senate signaled a rethinking of a philosophy of government that had held sway in Florida since the 1930s and the promotion of a new theory about how state government should be run. The following chapters discuss the changed political environment in Florida and describe the elements of the theory that guided Bush's behavior in a new philosophical context.

Notes

1. Interestingly, Bush himself was never able to bring about the execution of the killer featured in the ad, and as of February 1, 2009, he was still imprisoned in the Florida State Correctional System.

2. Before the campaign was truly underway, Sandra Mortham and her chief aide, Richard Hefley, came under fire for using the Office of the Secretary of State for political purposes. In the wake of the allegations, Hefley resigned and Mortham withdrew from the lieutenant governor's race. She was replaced by Secretary of Education Frank Brogan and was defeated by Katherine Harris when she ran for reelection as Florida's secretary of state.

Chapter 2

Bush and a New Political Environment in Florida

Introduction

All governors, indeed all public officials, are elected into a context of political, social, and economic circumstances that have profound implications for their activities and their performance. "Creative leadership may be rein-forced by favorable conditions, or overcome such conditions. Inept leadership may be helped by favorable events or swamped by them" (Hargrove, 2008: 7). In Florida, these governing conditions were changing dramatically as Jeb Bush was elected. Just as he came to office, Florida made the transition from a Democratic to a Republican government and the state's economy began a sustained period of substantial growth.

These conditions were unique in the political history of Florida and are rare in American politics in general. Stephen Skowronek's monumental work on the American presidency finds them only four times in American history; with the presidencies of Thomas Jefferson, Andrew Jackson, Abraham Lincoln, and Franklin D. Roosevelt. Called periods of reconstruction, they provide "the most promising of all situations for the exercise of political leadership" (Skowronek, 1997: 37). In Florida in 1999, opposition to the old Democratic regime held sway in the legislature and the governor was granted "an expansive authority to repudiate the established governing formulas" (ibid.). This chapter describes the nature of this reconstructive period in Florida history and how it conditioned Bush's political strategy.

Political Conditions: Control of the Executive Branch

In the 1998 gubernatorial election, Jeb Bush won 55.3 percent of the popular vote in Florida and all but six of the state's sixty-seven counties and brought the Republican Party to the governor's office for only the third time since Reconstruction. In addition, the Republicans, for the first time in the state's history, achieved parity with the Democrats in the state's cabinet, winning races for attorney general, treasurer, and secretary of education. With the Democratic commissioner of agriculture leaning Republican and subse-quently changing parties, Republicans were in a historic position of influence in the executive branch of Florida state government.

Despite the overall positive outcome for Republicans, Bush's personal performance was not the driving force in the election. He ran behind five members of the six-person cabinet, both Democrats and Republicans: attorney general, comptroller, treasurer, commissioner of agriculture, and secretary of education. His share of the vote was the third-lowest winning percentage in a governor's race in state history, exceeding only those of Democrat Sidney Catts in 1916 and of the state's first republican governor, Claude Kirk, who won with 55.1 percent of the vote. In the end, he won because Democrats dropped off from their support for his predecessor, Lawton Chiles and not because his popularity improved dramatically among Republicans over the time since the 1994 election.

In 1994 almost two-thirds of registered voters in Florida cast a ballot in the gubernatorial election; in 1998 turnout was less than 50 percent. Democrat-rich Broward and Palm Beach counties, which had turnouts in the 1994 elections of 61 and 67 percent, respectively, dropped to 50 and 44 percent, costing Democratic candidate Buddy Mackay hundreds of thousands of votes. In 1998, Bush's vote total improved by only 100,000 over that in 1994 even though the number of Republicans in the state increased by more than 500,000 during that time period. Nevertheless, this relatively modest personal showing was forgotten as the Republicans rejoiced in their first-ever control of the executive branch of government in Florida.

Political Conditions: Legislative Dominance

Although obviously important, Bush's election to the office of governor was only a part of the story of the reconstruction of politics in Florida in 1998. Equally momentous was the increased dominance of Republicans in the state legislature.

As late as 1986 Republicans held only 37 percent of state senate seats and 36 percent of the seats in the state house and were virtually irrelevant in both houses of the state legislature. Responding to this circumstance, the party initiated a massive organizational effort designed to challenge Democrats at all levels of state government. Aided to a large extent by the popularity of Ronald Reagan, the party increased voter turnout, was successful in the gubernatorial campaign of Bob Martinez and the U.S. Senate victory of Connie Mack, and began fielding candidates for almost all state legislative seats. By the early 1990s, these efforts began to pay off.

In 1992, Republicans elected an equal number of members to the state senate as did Democrats, twenty each, and shared leadership of that body under Democratic governor Lawton Chiles. In 1994, Republicans took over the majority in that chamber for the first time in the modern era and in 1996 increased their dominance. Lagging slightly behind their senate colleagues, Republicans in the house of representatives did not achieve a majority until 1996, when they elected sixty-one members as compared to fifty-nine for the Democrats. These developments foreshadowed the election of 1998 and set the stage for the reconstruction of Florida politics that was to come in the following year.

In 1998, the Republicans elected 70 representatives to the 120-member state house of representatives and 23 senators to the 40-member state senate. These numbers gave Jeb Bush the kind of majorities necessary to initiate his revolution of state politics.

The 2002 election saw additional increases in the Republican majorities in the state legislature and in Congress. To a large extent, this increase was a function of a Republican reapportionment plan that made all but a few of Florida's legislative and congressional districts completely noncompetitive, with, of course, more Republican than Democratic seats. In Congress only one seat was decided by less than 5 percent of the vote and one seat by less than 10 percent. All others were decided by margins greater than this and eighteen were declared landslides (victory by 20 percent–40 percent) by *FairVote.org*. Florida ranked forty-eighth in the nation on this organization's Democracy Index.

In the 2002 state house races, 78 of the 120 districts did not have candidates of both major parties and in the Florida Senate there were two-party races in only 14 of the 40 seats, as candidates sat out races in which their party was an overwhelming underdog. Ultimately only *4* legislative seats were decided by 10 percent or less of the vote, a traditional break point for competitive races. In the aftermath of the 2002 election, the Republicans controlled 26 of the 40 seats in the senate and 81 of 120 seats in the house, giving them an unbeatable majority, despite the intraparty squabbles that inevitably appear when legislative majorities increase. Although battles between house and senate Republicans were reasonably frequent in Bush's second term, they did not materially affect the governor's legislative agenda. (See Benson, 2007 for a more detailed account of the transition from Democratic to Republican control in the legislature.)

Unified Political Philosophy

Numbers alone did not make the legislative elections of 1998 and 2002 important to political reconstruction in Florida. More critical was the ideological composition of those elected.

The Republican legislative party that took power along with Jeb Bush was philosophically united and extremely conservative. Swept into office on the tides of the same conservative wave that Governor Bush rode to victory, it was composed of two groups, pro-business conservatives who were somewhat moderate or indifferent on social issues and right-wing ideologues with strong ties to the organized Christian Right. These groups were unified in support of the neoconservative political philosophy: fiscal restraint, small government, low taxes, "free market" solutions to public problems, and "family values." The groups were the central elements of the Jeb Bush electoral constituency and provided him an almost religious following in the legislature. Their fervor was described in this way by the house minority leader: "that first year, 63 lawmakers came on board [in the House] ready to jump off any cliff he asked them to. And they did it smiling, singing Kumbaya" (Stockfish, 2007).

The GOP's legislative leadership at the time of Jeb's election also represented the key elements of the Bush electoral coalition and reinforced his influence in the legislature. The senate president was Toni Jennings, a pro-business conservative from Orlando with close ties to and support from the Orlando Christian Right. She was later to become Bush's lieutenant governor. The speaker of the house was Daniel Webster, a state representative from Orange County (Winter Park) who was an original member of the ultrafunda-mentalist house caucus dubbed the "God Squad" and who allowed the director of the Florida chapter of the Christian Coalition to work directly out of the speaker's office. Both Jennings and Webster used philosophical agreement and control over the funds raised through a new policy regarding lobbyist donations to exert strict discipline in their respective chambers.

Unlike the leadership in most state legislatures, which serves at the pleasure of the majority party and can stay in power for years, the Florida legislature selects new leaders each term. Thus, over the course of Bush's tenure in the governor's office, nine people served as either speaker of the house or president of the senate. In the house, several of these leaders were close personal friends and political allies of the governor and worked assiduously to accomplish his goals. These included Tom Feeney, Jeb's first running mate as lieutenant governor, and John Thrasher, a close friend and a political ally "who would not move a muscle without checking with the governor" (Nickens, 2001). An editorial in a major newspaper suggested that "Feeney ran the House as if parliamentary rules were only for other people. And even though the Senate was conducted with proper decorum, the end game for both houses was the same: to give Gov. Jeb Bush powers that Huey Long might envy" (*St. Petersburg Times,* 2001).

Even when house leadership was at its weakest, with Johnnie Byrd in 2004–2005, and when it was not close to Bush personally—as was the case in 2005–2006 with Alan Bense—it clearly reflected his conservative governmental philosophy, thus reducing conflict to issues of priority as opposed to substance. Since ideology dictated the proper answer to policy questions there was little incentive for the legislature to debate the merits of an issue.

The state senate also shared the governor's political philosophy, although with somewhat less fervor, and generally went along with his proposals even when the leadership had reservations. In 1999, for example, the newly elected senate president stood up to say that he was voting for vouchers even though he was extremely skeptical of them simply because Bush had asked him to do so.

It was not until the last two years of Bush's second term that Jeb ever faced anything approaching "lame duck" problems, and here only in the senate. In 2005, the senate president told the governor to "watch what he says" in the heated final days of the legislative session and accused Bush of trying to "cannibalize and plagiarize" the senate's work in particular areas (Cotterell, 2005). Bush then complained that senators trying to write legislation involving oversight of state contracts were "meddling" in executive branch powers and threatened to veto the relevant bills (Lauer, 2005: 1A). Despite such exchanges over the course of his last years in office, the Senate, with one important exception, generally gave Bush the essence of what he asked for.

Over the course of his administration, the Florida legislature responded so positively to the leadership of Governor Bush that the house minority leader said that "the legislature is not its own branch of government anymore. We're Jeb's workroom" (Hylton, 2006). A prominent political columnist characterized the legislature's behavior during the two terms as running the gamut from "fawning to awe-struck" (Cotterell, 2005), and the governor himself called it "willing and compliant" (Robinson, 2007).

Other Legislative Conditions

During the period of Republican euphoria over their ascendancy in Florida government, legislative leaders also moved quickly to enhance their influence in state politics by adopting new policy regarding political contributions. This policy, modeled after the tactics inaugurated by Tom Delay, Republican majority leader in the U.S. House of Representatives, involved what was essentially a shakedown of lobbyists (Dubose and Reid, 2004). From the mid-1980s, special interests in Florida had generally donated fairly equally to both parties and to candidates from both parties. After their success in 1998, however, Florida Republicans announced that they expected donations of two dollars for every one dollar donated to Democrats. Lobbyists who did not comply were to be denied access to both the governor and the legislative leadership (deHaven-Smith, 2005: 208).

Finally, legislative term limits made legislators already predisposed to support Bush even more compliant. Term limits were enacted in Florida in 1992 and, by a stroke of good fortune for the governor, became effective just as Bush took office, forcing out of the 2000 legislature more than half of the experienced members. In 2001 there were 75 new lawmakers, 12 in the 40-member senate and 63 in the 120-member house of representatives. This change had an effect similar to that in other states, emptying the legislature of experience and forcing green legislators to struggle with issues so complex that by the time they began to understand them, it was time for them to leave.

Alternatively, seeing that they couldn't stay long, they arrived seeking headlines, rather than listening and learning. The permanent legislative staff, often an important counterweight to precipitous decision making, became marginalized. New members coming into the legislature were ill informed about the kinds of problems that long-term staff can help the legislature avoid and, given their short-time horizons, were not that interested in them. With most of the legislative "bull gators" who could mount opposition to a governor gone, lobbyists and the executive office were the real winners in this environment and term limits gave Bush additional influence over the legislature.

Economic Conditions

Substantial political science research suggests that the condition of a state's economy affects political activities within that state (Crew and Weiher, 1996; Crew et al., 2002). "Inflation, unemployment, fluctuations in personal income [and state revenues] and other economic conditions create demands for action" (Crew and Hill, 1995: 32) and establish parameters for governmental activities. The governors of Florida are particularly vulnerable to changes in economic conditions because of the state's reliance on a sales tax as the primary method of revenue. This tax system is designed to pass the burden of paying for state services onto tourists and lower income citizens and it "produces a revenue stream that is more volatile than the economy as a whole" (Grizzle, 1994: 211). Thus, while Florida's population growth has been close to three times the national average for the past several decades, its per-capita spending and revenue collection has been very erratic. This situation often forces governors to modify, or even change, their policy focus from year to year.

Jeb Bush took office at a point when the state's economy was in the best condition in its history and it continued to prosper through his term. Buoyed by the strength of the nation's economy, sporting record levels of unemployment, and profiting from a multi-billion-dollar settlement with the tobacco industry that had been engineered by his predecessor, Lawton Chiles, the incoming governor had a budget surplus of roughly $3 billion (Ormond, 2004) and an economic cushion that no previous governor could match. Further, consumer confidence when Bush took office was higher than it had been since July 1989, and the average consumer confidence during his first year in office was higher than the average from any year in the previous decade. Finally, and perhaps most importantly for his administration, Governor Bush profited throughout the entire eight years of his term from a long-running housing boom that powered an economy described later as a "windfall." "We were in a bubble," said the director of the Office of Economic and Demographic Research, the staff unit that estimates state revenue and expenditures for the legislature (Cotterell, August 2, 2007).

Summary

Jeb Bush came to the office of governor of Florida in what was arguably the most favorable set of political and economic circumstances for a governor in the state's political history. As one political commentator said, "things were just aligned" (Stockfish, 2007). Opposition to the long-dominant Democratic regime was evident in the election returns for governor, other executive branch officials, and the state legislature, and although these returns did not convey a specific mandate as to future direction, they did reflect widespread public agreement that something different would be welcome. For the first time in modern state history and for the first time in the twentieth century in the South, a Republican governor was elected concurrently with Republican majorities in both houses of the state legislature. In addition, and perhaps most important, these majorities were highly unified around a rigid conservative governmental philosophy that had been struggling for influence for several decades. Furthermore, the state's economy was in robust condition throughout the Bush administration.

These conditions obviously enhanced the governor's chances for political success. But it is worth noting that the "commanding authority [governor's] wielded at these moments does not automatically translate into more effective solutions to the substantive problems that gave rise to the crises of legitimacy in the first place" (Skowronek, 37).

Chapter 3

Promoting a Revolution

Introduction

In pursuit of their objectives, governors, like other public officials, are guided by political philosophies or theories of government. Some of these theories are more rigid or consistent than are others and governors vary in the extent to which they adhere to the tenets involved. Nevertheless, all elected officials take guidance from some set of ideas about the role government should play in the society and about how it should carry out its responsibilities. In his second campaign for governor of Florida, Jeb Bush changed both the message and the rhetoric he had employed in his loss to Lawton Chiles, downplaying his extremist views and his evangelical style. But he did not abandon his original, conservative vision for Florida's state government. Thus, once elected, the governor adopted a conservative and rigidly theoretical view of government that challenged the underlying principles upon which much public policy in Florida over the previous decades had been based. Arguing that adoption of this new governmental theory would revolutionize social and political conditions in Florida, Bush moved aggressively to put it and the associated policies in place.

Governing Philosophy and Leadership Style

The theory of government brought to Florida by Governor Bush's victory had emerged over the previous twenty years from organizations such as the American Enterprise Institute, the Manhattan Institute, the Reason Foundation, the Bradley Foundation, and others. Described as "neoconservatism" or "movement conservatism," the theory challenged the fundamental underpinnings of decades of economic, domestic, and foreign policy. (For an insightful analysis of the rise of this movement, see Saloma 1984.)

The theory drew inspiration from the writings of economists Friedrich von Hayek and Milton Friedman, relied heavily on a "theology" of free markets, and combined both social and economic principles. On the economic side the theory called for limiting the size and scope of government because this yielded lower taxes and, theoretically, led to long-term growth because fewer of society's resources were siphoned off to uses that did not contribute to the growth of capital. On the social side, the theory hypothesized that lower taxes and smaller government produced more individual liberty and fostered a climate of personal responsibility and self-determination. According to the theory, these attitudes reduce long-run demand for societal support for health care, retirement security, and other social programs, thus reducing demand for larger government and more taxes. The theory reflected an individualistic, anticommunitarian view of social organization that cut along economic lines.

The theory of conservatism adopted by Jeb Bush was relentlessly consistent and carried with it an almost canonical list of specific agenda items to be checked off, many of which were viewed as moral absolutes rather than options open to debate and alteration. They included tax reduction, fiscal restraint, reduction in the size and scope of government, industrial and environmental deregulation, and support for private property rights. The theory also promoted a variety of free-market strategies in government; school vouchers, charter schools, faith-based initiatives, tort reform, privatization of public services, tradable pollution rights, and deep reductions in antipoverty spending. Finally, "movement" conservatism contained elements of a particular social philosophy and expressed skepticism about multiculturalism and opposition to abortion, gay rights, and gun control.

Governor Bush took great pride in his reputation as a "wonk and nerd" who read widely and thought critically about both public issues and alternative ways of addressing public problems, and his staff claimed that he was usually the best-informed person among the participants in any discussions about issues of public policy that he faced. However, in his efforts to change Florida government, he minimized these critical capacities in favor of conservative governmental philosophy, and adopted it as his fundamental guide. In a November 2007 interview with Peter Robinson of the Hoover Institute, Bush conceded that his governmental strategy was created by "stealing ideas" from the institute and similar organizations and developing strategies to implement them (Robinson, 2007). He also said that "by trial and error, we've tried just about everything the Manhattan Institute has been advocating or talking about over this last generation" (Bush 2007).The governor's commitment to conservative theory and philosophy was evident in the selection of the problems he took as his priorities and in the solutions he employed as remedies. Furthermore, while very little, if any, evidence was provided over the course of his administration to show that these ideas about government and public policy were effective, his support for them was unflagging. He was committed to them as matters of principle. He was, in the words of both his supporters and others, a "true believer" (Smith, 2007; Gailey, 2005), willing to use all the institutions of government aggressively to accomplish conservative goals.

Leadership Style

Governor Bush married his philosophy of government to an "activist-visionary" theory of gubernatorial leadership that had been promoted by governmental reformers in the middle of the twentieth century. This theory, referred to as the "strong governor" or the "self-reliant" executive, cast the governor as the central player in state politics, with responsibility for identifying and resolving issues of public policy, for managing and controlling state government, and for directing its policymaking activities. Bush adopted this theory wholeheartedly, emphasizing big-picture priority-setting over careful administration—decisiveness over inclusiveness. He expropriated the language of 1990s management gurus James Collins and Jerry Porras and referred to his ambitions as BHAGS or "Big Hairy Audacious Goals." To pursue these goals, he adopted a confrontational posture that earned him the nickname "King Jeb" (Kleindienst 2007), and his aggressive pursuit of his objectives suggested that he saw political leadership as an individual responsibility rather than an interactive process between himself, other public officials, and the public.

In his day-to-day pursuit of his agenda, Governor Bush employed a top-down, command-and-control managerial style that by his own admission was highly opinionated and that limited input from his advisors (Fineout, 2005; Jones, 2005; Cotterell, 2006). In fact, he had no advisors in the conventional sense; people close to his age or older, more experienced or more able who could speak to him as a peer. Instead, he relied on what was described as "some real low-voltage hacks" (Hiaasen, 2006), a revolving group of young staffers, many recently graduated from college or law school, who were awe struck by the governor and unlikely and unable to challenge his actions. Motivated by his political philosophy and keeping his own counsel, the governor identified what *he* viewed as the important problems facing the state of Florida and proposed specific strategies to resolve them. In pursuing this strategy, he demonstrated a penchant for exceptionally hard work, but also developed a reputation for a "dictatorial style and reluctance to take advice" (March, 2005) and an "unwillingness to listen to people who disagree with him" (Howard 2006). In essence he operated with a constituency of one; his own conscience.

The governor took pride in his assertive style and claimed to "have a sense of urgency that others don't share" (Rushing, 2006). Gubernatorial scholar Richard Scher (Scher, 1994) has identified a number of energetic administrations in Florida—Democrats Bob Graham, Reubin Askew, and LeRoy Collins, and Republican Claude Kirk, the self-styled "tree shaking son-of-a-bitch" (Simons, 1968: 12) who served in the 1960s—but Governor Bush suggested that it was *he* who had "shown that governors can be activists" (Rushing, 2006).

Policy Priorities and Governing Strategies

In his campaigns for Governor of Florida, Jeb Bush focused primarily on the issues that had been publicized and promoted by the conservative thinkers from whom he drew much of his inspiration. These issues were governmental downsizing, reform of both public education and the social welfare system, tax reduction and public finance, crime and criminal justice, and economic development. Given this focus, many issues that were arguably more important to the state were downplayed; issues such as transportation gridlock, soaring property insurance and property tax rates, heavy dependence on oil as an energy source, sprawling development, and the need for mass transit in heavily urbanized Central and South Florida. Conservative philosophy drove Bush to focus as much on the way in which his administration would run state government as on what he would do substantively. And it was in running state government that Bush promised a revolution.

In order to manage the affairs of state, governors employ both financial and organizational/managerial strategies. Their financial strategies involve choices about whether and how to generate revenue, and about the level of monetary resources devoted to particular policy arenas. Alternatively, and usually in conjunction with their financial strategies, governors also propose changes in law and utilize organizational and/or managerial tactics to bring about new requirements or new directions in the delivery of public services.

Declaring that "we must learn from the examples of other states that have tried [and failed] to tax and spend their way to prosperity" (*State of the State Address,* 2003) Governor Bush followed conservative theories and downplayed the importance of financial resources to the resolution of public problems, concentrating instead on changing law and on organizational and managerial reforms in order to achieve his objectives. The following paragraphs describe the primary features of the Bush policy agenda, both fiscal and otherwise, in some detail. In subsequent chapters I analyze the implementation of these policies and describe their policy effect.

Fiscal Policy

A fundamental component of the conservative political philosophy that Governor Bush adopted as his guide was to drastically limit the government's ability to raise and spend money. To accomplish this goal required the use of a variety of strategies.

Restricting Growth in Spending

An overarching principle for governmental conservatives and for Jeb Bush was restraint in state spending. For Governor Bush this principle was defined as holding spending growth below the growth of personal income in the state. As the governor said, "the system is geared toward spending money. That's what this whole process is about. I just don't think government, as a matter of course, should grow faster than people's ability to pay for it." Thus, keeping state spending below growth in income became a primary policy goal for the governor and a standard against which he measured his success. Bush pursued this goal relentlessly, using a wide variety of strategies: pressure on agency heads to limit annual budgetary requests; arbitrarily capping the monies that could be raised from service fees that were to be used for dedicated purposes such as affordable housing; and simply refusing to fund requests from agency heads for particular services, for example, beds for county jail inmates who had severe mental illnesses.

Tax Reduction

A second principle was intimately intertwined with slowing spending growth. The principle was that Florida state government could be run without an increase in state taxes, indeed the state would benefit from having fewer *sources* of revenue than had been the case in previous administrations. The rationale underlying this premise went back to the economist Arthur Laffer's famous curve showing the relationship between tax rates and tax collection—a relationship that the governor's father once called "voodoo economics." Governor Bush's argument was that reducing taxes would stimulate the economy and produce greater revenues within a smaller tax structure, or as he put it "tax cuts generate consumer spending, which generates job growth, which generates more success among Floridians" (*Orlando Sentinel,* 2006; *St. Petersburg Times,* 2001). Although this argument had been undermined by, among others, President Bush's Council of Economic Advisors (Economic Report to the President 2003; Mankiv and Weinzierl, 2004), Governor Bush used it throughout his administration, even in the face of declining state revenues and increasing budget deficits.

Only nine states bore a tax burden lower than that in Florida when Jeb Bush came to the office of governor (Tax Foundation, 1995). Furthermore, in the seven years prior to Governor Bush's ascension to office, surveys conducted by researchers at Florida State University showed that more than 70 percent of Floridians deemed the level of the state's primary tax, the sales tax, to be neither too high nor too low, but "about right" (Florida State University, 1999). Not surprisingly, therefore, there was no general public clamor for tax relief in the state, and during Bush's tenure as governor this issue never ranked in the top ten on the list of the "most important issues facing the state" compiled yearly in Florida State University's *Annual Policy Survey.* Indeed, in a poll taken just months prior to his first call for tax relief, fewer than 1 percent (.4 percent) of Florida's citizens thought that taxes were "out of hand" and needed reduction (*Annual Policy Survey,* 1999). Nevertheless, Governor Bush made tax reduction the centerpiece of his administration and continued to pursue this goal throughout his time in office.

Since Florida has no state income tax, Bush's plan for tax relief focused on rebating taxes on utilities, cutting property and business taxes, reducing the unemployment tax, providing sales tax holidays, and eliminating entirely the state intangibles tax, Florida's only tax based on ability to pay. Although there *was* concern from some quarters about the fairness of the state's primary revenue source, the sales tax (Florida TaxWatch, 2002). Bush resisted calls for its modernization through elimination of loopholes that allowed many activities and products (ostrich feed, tanning salons, and others) to avoid paying the tax (*St. Petersburg Times,* 2002). Instead he proposed to add new activities and materials to the list of exempted items (James, 2004).

Growing the Economy

The tax and spending policies described above were fundamental to Governor Bush's effort to improve Florida's economy, which, along with improvement of public education, was the top priority of his administration. But the governor did not depend exclusively on these indirect efforts to grow the state's economy. Instead, he promoted business development relentlessly, claiming to have made at least one business location telephone call per day, traveling widely both inside and outside the United States to promote the state's economy and touting the state's "business friendly" climate at every opportunity. Like other governors, he employed multiple economic development strategies that were based on a variety of economic theories: infrastructure development, locational incentives and entrepreneurial activities. The rhetoric surrounding Bush's business development actions focused on the importance of creating a more diverse economy in a state that had traditionally relied very heavily on the low-paid, low-skill tourist and leisure industries.

The infrastructure development approach draws upon the economic theories of Maynard Keynes and emphasizes the construction and maintenance of a state's physical infrastructure such as roads and highways, seaports, waste treatment facilities, and so forth to encourage and support economic growth. Jeb's budget routinely supported increased expenditures for these activities and he claims that his 2005–2006 transportation budget represented a 96 percent increase over his first budget, eight years prior (Florida Department of Transportation 2006). These funds supported efforts to construct new state road lanes, to reconstruct and rehabilitate existing lanes, to replace bridges for the state, and to support individual projects at the county level. These activities were typically justified as necessary in order to diversify the state's economy and to enhance economic prosperity. His 2006–2007 budget included a "25% increase in the state's capital outlay budget" that went to education infrastructure, environmental infrastructure, transportation, and emergency-preparedness infrastructure.

The governor also adopted a locational incentive strategy when trying to bolster economic activity in the state. Using a mixture of tactics, the state promoted the use of low-interest financing for businesses, tax exemptions, subsidized employee training, and other activities that promote the creation of a "positive business climate." By far the largest of these efforts took place in 2003 with the use of $310 million from one-time federal economic stimulus monies to entice Scripps Research Institute of Lo Jolla, California, to create a major biomedical research facility in south Florida. This amount was combined with $200 million in local subsidies. Calling the Scripps investment a "seminal moment" in Florida history, Bush claimed that it would create 6,500 jobs, generate about $1.6 billion in additional income to Floridians, and boost the state's gross domestic product by $3.2 billion in the succeeding fifteen years.

Two other similar organizations, the Torrey Pines Institute for Molecular Studies and the Burnham Institute for Medical Research, were also lured to the state with the investment of $80 million and $300 million, respectively, in land and tax incentives. When combined with the Scripps project, the state hoped to create biotechnology hubs similar to that in San Diego where Scripps, the Salk Institute, and the University of California at San Diego are the driving forces. While state university officials felt that the money would have been better spent augmenting already established research facilities at the University of Florida, the University of Central Florida, and the University of South Florida, the governor went for a more dramatic strategy and claimed that an additional forty thousand jobs were to be created as a result of the industry clustering expected to take place around the new facilities.

In addition to trying to influence the *location* of businesses, Governor Bush also sought to enhance existing markets and to encourage new economic ventures, in effect to use public resources to become an entrepreneur. By some measures the entrepreneurial spirit in Florida was not high—*MoneyTree* reported in 2005 that Florida companies had collected just 0.5 percent of $5.8 billion of investment dollars distributed nationally—but Bush pressed forward in 2006 with a recommendation for a publicly supported $75 million venture capital fund designed to attract "start-up" companies to the state. This proposal, dubbed the Florida Capital Formation Program, was proposed in his last budget recommendation.

The governor also utilized $55 million in state funds to support activities aimed at strengthening Florida's commercial space industry located at the Kennedy Space Center and to luring new activities to the state that would integrate space, aeronautics, and aviation technology. Oddly, while the space industry had been a pillar of the state's economy for more than fifty years, Governor Bush had to be pushed into this venture and committed the funds only after business leaders in the state criticized him for ignoring "a changing landscape and charting a course of neglect" (Floridatoday.com., 2006). Even then the amount of money dedicated was judged to be inadequate. As a result of the governor's reticence, the state of New Mexico was able to cut into Florida's dominance in this area. Newspapers in New Mexico were jubilant at Florida's lack of interest in and support for this industry, saying that "at every turn, Bush, lawmakers and state officials have been out-thought, out-maneuvered and out-hustled on this issue, in what amounts to an inexcusable failure" (Homans, 2006).

Changing the Organization and Management of Florida State Government

The primary focus of Governor Bush's attempts to deal with the problems that he thought the state of Florida faced was organizational and managerial change. Revenue was obviously required to finance governmental activities, but the governor made it clear that "throwing money" at public problems was not the way to solve them. Thus, most of his major initiatives focused on changing both the structure of Florida state government and its managerial policies.

Downsizing, Privatizing, and Contracting Out Public Services

Like other governmental conservatives, Governor Bush disliked and distrusted government and promoted the idea that smaller government—combined with more privatizing of governmental services—was more efficient government. He argued that "the most efficient, effective and dynamic government is one composed primarily of policymakers, procurement experts and contract managers" (Bush, 2007). He expressed his general philosophy about government in his 2003 Inaugural Address when he stated that "there would be no greater tribute to our maturity as a society than if we make these [governmental] buildings around us empty of workers…monuments to a time when government played a larger role than it deserved or could adequately fill."

With this philosophy guiding his actions, Bush worked to diminish the credibility of government in Florida, to reduce its size and scope, and to make it more accountable to political overseers. In pursuit of his reduction in government goals Governor Bush first reformed, or "modernized," Florida's personnel system and then employed an array of free-market solutions proposed by conservative think tanks to reduce the role of government. These included "downsizing," contracting out, and privatization.

Modernization and Downsizing

The governor's personnel modernization effort was initiated in his first year in office and took the form of a fundamental change in the underlying basis for public employment in Florida. Following up on the recommendation he had made when he served as secretary of commerce under Governor Bob Martinez, Bush proposed legislation that changed the Florida personnel system from one in which employment was based primarily on merit to one in which more state employees served at the will of their employer. When this legislation was adopted, the governor removed a large number of state employees from the "protected" service and moved them into select exempt or "fire-at-will" job categories. This statutory change also made possible two additional personnel strategies that furthered the governor's goals of diminishing the role of government in Florida.

The first of these strategies was simple reduction in the number of persons employed in state government. With the flexibility to eliminate and move employees around within an agency, the governor issued budget directives to state agency heads requiring that staff reductions of 25 percent be submitted to him during the preparation of the budget. Based on these recommendations, employee reductions were begun throughout Florida state government and Florida's already small government workforce was made even smaller. The recommendations also became the foundation for decisions to leave unfilled many vacant positions as they emerged.

Privatizing

The second strategy, which became the signature of his administration, was to privatize and contract out large segments of Florida state government, thus reducing the size of the state's workforce. Bush's efforts extended far beyond the traditional areas of privatization and into the areas of criminal defense, provision of welfare benefits, child protection services, public education, staffing of nursing homes for veterans, and Medicaid. Under Governor Bush, privatization of public services was thought to have been employed in Florida more broadly than in any other state in the nation. These efforts are described in some detail later in this chapter, and in chapter 7 I assess the impact of this strategy.

Reforming Public Education: Accountability and Choice

When Jeb Bush came to the office of governor of Florida, the state's secondary school system, by many measures, was among the weakest in the nation. Over the course of his administration, Governor Bush made improving this system his number-one substantive priority, and he devoted sustained attention to bolstering its quality. His focus on the problem continued into the last year of his administration and beyond, and he claims to have sparked a "renaissance" in public education in Florida.[1]

The problems of public education in the state were varied—underpaid teachers, poor facilities, large, overcrowded schools and classes, and large numbers of people teaching out of field. The Bush remedies, however, focused almost entirely on two broad administrative changes promoted by conservative theory. These changes were designed to improve *accountability* for student performance and to provide students and parents more *choice* in selecting the school they were to attend. He also lobbied throughout the full course of his administration *against* a specific effort to reduce class sizes.

Educational Accountability

The centerpieces of the Bush effort to improve school quality in Florida were "accountability" and "school choice." Saying that "we believe in educational choice as a matter of principle and we believe in school account-ability as a matter of principle as well" (Hoover Institution, 2003), the governor adopted multiple strategies to put these concepts into place.

The governor's program of accountability was introduced in Bush's first State of the State Address in 1999 and labeled the "A+ Plan for Education." The plan called for "accountability for school performance, teacher training, school improvement, school recognition, and assessment of the performance of teachers and school administrators" (Floridians for School Choice, 1995). The central feature of the Bush proposal was the innovative use of the standardized tests on math, English, and reading that had been in place in Florida since the 1970s. In the Bush proposal, the results of these tests, administered to children, were aggregated in order to assign grades to *schools*, and thus to hold schools accountable. The school grades were then used as a basis for the award of vouchers to those students who were enrolled in "F" schools. In this manner, accountability and choice were joined.

School Choice

Following the neoconservative principle that policy positions are moral absolutes rather than options that might be open to debate, Governor Bush supported school choice both as a "moral imperative" and "because the competition of choice drives positive change in our public schools" (Bush, March 7, 2006). His plan to provide this choice in Florida was implemented through a series of voucher programs and with charter schools.

The first and most prominent of the voucher programs, the Opportunity Voucher, was the first statewide school voucher program in the nation and was a fundamental element of the A+ Plan. Beginning in 1973, students in Florida's public schools had been tested on a variety of subjects, with the results of the tests used for diagnostic purposes. Governor Bush's innovation was to aggregate the results of these tests, known as the Florida Comprehensive Assessment Test (FCAT), to the school level, publicize their results with a grade, and utilize the grades as the basis for a voucher program that permitted students to leave "failing" schools and to go to other public or private schools, simultaneously achieving both accountability and choice.

In the Bush plan, schools were awarded grades from A to F and students who attend a school awarded a grade of F in any two out of four consecutive years were offered vouchers (or "opportunity scholarships" as Bush called them) to be used to attend another, "better," school of their choice, including private and religious schools. The vouchers were paid for with the per-pupil expenditure of funds provided by the state for each student in the school district in which the "F" school was located. These funds traveled with any students who chose to use the voucher to the new school in which the student enrolled. During the school year 2004–2005 alone this program shifted over $3 million of public money into the state's private schools.

The Opportunity Voucher Program was subsequently augmented by three others: one for children with learning disabilities (McKay Vouchers); a second for low-income families, the Corporate Income Tax Credit Voucher Program; and the third for pre-kindergarten students. The Corporate Income Tax Credit Voucher Program was supported by tax-free contributions from corporate sponsors.

Bush also promoted another "choice" mechanism as a tool to improve public education in the state: charter schools. Charter schools could be created outside the regular public school system by groups of individuals or by governmental or private or nonprofit organizations. Existing public schools were also permitted to transfer from regular to charter status. Once created, these schools were freed from many of the requirements and standards of the regular public school system.

Although less highly publicized than the voucher programs, this system found great favor in Florida. Through his Foundation for Florida's Future, which was created to keep him politically visible after his defeat by Lawton Chiles, Bush sponsored one of the first charter schools in the state, and his support for them remained consistent throughout his administration. By the end of his term he had succeeded in creating an entirely separate system of such schools, one with its own independent governing board appointed by the State Board of Education upon recommendations from the governor, senate president, and house speaker. In 2006, 206 charter schools in Florida serving ninety-two thousand students were operating in this system. While these schools also drew criticism from opponents whose political ideologies clashed with that of the governor, they were not subjected to the visceral hostility that accompanied the debate over vouchers.

Additional Educational Strategies

It was not until the final year of his tenure as governor in 2006 that Governor Bush proposed educational reforms that did not focus on school choice or the rewards and sanctions approach underlying his school accountability program. Dubbed the A++ plan, his final strategy required high school students to take additional courses in mathematics and to declare an academic major like college students. The academic major portion of the law required every ninth grader to select a major in one of more than four hundred approved subjects, ranging from world cultures to fashion design to family and consumer services. The proposal also required middle-school students to pass three years of math, science, social studies, and English before moving on to high school. Although Democrats in the state legislature opposed the plan on the grounds that it used the FCAT as the barometer for determining whether or not schools were improving, this proposal suggested that the governor's thinking about how to improve the quality of public education in the state had evolved beyond strategies based exclusively on rewards and sanctions for academic performance and on to efforts that focused on academic substance. Nevertheless, a spokeswoman for the Association of American Colleges and Universities called the program a "colossally bad idea" (Hu, 2006).

Reforming the Social Services System: More Privatization

From the earliest days of his entry into Florida politics, Jeb Bush took an ambiguous stance toward the state's social services system. Like other conservatives, he roundly denounced the cash assistance portion of the state's public welfare program and joined enthusiastically in the reforms that came about as a result of the federal government's passage in 1996 of the Personal Responsibility Act. However in many of his State of the State addresses, Governor Bush also made reference to his concern for what he called the state's "most vulnerable citizens"—seniors needing community care, children needing health insurance and foster care, and individuals with developmental disabilities—and pledged attention to their problems.

As was the case in his efforts to reform other areas of public policy, Bush relied most heavily on legislative and managerial changes to accomplish his social policy goals. And the managerial changes he proposed were based on conservative governmental theories; taking the responsibility for providing social services away from state government and entrusting it to private or religious or nonprofit community-based organizations through privatization and contracting out. He privatized a majority of the public welfare system, the state's child protective services program, and the developmental disabilities program. He also initiated a similar effort with regard to the state's Medicaid program. Thus, over the course of the Bush administration, the role that Florida state government played in providing a social safety net for its citizens was substantially altered and diminished.

The Faith-Based Initiative
In the social policy arena, Governor Bush embraced with great enthusiasm the use of religious organizations to take over activities traditionally provided by governmental agencies. Florida has a long history of working with religious-based organizations such as Catholic Charities, Lutheran Social Services, and the Salvation Army to provide social services to disadvantaged citizens in Florida and Bush's enthusiasm for enlarging the pool of such entities was viewed by some simply as an effort to pander to religious conservatives in the state.

To pursue his strategy, Bush created in the Office of the Governor a Faith-Based Advisory Board designed to mobilize additional religious organizations and to encourage their participation in his efforts to make nongovernmental organizations the primary mechanism for delivering public services in Florida. The board also provided direction to state agencies in their use of religious organizations in their work and technical assistance to the organizations in securing grant funds from both the federal and state governments. Bush also required state agencies to create official positions—called faith-based liaisons—to help eliminate internal obstacles to the receipt of funding for religious groups.

The governor felt that groups and organizations recruited through these mechanisms could be used to support a variety of governmental activities: delinquency prevention programs for youth, services for children with disabilities, AIDS prevention programs in inner cities, and other such activities. Programs in state prisons were also to be managed by faith-based organizations.

Privatization and Developmental Disabilities

The election of Jeb Bush in 1998 is viewed by many within the social services community in Florida as a watershed event for the program that provided services to Floridians who suffered disabilities such as autism, cerebral palsy, and mental retardation. In Bush's first year as governor, the budget for this program was $216.5 million of state and federal tax dollars. Within two years the total jumped to $494.2 million and by the end of the Bush term the figure was about $950 million. To some extent, these increases undermine the argument that Governor Bush did not want to spend taxpayer money on social services.

As is the case in other states, the developmental disabilities program in Florida is designed to help the affected individuals stay out of institutions, and most of the money expended on the developmentally disabled in Florida is spent on "home and community services" which are intended to help people live with their families or in small facilities such as group homes. In reforming this system, the governor and the legislature duplicated their strategy in other areas of public policy and stipulated that "private businesses, not-for-profit corporations and other organizations capable of providing needed services to clients in a cost-efficient manner shall be given preference in lieu of services directly provided by state agencies" (Florida OPPAGA, 2000: iii). Thus, over the course of the Bush administration private contractors of varying kinds were enlisted in efforts to provide support services to over thirty-two thousand people in Florida who needed help in maintaining a modest amount of independence in their daily lives. In a later chapter, I review the effects of this privatization effort.

Privatizing the Welfare System

The food stamp, Medicaid, and cash assistance programs managed by the Florida Department of Children and Families and by the Agency for Health Care Administration were high-profile social services programs. They were the focus of the welfare reform movement begun nationally in 1996 and that Bush supported so aggressively during his campaign against Lawton Chiles and once he became governor. Saying that taking welfare should be more shameful than working and that the state should limit welfare benefits, Bush embarked on a massive effort to reform both the content of these programs and the manner in which they were administered.

The agency responsible for administering Florida's programs of social services was transformed over the course of Governor Bush's administration from an organization whose own employees provided child welfare, mental health, substance abuse, and economic self-sufficiency programs such as food stamps, Medicaid, and cash assistance to one that oversaw the provision of these services through contracts with private or nonprofit entities. Although the impetus for privatization in the social welfare arena began prior to Jeb's ascendancy to the office of governor, Bush quickly embraced the concept and moved perhaps farther than any governor in the nation toward privatizing the state's social services system and shifting responsibility for delivery of these services away from a state agency.

Governor Bush placed control over welfare policymaking in a highly decentralized governance system—a group of twenty-four public/private partnerships called Regional Workforce Boards. These boards were composed of representatives of private, public, and not-for-profit organizations that used public funds to contract with case management providers who were responsible for helping welfare beneficiaries find employment and for assisting them in accessing related services such as child care, transportation, and the like. The case management providers were private companies and nonprofit organiza-tions. The Florida Department of Children and Families simply received the federal TANF bloc grant that supports the state's welfare program and main-tained responsibility for eligibility determination regarding cash assistance, food stamps, and Medicaid (Crew and Davis, 2000). As of January 2006, the Department of Children and Families had 1,166 contracts with a total (multiyear) value of approximately $3.69 billion (Florida OPPAGA, 2006). In that year, the majority of the department's budget was used to pay private contractors for program services or for direct payment to clients.

Reflecting his skepticism about government, the governor had hoped to remove the Department of Children and Families entirely from direct contact with applicants for welfare benefits and made an effort to turn over to the private sector the job of determining eligibility for welfare assistance. When this effort was rebuffed by the federal government, he initiated an effort to automate this process and to require applications for the services involved to be made electronically. Underscoring his position that welfare cash assistance should be the last alternative for Floridians facing economic privation, the governor also pushed for some of the nation's most stringent laws enforcing compliance with the rules related to receipt of cash benefits.

Through the actions described above, Governor Bush created a new public welfare delivery system in Florida, took the state's government almost entirely out of the business of providing a social services safety net to its most vulnerable citizens, and turned the provision of these services over to the private and the nonprofit sectors.

Child Protective Services

One of the biggest crises of Jeb Bush's administration took place in 2000 and 2001 with the disappearance of a child from the state's child welfare system. This widely publicized case provided an impetus for Bush to intensify an effort begun under his predecessor, Lawton Chiles, to reform the state's system of foster care and related services to abandoned and neglected children. In August

2001, Jeb Bush asserted that "Florida is leading the nation in the quiet revolution of child welfare reform" (Office of the Governor, 2001). Part of the revolution that Bush referred to was a doubling of funding for child welfare services over the first two years of the Bush administration. But the larger revolution was another of conservativism's objectives: privatization of the state's child welfare system.

In 1999 the Florida legislature responded to the urging of Governor Bush and enacted legislation that took from the Department of Children and Families (DCF) responsibility for providing foster care and related services to abandoned or neglected children and turned it over to a group of private and nonprofit organizations under the supervision of "Community Alliances" that served the state's sixty-seven counties. Like the Regional Workforce Boards described above, the Community Alliances, represented by a nongovernmental "lead agency," hired private and nonprofit organizations as subcontractors to provide the services involved.

The theory upon which Bush made this shift was that the organizational structure of a state government agency was too rigid to adapt to the huge variety of circumstances and needs faced by at-risk children throughout Florida; that DCF needed the assistance of multiple community groups in providing safe and permanent homes for vulnerable children; and that the agency did not have the leverage to influence the performance of all the necessary groups. These problems were to be resolved by providing funds directly to a group of community-based organizations who would take responsibility for the provision of care for those children who were victimized by abuse, neglect, and/or abandonment. The groups included private companies, nonprofit organizations, and faith-based groups.

Medicaid Reform

The Medicaid program is one of the largest social programs, indeed one of the largest programs of any kind, in Florida and in any other state. In Florida in 2005, the program helped insure 2.3 million people, over 1 million of them children, paid for health care for much of the state's blind and disabled population, and covered the costs of two-thirds of nursing home care in the state. The costs involved in the program in 2005 were about 18 percent of the state's budget. Financing and managing Medicaid is a serious problem for all states and is the subject of heated debate throughout the nation. Throughout his administration Governor Bush expressed great concern about the financial effect of the Medicaid program, and his early interventions were policies to identify and root out waste, fraud, and abuse within the system and to curtail the costs of drugs utilized in the program. In 2005, however, he moved beyond these efforts and offered an initiative that took much of the decision making about the scope and extent of services to eligible beneficiaries away from government and moved it into private hands. The underlying theory was that "turning the program over to the private sector would save the state money and improve access (and quality) through competition" (Weissert and Weissert, 371).

Announced in his next to last State of the State Address, Governor Bush proposed an overhaul of Medicaid that reflected another major philosophical shift in the state's program, moving it from a "defined benefit" to a "defined contribution" basis. The proposal had two significant features. The first was acceptance of a lump sum of money from the federal government to fund the state's program in exchange for flexibility to determine eligibility and benefit levels. The state took on the responsibility for meeting the health-care needs of its residents regardless of whether the costs to do so exceeded the amount negotiated between Tallahassee and Washington. If costs exceeded negotiated levels, Florida would be able to use the flexibility granted by the federal government to impose benefit restrictions and cap program enrollment in order to contain costs. This provision was designed to permit the state to more accurately predict and control its costs.

The second major change in the governor's reform was to provide each person enrolled in the program with a risk-adjusted allotment of funds (a voucher, which the state called a premium) with which to purchase health care. Using this voucher, enrollees were required to purchase a health-care plan from a participating managed-care organization. The only requirement for these plans was that the benefit package offered had to be actuarially equivalent to the value of the existing Medicaid benefit package for an average member of the population. Once an adult reached a yet-to-be-determined annual maximum benefit limit, he or she is responsible for all health costs.

To entice insurance companies to insure some of Florida's sickest and poorest citizens, the state proposed to cap Medicaid benefits, as would private insurance companies, and set a ceiling on spending for each recipient. Managed-care companies and other health-care networks would design alternative health plans that Medicaid patients would use. Basic services and emergency services then covered by the state's mandatory and optional Medicaid programs would be automatically covered. Beyond that, different managed-care networks could attract patients by offering additional services. However, patients would have a choice only among managed-care plans and no longer have access to traditional fee-for-service health care. In addition, health-care scholars at Florida State University suggested that "oversight and efforts to assure accountability from the private entities that would be providing this key health care service to a vulnerable population seemed to be missing" (Weissert and Weissert, 372).

The Bush strategy for Medicare reform represented a substantial break from existing governmental theory and the governor assumed that the conservative premises that formed the basis of his new program were valid. Reflecting his aggressive leadership style, he proposed this replacement for one of the state's largest and most complicated programs as a single package, to be adopted and implemented throughout the state simultaneously.

As public hearings on this reform began around the state, questions were raised about the Herculean task involved in such a change and, for one of the few times during the Bush reign, the governor's Republican allies in the legislature balked. They rejected full-scale implementation, calling instead for "small pilot projects, feasibility studies and smaller money-saving plans that could save a couple of hundred million dollars, not the billions, as Bush wanted" (Ulferts, 2005). In the end, the legislature authorized the governor's managed-care Medicaid program as a pilot project in only two of the state's social service regions, required that any expansion in the program be contingent on review and approval by the legislature, and reserved the right to approve implementation of any waiver of existing Medicaid rules negotiated between Florida and Washington. In October of 2005, Florida was granted the first Medicare waiver of this sort in the nation. Bush called the state legislature into special session and was given authority to initiate this reform. It was implemented in 2006.

Protecting Florida's Environment

In his first campaign for governor, Bush did not have a positive environmental platform. Instead, he identified Florida's highly regarded land-conservation program, Florida Forever, as a likely target for budget cuts and also criticized the state's development regulations (*St. Petersburg Times*, 1999, July 10) However, in the aftermath of his defeat by Lawton Chiles he "greened considerably" (Barnett 2007, 82), and in his second campaign for governor and throughout his administration Governor Bush proclaimed his commitment to preserving Florida's natural environment. In his first State of the State Address he said that "there is no more valuable legacy we could leave [to Florida families] than a clean and beautiful natural world."

The governor's activities in the environmental arena were framed by an inherent tension between growing the state's economy and conserving the natural resources that are the basis of the economy. Bush's policies to resolve this tension fell into two categories: (1) conservation of existing natural resources through the purchase and/or protection of land and other natural resources; and (2) efforts to influence the impact that the state's population growth has on these resources.

In the conservation arena, the governor strayed from strict adherence to conservative doctrine and supported policies that were based on a variety of economic and governmental theories. In fact, some were "big government" efforts of the kind generally derided by conservatives. These included support for substantial state funding of Florida Forever, the state's program for purchasing environmentally sensitive lands, and for state and federal financing for the renewal of the Everglades. He also initially supported government regulation to prevent offshore oil drilling. There was wide agreement among Floridians about the value of these resources, and his actions found support from large majorities of the citizens of Florida.

Florida was one of the first states in the nation to address "growth-management" problems and in 1985 adopted one of the country's first statewide growth-management policies. This system gradually became ineffectual in the face of huge population growth and relentless pressure to water down restrictions on growth in order to maximize economic development. As described above, Governor Bush was sensitized to this problem in his first campaign, and in 1998 he ran on a promise to reform the policies that guided population growth in Florida and to support strong state efforts on their behalf.

Once elected, however, the governor began to vacillate as he became enmeshed in the long running fight over how much growth should be permitted in Florida. On one side of the controversy was the development community, which was a major constituency of Bush and the Republican Party. This constituency pushed efforts to grow the economy through land development. On the other side, the environmental constituency protested that too much growth was changing Florida for the worse. A developer himself, Governor Bush was caught in this crossfire. Thus, he employed a combination of conservative and more traditional strategies in pursuing his goals. These included initiatives to encourage more people to move to Florida and a revision to the state's growth-management law designed to force local communities to provide the schools, roads, and other infrastructure necessitated by the growth.

Summary and Conclusion

The gubernatorial administration of Jeb Bush was significant in Florida political history and we do not need to accept the validity of his theory of government to recognize that he identified major problems, proposed controversial solutions and acted aggressively to put them into place. Embracing a highly consistent theory of government, Bush undertook what he thought of as a revolution designed to transform both Florida's governmental structure and the nature of state public policy. As will be seen, he achieved considerable success and persuaded the state legislature to adopt a large portion of his policy agenda. These policies created substantial change in Florida; they reoriented state priorities, replaced traditional instruments of service delivery with new ones and reduced the state's ability to generate new resources to be used in governing. The governor and his supporters claimed that these changes produced substantial progress in solving public policy problems in Florida.

The great English philosopher Bertrand Russell once declared that "change is one thing, progress is another. Change is indubitable. Progress is a matter of controversy" (Russell, 459). Governor Bush and his Republican allies in the state legislature undoubtedly brought about change in the governmental system of Florida. Whether these changes led to progress is much less clear and in some respect is a value judgment.

Later in this book, I will attempt to assess the nature and extent of the progress Bush achieved by addressing a series of questions about the changes involved. The most general of these is, "were the outcomes and improvements anticipated by Bush's theory of government achieved?" More specifically, is Florida state government more efficient than it was in the past? Are students better educated? Is the state's economy in better condition? Are the state's most vulnerable citizens healthier or more secure economically? And, equally important, which groups of Floridians bore the burden of the changes initiated and which benefited from them? Answers to these questions will provide the basis for an assessment of the validity of the governor's theory of government and of the quality of the governor's revolution and of his administration.

Note
1. While the state's system of *higher* education was also beset with problems and with low rankings on national scales, Bush devoted almost no attention, aside from changing the system's governance structure, to remedying the problems involved there.

Part II
Consolidating Power and Pushing the Agenda

Chapter 4

Seizing the Levers of Power

Introduction

The political and economic conditions described in an earlier chapter provided Governor Bush an ideal political and policymaking base. He had large, almost fanatically loyal, majorities in both branches of the legislature and an economy that gave him great policy flexibility. Nevertheless, his ability to capitalize on these conditions was limited by comparative weakness in the formal power of the Office of the Governor of Florida.

The governmental reformers whose efforts in the middle of the twentieth century produced great changes in American state government were successful in persuading the states to adopt an aggressive theory of gubernatorial leadership that made the Office of the Governor the primary focus of government. In adopting this theory, states focused on the formal power necessary to high performance in this role. Changes were made in state statutes and in state constitutions making governors more visible, enhancing their formal authority, and providing them the tools for political and administrative control. They were granted longer terms in office and improved opportunities for succession. Statewide elections for competing executives in state government—chief state school officer, commissioner of agriculture, and the like—were reduced in number or eliminated altogether. Appointment and removal powers were increased and governors were given a greater role in the budget process. These changes allowed the reformers to argue that governors now had the political visibility and the formal tools necessary to become chief executive and to direct state government (Sabato, 1983). As a consequence they were expected to have a policy agenda, even if it was controversial, and to reach out to the electorate and to public officials, explain their positions, and gain their acceptance.

At the time of his election to the Office of the Governor of Florida the "strong governor" theory had not been completely established in the state, and the office Bush inherited had been denied many of the formal powers called for by the theory. In the year before Jeb Bush was elected, Florida's Executive Office outranked that of only six other states in terms of formal power—that is, control of the budget, appointment powers, independent control over the Executive Office, and other instrumental powers (Beyle, 1999, 204).

Earlier governors had complained that this structural weakness inhibited their ability to govern effectively and had sought a variety of changes designed to give them greater control over the formal levers of policymaking. And while

Governor Bush publicly claimed that "the structural power, the power granted by the constitution is secondary, I think, to the use of the office" (Lauer, 2003), he and his Republican allies in the legislature aggressively pursued formal control of government by the executive office. By the time Governor Bush left the job, he had turned the office of governor in Florida into a point of centralized control for state policymaking, justifying the changes by saying that "a weak form of governorship is not appropriate for a dynamic state like Florida that is ever-changing" (Rushing, 2006). The following sections describe the activities that contributed to this change, beginning with a description of the governor's efforts to gain influence in the budgetary process.

Gaining Control of the Budget

The ability to control the budget is widely viewed as critical to executive leadership, but rankings of the Florida governor's power on this dimension placed the state at the bottom in the nation when Bush came to power (Beyle, 2004: 213; Barrilleaux and Beckman, 2003: 409–417). Since a fundamental element of the governmental theory upon which the Bush administration was based called for limiting governmental spending, it was imperative for the governor to gain control of the state's budgetary process. Thus, Bush moved smartly to initiate strategies to redefine the role of the governor in state budgeting and to shift powers away from the legislature and toward the executive branch. Oddly, and seemingly in defiance of the theory underlying the separation of powers in American government, the Florida legislature was complicit in these efforts.

New Leadership in the Budget Office

Jeb Bush came to the office of governor of Florida with a background in real estate deal making and with virtually no experience in budgetary management, one of the primary responsibilities of a governor. His inexperience was combined with skepticism about existing budget professionals in Florida state government who had long worked for Democratic administrations. In order to make the changes he thought necessary to his revolution, he needed a budget director who was an experienced and skillful technician, but who also shared his budgetary philosophy and who was psychologically prepared to cut the budget. Relying on his contacts with conservative activists throughout the nation, he found such a person in Donna Arduin, a well-known budget analyst who was widely traveled within national Republican circles.

Ms Arduin had worked for Patti Woodward at the Office of Management and Budget in Ronald Reagan's administration in Washington, had moved on to Michigan to serve as chief deputy budget director for Republican governor John Engler, and from there to budget director for George Pataki, a Republican in New York before coming to Florida. After Florida she moved on to California to become budget director for Arnold Schwarzenegger. She then went into partnership with Arthur Laffer (godfather of Ronald Reagan's voodoo economics) and Stephen Moore, director of Fiscal Policy Studies for the Cato Institute, a core intellectual institution for movement conservatism. In 2006 and 2007 she reappeared in Florida as fiscal advisor to the incoming Republican speaker of the Florida House of Representatives.

An acknowledged fiscal expert, Arduin was described as both autocratic and as a "good person with a good heart." It was also said that she was willing "to make recommendations to close Florida's state library, to eliminate money for eyeglasses, hearing aids and dentures for poor seniors and to force 55,000 low-income children onto health insurance waiting lists" (Furillo, 2003).

Arduin became a major asset to the governor and his efforts to remake Florida state government. She shared his governmental philosophy, was technically competent and politically loyal. Relying on her expertise, the governor undertook a remake of the state's budgetary process in order to gain policy influence in Florida.

A New Budget Process

In Florida, Arduin and Governor Bush were introduced to a budgetary process that the legislature had learned to manipulate in its favor and that Bush wanted to reform.[1]

In the aftermath of a new constitution in 1968, Florida had adopted an executive budget procedure in which the governor and his staff relied on estimates from the state's executive agencies to create an annual budget that was then submitted to the legislature for consideration. Typically the legislature downplayed this document, and employing a subterranean process, prepared its own, using lobbyists, cabinet officials, its own staff, and state and local elected officials for guidance. The governor then had fifteen days in which to consider and decide the extent to which he would agree with the budget, maintaining the veto as a threat. Under usual circumstances the veto was exercised sparingly for fear of antagonizing future legislatures and the legislative budget ordinarily prevailed over that of the governor.

The Bush strategy sought to change this process and to allow the governor to exert his will. His approach was composed of four separate elements.

First, beginning in 2000, Bush changed the traditional budget format in a substantial way. Rather than present activities in line-item fashion, he "bundled" them into large programmatic areas. This design made it much harder for legislators to "bury" special, local projects somewhere in the bowels of the budget where it would escape notice and made it easier for the governor's budget staff to see and bring them to his attention on final review. It also eliminated the need for the ten-year history of appropriations that had been published by the state for years and that had allowed generations of legislators and other public officials to see how contemporary figures compared to earlier ones. Critics of the governor's new procedure claimed that it was adopted intentionally in order to make it difficult for those who wanted to track change in spending over time to do so and to prevent invidious comparisons of Bush appropriations to previous administrations.

Second, the governor began to submit his budgets on line and on electronic disks. The resultant visibility reduced substantially the air of secrecy surrounding legislative budget construction and made it easier for those following the budget process to compare what the legislature did to what the governor had proposed. Special interest and pet projects were therefore easier to detect.

Third, Bush made explicit his criteria for making budget judgments in advance of the legislative session. Legislators and lobbyists were thus put on notice and items they included risked veto if the criteria were ignored.

Finally, and most important, Bush exercised the line-item veto liberally and resolutely. In 1999, he vetoed over 550 individual items, totaling nearly $313 million. This created a firestorm of protest, and some legislators and legislature watchers expressed the view that the legislature would not be so cooperative in the future. Nevertheless, Bush continued his actions in both 2000 and 2001 when he vetoed a total of over $600 million and had no difficulty in shepherding his agenda through the legislature. The *St. Petersburg Times* reported that over his eight-year tenure, Bush vetoed more than $2 billion in legislative spending (Bousquet, 2006). In each of these years, the ideologically cohesive Republican majority acceded to these vetoes with little complaint, seemingly more interested in following Bush's philosophical lead than in protecting legislative independence and their own projects.

The Bush strategy was successful in shifting power long held by the state legislature back to the executive branch. His use of substantial numbers of line-item vetoes sent a message to individual legislators, legislative leaders, and lobbyists that the time of special projects, or "turkeys" as they are called in Florida, was over, or at least sharply reduced. Nevertheless, the strategy could not have been so successful in the absence of complicity on the part of his ideologically sympathetic allies in the legislature.

Governor Bush also found other ways to use the budget process to advance his governmental philosophy. They included limiting budget requests from state agency heads, using nonrecurring money to fund ongoing activities, and modifying the state's revenue and expenditure estimating process.

Limiting the Influence of State Agency Heads in the Budget Process

Florida statutes require that state agency heads submit budget requests to the governor and to the legislature that are based on an *independent* judgment of agency needs. While the governor uses these requests to develop his budget, they are also submitted separately to the legislature as a basis for its own deliberations. The statute is designed to ensure that the legislature is provided a picture of the needs of the state unclouded by gubernatorial priorities.

In preparing his initial state budget, Bush adopted a strategy that succeeded in limiting the effect of this statute and thereby increasing his own influence in the budgetary process. The strategy was to instruct his budget director to transmit the message that state agency heads were not to ask the legislature for more money in the following year than they had received in the previous year, regardless of assessed need (Becker, 1999). This action was seen as a direct attempt to overrule state law on this topic and led the Republican chair of the Senate Budget Committee to demand that agency heads submit letters stating that they complied with the law requiring an independent assessment of need. When questioned by reporters on this issue, Donna Arduin said that the governor's letter was "simply guidance" and no one "dictated" anything to agency heads. Not surprisingly, however, the agency heads appointed by Bush complied with the governor's "guidance." By thus screening the information that agencies were able to provide the legislature and by limiting agency budgets to a previous year's figures, Bush was given greater leeway to impose his own budget priorities on the legislature.

The governor's office utilized this tactic repeatedly and it was an open "secret" throughout the Bush administration. It erupted into public view late in 2005 in a dispute over funding for the State Department of Juvenile Justice (DJJ). In a hearing between lawmakers and officials of that department, legislators asked why agency guards were so poorly trained and equipped and criticized DJJ officials for not seeking money to resolve the problems involved. Rising to the defense of the agency's secretary, the governor's staff representative asserted that the secretary was "limited in his legislative budget request to what the governor says he can put in it. His hands are tied." He then went on to say that neither the legislature nor the DJJ secretary had the right to meddle in the agency's spending plan. Challenged on this statement, others in the governor's office responded by saying that "the governor's office has always conducted the legislative budget request process based upon the laws which guide these procedures" (Miller, 2005).

Inexplicably, while even Republican legislators suggested that the budget requests they received were more a reflection of the governor's political goals than a statement of Florida's real needs, they acquiesced in this behavior, thus further reducing their own influence in the state's policymaking process.

Using Nonrecurring Funds

Like most states Florida has set aside funds in a variety of trust accounts to support specific activities. These funds come from taxes, bonds, or fees from related activities. Thus the State Transportation Trust Fund in Florida is supported by gas taxes and vehicle registration fees and is dedicated to the support of projects to improve the state's system of transportation. Several trust funds established within the state's Fish and Wildlife Conservation Commission, which are funded by the sale of duck stamps and specialty license plates, are dedicated to support for non-game wildlife and manatee protection. The Sadowski Affordable Housing Act has provided thousands of low-income Floridians with affordable homeownership and employment opportunities and the Florida Communities Trust Fund helps cities create community parks, open spaces, and greenways. Sadowski monies come from a documentary stamp tax paid on the transfer of all real estate in Florida. Florida Communities funds are provided by the sale of Florida Forever Bonds.

Funds such as these are especially tempting sources of revenue for governors who have committed themselves to either reducing taxes or to not raising them. Governor Bush argued that such funds violated "the executive power" by placing funds outside his control (Hollis, 2006) and his budget director, Donna Arduin, suggested that "we [the governor] need to consider the limitations of your [the legislature's] authority" here (St. John, 2003). On this issue she clashed with state economists who had a long-standing commitment to paying recurring expenses—teacher salaries and medical costs for the poor—only with recurring funds. Arduin argued that one-time cash should be used for recurring expenses and that the funds could be used to supplement the state's general fund account.

Operating on a commitment not to raise taxes, Governor Bush could not resist the temptation to utilize these funds to support ongoing needs for schools, health care, and like public services in years, such as 2001, when existing state revenues were short. And in 2005 the governor asked the legislature to cap the amount of money in one of these accounts—the affordable housing fund—in order to give him more say over where the monies were to be spent. Thus, while the lack of affordable housing in Florida grew, and funds dedicated to dealing with the problem accrued, Bush spent the money on more immediate purposes in order to help balance the budget without raising taxes. By 2006, the governor had shortchanged reduced-cost housing by more than $600 million.

Critics claim that using these funds to support ongoing state needs was "like budgeting your annual bonus for the rent" (Dyckman, 2004), and even Republican legislators found it alarming. Republican senate president Jim King said, "We're supposed to be fiscally conservative. No one can argue that the way we've spent money in the last five years meets that test" (ibid.). Further, local officials complained that these raids shifted pressure onto cities to "pick up the slack—and the tab—when there isn't enough money to build affordable homes or when Florida's transportation system begins to buckle under population growth" (Reder, 2004: 4E). Nevertheless, between 2001 and 2005, Bush expended more than $4 billion in funds that had been set aside for specific policies on activities that the state supports on a regular basis. His 2002 budget alone relied on $1.5 billion from thirty-four separate trust funds. While use of these funds permitted Bush to satisfy his pledge not to raise taxes, it left the state with a $4 billion deficit that a future governor and legislature were required to address.

Estimating State Revenues and Expenditures

Over a period of years, the Florida legislature had developed a somewhat unique and highly regarded mechanism for estimating the costs associated with services such as juvenile justice, early learning, and K–12 education, to estimate the fiscal impact of constitutional amendments, to predict the revenue and expenditures that were necessary for preparation of the state budget, and to estimate the economic implications of legislative actions. This mechanism involved a series of "consensus estimating conferences" made up of professional staff from both the house and the senate, from the governor's office, and from the Office of Economic and Demographic Research, a staff arm of the legislature working under the Joint Legislative Management Committee.

The conferences and the estimating process are open to the public and are designed to provide a professional, objective, nonpartisan approach to forecasting. For most of the life of this process, the professional staff involved had been encouraged to "speak truth to power" on these highly important matters and had been shielded from political influence brought by the governor or by individual legislators. This circumstance changed with the rise to power of the Republicans, and both senior legislative staff and journalists who had covered the legislature for years say that pressure from Governor Bush contributed to a substantial shift in the culture that structured the fiscal behavior of the legislature. In the aftermath of the change, legislative staff and estimating activities began to succumb to the political influence of the governor and of the legislative leadership and to be driven as much by political ideology as by objective economic or fiscal criteria. A series of examples were offered to support this claim.

A preview of the changing attitude regarding the importance of objective analysis was offered in the governor's first term when federal laws were passed to provide corporate tax breaks. Governor Bush defended these breaks on the grounds that they would stimulate the state's economy. However, an analysis by Economic and Demographic Research demonstrated that the cuts would have a negative effect on the Florida economy. The governor "blew up" and was overheard in the rotunda of the capitol saying that the chief economist needed to "get out in the private sector" and "see how the real world works," and the analysis was ignored. Recognizing the comments as a threat to fire the bearer of what the governor saw as bad news, other legislative staff sprouted lapel buttons that read "Don't Privatize Ed." Anticipating the likelihood that these pressures were to be a continuing issue, the chief economist retired in favor of graduate school at Florida State University.

Republicans in the legislature also either ignored or attacked the results from several other Economic and Demographic Research fiscal analyses with which they disagreed. One, conducted at the request of the Democrats, questioned the underlying economic assumptions of Governor Bush's proposal to provide $500 million in economic stimulus funds to the California-based Scripps Institute to start a biological research facility in Broward County. A second showed that Florida would get less economic benefit from a $262 million tax break the governor and house leaders wanted than from spending the money on public services; and a third undermined the estimates made by the governor's budget director regarding the costs associated with the implementation of the constitutional amendment to create a high-speed train between Orlando, Miami, and Tampa. The governor wanted to repeal this amendment and used extremely large projected costs as the justification. His estimate was so inflated that it was subsequently rejected by the state supreme court, which is charged with review of proposed amendments.

Opposition to objective analysis that challenged another of the governor's attempts to change the state's constitution ultimately led to an effort on the part of the Bush administration to change the rules guiding the estimation process.

Much of the integrity of the estimating process in Florida was based on an understanding that all members of the conference had to agree on the estimate. Thus the process employed consensus voting that mitigated the ability of political factions to influence the outcome. Governor Bush came up against this process in his efforts to undo another constitutional amendment with which he disagreed and, in this instance, he simply got the rules changed.

The amendment related to class-size reduction in the state's public school system. Adopted just before Bush was first elected, the governor fought it throughout his administration. In the waning years of his term, Bush secured the support of Republican legislators and made a last effort to nullify this amendment with one of his own. To justify the change, Bush produced an analysis that specified extremely high costs. The representatives from the house, the senate, and governor's office quickly agreed with the estimates provided, but the representative from Economic and Demographic Research would not concur, suggesting that the costs were lower than the estimates from the other participants. In order to by-pass this problem, legislation was enacted which stipulated that, for purposes related to constitutional amendments, estimating decisions were to be made on the basis of majority rule. The proposed amendment thus passed this fiscal test but for other reasons failed to get out of the senate.

Political pressures to influence the estimation of the costs associated with legislative decisions, staff changes that removed seasoned budgetary professionals in favor of those with political connections, the placement of legislators with no appropriations experience into positions of leadership on appropriation committees in both the house and the senate, and close cooperation between the governor and the leadership in the Florida state legislature, and particularly in the house of representatives, gave new influence over the budgetary process to the governor.

Consolidating the Executive Branch

Throughout Florida's history, the executive branch of government in the state had been characterized by substantial political decentralization. That is, many of the major agencies of state government were under the control of individuals who were elected to their positions and over whom the governor had little or no influence. These officials could even include members of the opposing political party.

Further, in addition to managing their own agencies of state government, these same officials were automatically members of an executive "cabinet" that had oversight authority for seven additional state agencies. This entity was not a governor's cabinet analogous to that of the president, but an institution with constitutional independence. While the governor was also a member of this cabinet, every other member's vote was equal to his, thus substantially reducing his influence in state policymaking. The governor could not even grant clemency to prisoners without the support of other members of the cabinet.

Criticism of this cabinet system of government was widespread and several attempts were made during the 1970s to change it. Resistance from the individuals who held the offices and from the interests they represented had prevented such changed. Finally, in 1998, in the same election in which Jeb Bush was first elected governor, and when pending term limits reduced the incentives for the incumbents in these offices to resist change, a constitutional amendment consolidating the executive branch of government was proposed and adopted. The new cabinet was put into place in 2003.

The new structure greatly increased the governor's influence over the executive branch of Florida state government. It decreased the number of executive officials elected directly by the people from six to three and created a new cabinet composed of these three and the governor. It gave appointment power over the Department of Education and the Department of State to the governor. It also gave the governor new executive authority over the Department of Elder Affairs and the Florida Fish and Wildlife Conservation Commission.

When first elected, Governor Bush downplayed the importance of these new powers, pointing out that Florida still had less executive power than many other states and saying again that formal powers were not as important as informal use of the office. Nevertheless, the governor took advantage of this consolidation to increase political control over Florida state government and to use this control to further his policy goals.

His actions in this regard were consistent with the theory of a "strong" chief executive, but the governor's use of his increased authority demonstrated that consolidated executive power can be used for a variety of purposes and Bush often left the impression that he was using executive power for purely partisan reasons.

An Appointive Secretary of State

Bush's first action to utilize his new appointive power was to select a new secretary of state of Florida. One of only seven such officials in the United States who is not elected, the incumbent is second in the line of succession to the governor's office and, among other things, is the state's chief elections official.

Those who had pushed the decision to make the secretary of state an appointive position had hoped it would depoliticize an office that should have the complete trust of all citizens. This concern became particularly acute in the aftermath of the actions of the elected secretary of state in the 2000 presidential elections when Katherine Harris served simultaneously as secretary and as co-chair of the George Bush presidential election committee and engaged in actions that generated widespread criticism throughout the United States. However, after this change took place and the Jeb Bush administration took control, the president of the Florida chapter of the American Civil Liberties Union said the move "was a mistake. We've gone from bad to worse" (Roig-Franzia, 2004). This view was generated by a series of actions taken by secretaries who served during the Bush term.

Governor Bush's first appointee to the position was a former Republican mayor of Orlando, Glenda Hood, who had campaigned for George Bush in 2000, and when replacing Hood in 2004, he appointed another longtime political activist, Sue Cobb, former Republican-appointed ambassador to Jamaica and for almost twenty years a campaign fund-raiser and contributor to the Bush family. A member of Jeb's transition team in 1998, she and her husband contributed $130,000 to Republican candidates in the three years prior to her appointment, including $75,000 to the Republican National Committee.

In concert with these appointees, Governor Bush sought to consolidate power over the state's electoral system into the hands of the secretary of state and to utilize the position for what were viewed by many observers as his own partisan purposes. Numerous accounts of both the 2000 and 2004 presidential elections argued that the governor employed the office to Republican advantage and that the secretaries engaged in a number of activities related to the state's voter rolls and to the recount of the presidential ballots that were questionable (Tapper, 2001; Palast, 2003; Stuart, 2004; deHaven-Smith, 2007). And after the 2004 elections the governor introduced legislation that would have given the secretary of state even greater control over Florida elections, including final authority about who should be purged from voter rolls, a subject at the center of the dispute in both the 2000 and 2004 presidential elections. Even Republican legislators objected to this move and refused the governor's request. And the Republican supervisor of elections in Okaloosa County, Pat Hollarn, said it "is unquestionably the strongest attempt to exert power and manipulation of duly elected constitutional officers that I've seen in the 35 years I've been in Florida" (*Tallahassee Democrat,* 2005, 1B).

Other controversies involving voting technology and the absence of a paper trail for touchscreen voting machines also emerged during Bush's term and took on partisan connotations. Thus, even before Glenda Hood resigned her position, a former president of the state's elections' supervisors said placing a political appointee over the state's elections department was "the worst thing that ever happened to elections in this century" and expressed concern "about the bias that continues to surround every major decision" regarding the department (Fineout, 2005: 6A).

The actions described above cast a partisan spotlight on elections administration in Florida and hung a cloud of suspicion over the secretary of state's actions. It also brought criticism in forums ranging from the U.S. Supreme Court to late-night talk shows. Responding to a question in 2004 which asked him to explain the serious problems with elections in Florida, former president Jimmy Carter, who along with former president Gerald Ford had recently completed a study for Congress to recommend changes in the American electoral process, had this to say about the state: "Florida officials have proved to be highly partisan, brazenly violating a basic need for an unbiased and universally trusted authority to manage all elements of the electoral process" (Carter, 2004: A19).

These criticisms of the management of the electoral system lingered as the succeeding administration took office and were significant enough to prompt the Republican who followed Bush as governor of Florida to take action in an attempt to bring back a feeling of nonpartisanship to the office of secretary of state. Governor Charlie Crist began his term by filling the job of secretary with a widely respected local supervisor of elections who had been the president of the supervisors' statewide professional association. When making the appointment, the new governor said that having public confidence in elections would be a top priority over the next four years and that ensuring the integrity of the elective process is "one of the most important things that exists that government performs" (Cotterell, 2006).

Gaining Control of Public Education

The new consolidation of the executive created by the constitutional amendment of 1998 also made a substantial change in the governance structure of public education in the state and placed this system squarely under the political direction of the governor. The amendment on this subject that was approved by voters in 1998 created a new seven-person State Board of Education to be appointed by the governor, changed the commissioner of education from an elected to an appointed position and charged these two with supervising the "state's system of free public education."

The amendment left to the Florida state legislature the job of clarifying the structure with which the oversight was to be implemented and with the cooperation of his allies in this body, Bush utilized this opportunity to create a structure that gave Florida's governor substantial influence over K–12 public education in Florida. Further, while there was a question as to whether the voters even meant to include higher education in the new reorganization, Governor Bush used his influence in the legislature to ensure that *university* governance was also placed under the jurisdiction of the state board and thereby under gubernatorial control.

Throughout his term, Governor Bush employed these institutions in a manner consistent with the theories of a consolidated executive and of a "strong" governor and relied on his appointees to the new Board of Education both to portray his educational reforms in a positive light and to refute criticism of his actions in this arena.

As might be expected, not everyone agreed with all his actions and several drew criticism for being an inappropriate use of the executive power. For example, critics say that the first commissioner, Jim Horne, a former Republican state senator, was routinely used by Bush to resist accountability for problems in the state's voucher programs, which were among the governor's pet projects. Democratic senator Ron Klein said that Horne was caught in the cross hairs of a political battle. "I think the governor has strong beliefs about these programs and even when everyone found problems with them, there was a lack of commitment to change" (Miller, 2004).

Control over the Board of Education also gave Bush an instrument to help the governor respond to criticism of educational policy proposals with which he disagreed, and Bush appointees to the Board of Education were also put to use in this manner. This was particularly evident after the citizens of Florida approved a constitutional amendment about education that the governor opposed. Adopted in 2002, this amendment put a cap on class size in the public education system that was to be fully implemented by 2010. In the intervening years the governor took every opportunity to criticize this amendment and to mitigate its effects. In separate statements over the time period involved, the governor's appointees on the Board of Education repeated the same criticisms of the amendment as had the governor.

The state's system of *higher* education was also affected by Bush's efforts to consolidate power. Prior to the passage of the constitutional amendment and its enabling legislation, Florida's university system had been under the direction of a chancellor and a State Board of Regents, both of which were appointed by the governor, but with Board members appointed from specific regions of the state for nine year terms. The chancellor and the regents were designed to provide direction to the full eleven-campus system, to protect the universities from political interference, and to prevent duplication of programs in the state's higher-education system. Early in the Bush administration, this system performed its role as a shield against political interference too well and Bush moved to bring it under more direct control. The story involved in the change illustrates key features of Jeb Bush's political leadership, willingness to alter effective institutional arrangements in order to strengthen his political power, and a disposition to turn on political allies when they opposed one of his policy objectives.

One of Jeb Bush's earliest gubernatorial appointments was the chancellor of the state university system. The appointee was Adam Herbert, former president of the University of North Florida, one of the few African Americans who had publicly supported Bush in his election campaign and chair of the governor's transition team. During the early years of the Bush administration the chancellor and the Board of Regents successfully resisted political pressure to create a separate law school at Florida A&M University, the state's historically black institution. However, the regents incurred the governor's anger when they resisted attempts by John Thrasher, speaker of the house of representatives and a close friend of Jeb Bush, to create a college of medicine for his alma mater, Florida State University. At dinner in Sarasota, Thrasher appealed to Bush with a diagram of a new university governance system that would circumscribe the role of the chancellor and the regents and increase that of the state's governor. The new system was drawn on a napkin and a new structure based on the drawing was subsequently put into law; one that gave to the governor new power over governance of the state's university system.

The Board of Regents and the position of chancellor of the university system were dismantled (Adam Herbert went on to become president of Indiana University) and separate Boards of Trustees were created for each of the eleven universities in the system. These new trustees reported to the new Board of Education, and the governor was given authority to appoint both the Board of Education and the Boards of Trustees for the individual universities within the Florida system. A small university staff—with a chancellor in name only—reported to the commissioner of education, who in turn reported to the chair of the State Board of Education, thus burying the university system in a morass of confusion about resources, responsibilities, and priorities.

The governor's efforts to change the university structure raised the ire of U.S. senator Bob Graham, who as governor had been a supporter of the system headed by the chancellor and the Board of Regents. When his efforts to discuss the matter with Bush were rebuffed, Graham mounted his own constitutional amendment initiative designed to reassert the authority of the Board of Trustees and a "battle of titans" in Florida ensued. Graham won, his amendment passed in 2004, and the Board of Regents (now called the Board of Governors) was reconstituted. Nevertheless, fourteen of the seventeen appointments to this board were also made the province of the governor, thus providing him substantial influence over all aspects of higher education in the state.

The structure that emerged from these actions proved to be extraordinarily confusing and complicated substantially the relationships between the Board of Education and the Board of Governors, between the university Boards of Trustees and the Board of Governors, and between the legislature and the various governing boards. The respective responsibilities were so ill defined that they inhibited university decision making and invited legal challenges throughout most of the Bush administration. The president of the state's premier school, the University of Florida, complained that "it means I have to get something approved three times" (Bierman, 2006). A report issued in the first year after Bush left office called the system dysfunctional, saying it was "haphazard and poorly funded, with its core mission of educating undergraduates lost as universities compete with each other for national status" (Pappas, 2007). Ultimately, resolution of the issue was left to succeeding officials. In 2008, the Republican senate president proposed a return to an elected commissioner of education and sought legislation to clarify the relationships among the respective organizations (Liberto and Van-Sickler, 2008).

Governor Bush followed the tenets of the strong governor theory and maximized his influence on higher education policy through the appointment of a group of well-connected political allies to the Board of Governors and, through them, on university system management. One example of his use of his new power came in 2005 when the board sought candidates for the position of chancellor. Rather than conduct a national search for this position, which is potentially one of the most influential in Florida state government, the board simply posted its job opening on a small number of Web sites. Not surprisingly it received no applications from candidates with world-class credentials. The board then chose the Provost of a minor Florida university for the job, a person who was recommended by Armando Codina, Bush's close friend and former business partner from Miami. The choice was made even though the candidate was never interviewed by the board or even the search committee.

Some observers of Florida politics found the governor's intrigue in these ventures somewhat surprising since higher-education policy proved to have little attraction for Governor Bush, and he made few substantial proposals during his term to address what were fairly visible problems in the state's university system. His reticence came despite the fact that no university in the state was ranked among the top 200 in the world by the *Times of London* in 2005 and the highest ranking achieved by any university in the state in the 2005 *U.S. News and World Report* rankings was 50. Thus the manipulations he engaged in on this matter created the perception that Bush assembled power over higher education for reasons unrelated to the governance of the university system. A former chancellor of the Board of Regents was reported to have said that the governor made these changes "because he could" (Date, 2004: 248).

Centralizing the Management of Social Services

The Bush administration took one additional step designed to enhance the power of the governor in the state's political system. This came in the form of legislation that removed local health and human services boards from both the policy advisory and the managerial processes involved in providing a wide range of social services to children and families. This power was consolidated under the secretary of the Department of Children and Families, who is appointed by the governor.

During the 1990s, Florida provided social services through a network of regional boards that were appointed by county commissioners after screening by a broadly representative local nominating committee. These boards were designed to provide policy recommendations regarding local service needs and to nominate the local district administrators for appointment by the secretary of the state department responsible for these programs, the Department of Children and Families. Under prodding from Bush in 2000, Republican lawmakers eliminated the district boards and gave exclusive authority over the appointment of newly created regional administrators to the secretary of DCF, who was appointed by the governor.

These actions were entirely consistent with the theory that a chief executive should have control over administrative agencies that are his responsibility. But criticisms from scholars of public administration in Florida illustrate the conflicting values in the theory. They argued that this change removed local input from the process of deciding how to deal with local social services problems and "prevented the natural development of an integrated system that might have better protected thousands of children and adults" (Jreisat and Wolfe, 2002).

Increasing Gubernatorial Appointment Power

If the ability to appoint administrative and other officials who are to carry out gubernatorial objectives is a measure of potential gubernatorial influence, the governor of Florida had long been in a weak position relative to other governors. Over the years, Florida governors have had very little independent appointing power. Most agency heads are appointed jointly by the governor and the state senate or by the governor and an oversight board. In the most recent comparative assessment of gubernatorial appointment power, Florida's governor was given a rating of 1.5 on a 5.0 scale and ranked only ahead of Georgia on this dimension (Beyle, 2003). Using the authority granted by the constitutional amendment passed in 1998 and their control of Florida state government, the Florida legislature responded to Bush's urgings and acted quickly to enhance this aspect of gubernatorial control over Florida's state government. This was done primarily in two areas, higher education and the judiciary.

Appointments in Higher Education

As noted earlier, the 1998 constitutional amendment regarding consolidation of the executive branch of government left to the legislature the power to determine the manner in which the consolidation should take place. Guided by the speaker of the house at the time, legislation enacted in 2000 gave the governor new power to appoint over one hundred members of the state universities' Boards of Trustees. Consistent with the self-reliant executive theory which argued that governors utilize their appointees to help them promote their policy objectives, most people who were put on these boards had explicit Republican credentials and a large percentage of the remainder came from within the business and corporate sectors that were Bush's core constituencies. Bush also included five Republican lobbyists among his appointments, in spite of a 2005 law that banned such people from serving on these boards (Kimberly Miller, 2006). In making replacements to these boards over the years, these same credentials were decisive.

Given the public's perception that university trustees are prestigious positions, Bush's ability to appoint them gave him an important mechanism by which to reward campaign contributors and to provide high-visibility, high-paying jobs to his friends. One example of this occurred during the process of selection of a new university president at Florida Atlantic University in Boca Raton, Florida.

The presidency of Florida Atlantic opened in 2002 with the resignation of its president of twelve years. The Bush-appointed Board of Trustees created a search committee to find a replacement. The committee was chaired by George Zoley, vice chairman and CEO of Wackenhut, a company that had donated $260,000 to the Republican Party over the previous six years. The committee hired a consultant who spent more than $100,000 during a seven-month search process, screened and selected a set of finalists, set up interviews for them, arranged hotel rooms, and purchased them plane tickets. At this point Zoley had a change of heart. He sent an e-mail to the committee canceling the interviews, using the argument that they were moving too fast. While some members of the committee objected to this procedure, the Board of Trustees went along.

Three days after this maneuver, a previously unannounced candidate for the job appeared, Frank Brogan, Bush's lieutenant governor. Although Brogan waited to make his candidacy official until the day after he was sworn in for his second term as lieutenant governor,[2] he immediately became one of three new finalists, along with the sitting engineering dean at the University of Louisville and Stanley Fish, a literary scholar at Duke University who had an international academic reputation as well as administrative experience as dean of the College of Arts and Sciences at the University of Illinois, Chicago. When informed of Brogan's candidacy, Fish removed himself from consideration, saying, "there's politics within a university and politics from outside that involve it. This was all politics" (Barton, 2003). No one was surprised when Brogan got the $368,000-a-year job despite vehement objections by the Florida Atlantic faculty.

Two other prominent political figures, former Jacksonville mayor John Delaney and former speaker of the Florida House of Representatives T. K. Weatherell also found their way into university presidential office when Bush gave them his imprimatur. Delaney, a longtime Bush supporter, became president of the University of North Florida and Wetherell, a former business partner of John Thrasher, is president at Florida State University.

Judicial Appointments

Critics of Governor Bush, including his successor, argued that Jeb circumscribed the effectiveness of the state's courts by "neglecting" them financially and Governor Crist said, "we all know that they [the courts] were not a priority in his [Bush's] administration" (Klas, 2008). Bush did, however, devote attention to the appointment of state court judges, and gubernatorial power over the appointment to these positions was increased during the Bush term.

In large part the governor's effort to improve his influence over the appointment of Florida judges was driven by a desire to change what Governor Bush believed was an improper, liberal judicial philosophy in Florida. But there was also ongoing hostility among Florida Republicans about the role played by the judiciary in the American system of checks and balances. Bush and other Republicans regularly lamented the fact that public policy was made not only in the executive and legislative branches, but also in the judicial branch of government. And in numerous comments over the course of his administration, Bush personally distanced himself from the position held by generations of constitutional authorities that the three branches of government were co-equals. Governor Bush pushed his position so intensely that the president of the Florida Bar questioned whether he believed in the separation of powers doctrine, and a former supreme court judge said, "This particular administration has not yet understood why we have the separation of powers. They seem to believe that the governor and the legislature can do whatever they want and the courts should not interfere" (Crowley, 2003). Pursuing his own version of this doctrine, Bush promised to appoint judges who would respect "the primacy of the legislative and the executive as policymakers" (Ulferts and Bousquet, 2002).

While county court and circuit court judges are elected in Florida, vacancies are filled by gubernatorial appointment. Judges of the district courts of appeal and justices of the state's supreme court are also appointed. Until Governor Bush and the Republicans gained control of state government, the appointments were made by the governor from lists of candidates provided by nine-member, nonpartisan judicial nominating commissions (JNC) appointed by three separate entities. Three members of the JNC's were appointed by the Florida Bar, three members were appointed by the governor, and three members were selected by the other six members. The commissions were inspired by unethical and corrupt appointees made during the 1960s, were created in 1971 by Governor Reubin Askew, and were designed to limit the power of the governor to use judicial appointments as patronage.

In 2001, in the aftermath of the presidential election in which the Florida Supreme Court sided with Al Gore's position regarding the recount of ballots and at the bequest of the governor, the legislature revised the state statute to permit the governor to select all nine members of the nominating commissions. In the revised statute, the Florida Bar Association recommends five persons, all of whom can be rejected by the governor. The governor separately selects four members, thus giving the governor complete control over the selection process. With a total of twenty-six JNCs, this change opened up over two hundred new appointments for the governor and severely reduced the influence of the state bar and any other entity not connected directly to the governor. Subsequently, when filling judicial positions, Governor Bush and his appointees were criticized for using criteria unrelated to fitness to serve on the bench as standards for appointment.

Several judicial candidates complained to a Miami newspaper that they had been subjected to a series of inappropriate questions by one of these commissions, including whether they were active in their church, whether they thought they were "God-fearing people," how they felt about the U.S. Supreme Court's 2003 ruling striking down a Texas law criminalizing homosexual activity, and how they would feel about having the Ten Commandments posted in their courtrooms (*South Florida Sun-Sentinel,* 2003). One candidate, an assistant county attorney, was also asked whether she "would be able to balance her duties as a single mother of twins with her duties as a judge" (Kay, 2004).

While the JNC for the Fifteenth Judicial Circuit may have been unusual in its efforts to include what many saw as irrelevant criteria in its search process, reports from others throughout the Bush administration suggested that the search for new judges who were ideologically compatible with the governor was highly organized. A reporter for the *St. Petersburg Times* discovered an e-mail from the governor's assistant general counsel, Frank Jimenez, outlining a plan to create a shadow system of "unofficial regional panels" made up of Bush supporters who would recruit applicants for judgeships, and admonishing those involved that "I will be a pain-in-the-you-know-what if the recommended person is not ideologically compatible with the governor" (Hauserman, October 1, 1999). The response to this plan was somewhat predictable, with Bush supporters saying that a judge's values were important and should be taken into account, defending it, and critics arguing that it undermined the whole purpose of the JNC. The director of the Florida Christian Coalition said, "I think what Bush is doing is great," adding that the Bush administration had assured him that religious conservatives would be heard in the judicial selection process. Alternatively, a former supreme court justice suggested that the whole plan behind the Judicial Nominating Commissions was not to make candidates ideological clones of the governor. A former president of the Florida Bar com-plained that "many people are not willing to apply to go through the [screening] process...they believe they are the wrong party" (Fineout, 2005). And one of the most highly respected attorneys in Florida, who was the general counsel for former governor Lawton Chiles, said, "I think the system has become absolutely politically oriented and is destroying the concept of the independent judiciary" (ibid.).

In the end, many candidates that the JNCs produced for the governor satisfied his desire for more conservative judges as well as his need to reward important political constituencies, a tradition long honored at both the federal and state levels of government in the United States. Bush's first two appoint-ments to the Florida Supreme Court are illustrative.

In June 2002, Governor Bush had his first opportunity to fill a vacancy on the seven-person Florida Supreme Court. From a list of five names submitted by the JNC, he chose Raoul Cantero III, a Cuban American, Harvard-educated corporate lawyer from Miami and grandson of former Cuban dictator Fulgencio Batista. Cantero was the only candidate who had not been a judge, but Jeb and Cantero had worked together in the 1980s on a high-profile project involving a notorious Cuban American terrorist named Orlando Bosch. Bosch had been deported from the U.S. for his involvement in the bombing of a Cuban passenger plane that killed seventy-three people and was seeking to have the deportation reversed. Cantero, who was a primary spokesman for Bosch, and Bush, who was serving as the campaign manger for Congresswoman Ileana Ros-Lehtinen, who lobbied to have the deportation reversed, coordinated the effort to allow Bosch to return to the United States.

This appointment fit perfectly for the governor. It allowed him to appoint a judge who professed the same political philosophy as did he, and it gave him an opportunity to reward one of his most important political bases, the Cuban Americans.

His second appointment, also in 2002, gave Bush the opportunity to put on the bench a person who explicitly subscribed to his own notion of the judiciary as a secondary institution in Florida state politics. In his application for the post on the supreme court, Kenneth Bell said that the courts "must recognize their role as the weakest branch of government and pay due deference to the legislative and executive branches." Bell was also described as a man of "very strong religious beliefs," and his campaign for election to the circuit court in 1990 was tinged with charges of anti-Semitism. His support within the Christian religious community also played well with Bush.

Bush's appointment of Bell represented a dramatic change in judicial philosophy from the person he replaced, Leander Shaw, an African American who was an outspoken opponent of the death penalty. In describing the change that occurred with the selection of Bell, a Pensacola trial lawyer who had appeared before him said, "I think you go from a moderate liberal, which I think Leander Shaw was, to the extreme right. There's no stopping in between. The problem is that Bush has no respect for the judiciary. He never has" (Ulferts and Bousquet).

By the end of his term, Jeb Bush had appointed more than one-third of all Florida judges and most of these people, appointees to the lower courts such as the courts of appeals, represented the most conservative constituencies in the state. They included Charles Canady, a former congressman who was one of the floor managers in the U.S. House effort to impeach Bill Clinton; Paul Hawkes, a former state legislator and top aide to Tom Feeney, the governor's running mate in his first campaign for governor and winner of the "Conservative Legislator of the Year" award; Brad Thomas, one of Jeb's own aides who helped create the plan to privatize death-row appeals that became the subject of substantial criticism for poor-quality work; Leslie Rothenberg, who as a candidate for state attorney signed a pledge from the Miami-Dade Family Christian Coalition that she would oppose gay marriage and domestic partnerships with "my votes, powers and privileges of public office"; and Frank Shepherd the state's senior attorney for the conservative Pacific Legal Foundation, an aggressive advocate of private property rights.

Bush defended his selections to the court, saying that he wanted to "establish a bench that reflects the vibrant diversity of Florida" (Ramos, 2005) and that the selection process yielded a diverse group of candidates. Most of the Bush appointments were male and white, but the governor did increase the number of minority appointments on the bench. By the end of his term, Bush had appointed 343 judges. Sixty-eight percent were male and 77 percent were white. But Bush also chose 46 African Americans, 68 Hispanics, and 109 women among his appointments. Thus the total number of minority judges in Florida rose from 85 to 144 during the Bush term.

Minimizing the Influence of the Legislature

Throughout history, the state legislature has been viewed as the dominant political institution in Florida and in the 1980s was described as "one of the strongest legislatures in the nation" (Rosenthal, 1986: 418; see also Turnbull and Phelps, 1994: 107; Dauer, 1986). Within a few years of Bush taking office, this dominance was reversed, and the legislature was reduced to what the *Tallahassee Democrat* called "the governor's shadow" (*Tallahassee Democrat,* 2005, 4E). While this branch of government, particularly the senate, exhibited mild signs of revival in the last two years of Jeb's term, it lay supine for almost the entire Bush term and took on the role as a supporting player in a Florida version of parliamentary government.

The transformation from dominant to subsidiary institution came about for reasons of party loyalty, philosophical agreement, fear, and awe. It was aided by term limits, Bush intimidation of individual members, and direct attacks on the institution.

In his interactions with the Florida legislature Governor Bush seemed to reject the argument that (gubernatorial) power is the power to persuade (Neustadt, 1960) and played down the specific behaviors thought necessary to success in the complex interactions between co-equal political institutions: the need to explain, to justify, to convince, to get people on board, to compromise. Instead, the governor exhibited impatience and even arrogance with members of his legislative party. A common Bush strategy with regard to the legislature was to propose something that he and his staff, or the business community, had developed without consulting any others, expect the legislature to adopt it, and to exhibit frustration or anger when it was not quickly approved. The senate majority leader lamented that "it's almost like we're not allowed to have an opinion" (Bousquet, 2003). And the house minority leader said, "A lot of Jeb Bush's proposals were ultimatums that the legislature had no choice but to capit-ulate to" (Deslatte, 2007).

Term limits and the part-time nature of Florida's legislature made legislators already predisposed to support Bush even more compliant. Term limits in Florida had a similar effect as in other states, emptying the legislature of experience and forcing green legislators to struggle with issues so complex that by the time they began to understand them, it was time for them to leave. Alternatively, seeing that they couldn't stay long, they arrived seeking headlines rather than listening and learning. Lobbyists and the executive office were the real winners in this environment and term limits gave Bush additional influence over the legislature.

So too did the part-time nature of the legislature. Florida's legislature meets each year for sixty days. In the interim, the average legislator goes back to his or her district to engage in their own business and professional activities. They are not able to stay directly involved in either the politics or the substance of issues facing the state and are therefore at a disadvantage in comparison to the governor and his agency heads when forced to address public problems.

Governor Bush attempted to exploit these institutional weaknesses from the outset of his administration, using both "carrot" and "stick" methods. Employing an incentive, the governor offered to hire people on his own staff who would be trained and subsequently work for new house speakers and senate presidents once they assumed these positions. (By tradition, legislative leaders in Florida serve only one term.) This strategy was obviously designed to interject Bush administration political ideology directly into the legislature and was characterized by Democrats as "indoctrination without a doubt" (Gomez, 2006). As his tenure ended, this strategy was adopted by an incoming house speaker, who fired veteran legislative staffers to make room for eighteen members of Bush's policy and budget staff. This new speaker also hired Bush's first budget director, Donna Arduin, to serve as a private consultant on tax and spending matters (Kennedy, 2006;Leary, 2006).

The governor also engaged in more aggressively hostile actions to bring the legislature under his influence. In 2002, in 2003, and in 2005, Bush proposed to weaken the legislature by eliminating legislative entities that provided it the staff capacity to conduct independent oversight of governmental programs, a crucial element in a part-time, term-limited legislature. One of the organizations was the Office of the Auditor General; the second was the program evaluation arm of the legislature, the Office of Program Policy Analysis and Government Accountability (Florida OPPAGA). The third was the Council for Education Policy.

In 2002 OPPAGA had been cited by the National Conference of State Legislatures as "among the best of the legislative program evaluation offices around the country," and in 2005 the Government Performance Report by the Pew Charitable Trust said that "it may be the best in the country." Bush demeaned it, saying, "I'll be honest with you, I'm not aware of a single penny of savings that we have found by adopting an OPPAGA recommendation" (Lauer, 2003). Most observers of Florida politics attributed Bush's animosity for the above named organizations to the fact that they had pointed out problems in Bush agencies, some of which had led to firings and restructuring. His proposal to abolish them was so perplexing that even one of his strong supporters, the president of the pro-business Florida TaxWatch, suggested that eliminating agencies with governmental oversight capability was "penny wise and pound foolish." In the end, the legislature did not adopt Jeb's proposal but, indicative of its awe of the governor, did make some changes in OPPAGA staff and procedures to mollify him.

Bush was more successful in abolishing the Council for Education Policy, which had been created in 1980 and whose mission was expanded in 2001. This organization also reported to the legislature and provided independent review of Florida's education programs. When Bush pushed for its elimination, critics claimed it was in retaliation for recommendations that had countered those of the governor. Nevertheless, the legislature agreed with the governor and refused to continue its funding, thereby weakening its own ability to conduct independent analysis.

In attempting to turn the legislature to his own uses, Bush also demonstrated a willingness to "punish" individual legislators who opposed him. In 2003 when disagreements over medical malpractice reform developed between Bush and Republican senators, his deputy chief of staff e-mailed Bush supporters with suggestions about running more sympathetic people against the recalcitrants when the Republican primaries began. In 2006 he also worked aggressively for the primary opponent of an incumbent Republican state senator who had voted against his effort to place vouchers on the ballot as a constitutional amendment, sending campaign letters to constituents saying that the incumbent had "abandoned our party's principles and lost his way." Displaying his displeasure with the senator's "betrayal," he and his business allies raised $7 million for his opponent (Cotterell, 2006).

Actions such as these continued throughout the Bush administration and it was not until midway through his final term that some legislators began to take umbrage at the governor's efforts and to engage in efforts to reassert their role in Florida state government. But even here, it was almost exclusively in the senate.

As the 2005 legislative session was about to begin, the president of the senate put away $1 million to pay for television ads or a direct mail campaign to defend himself and the senate in the event of attacks during that session (John Kennedy, 2005). The senate president also refused to confirm the staff member who in 2003 had suggested running Bush supporters against incumbents who did not support the governor when this staffer was nominated by Jeb to run an agency of state government (Ulferts, 2005).

Also in the 2005 session the senate attempted to interject itself fully into the state's privatization and contracting process. Embarrassed by major problems in this process and accused by the governor of meddling in executive branch rights when it sought greater oversight, the senate tied provisions regarding contracting to their appropriations, hoping to force the governor to keep them involved or risk losing funds. While this strategy had been declared illegal on previous occasions, its adoption was an indication that the senate in 2005 understood that it was a separate branch of government and not an arm of the executive. Jeb vetoed this legislation.

In spite of this last-minute show of resistance on the part of one house, most observers of Florida politics thought that the legislature during the time Jeb was governor was much less independent than it had been under previous governors, even legislatures that were dominated by the party of the incumbent governor. The Florida legislature during the period 1999–2006 seemed to see itself as a junior partner to the governor rather than an independent branch of government.

Alan Rosenthal, arguably the nation's preeminent scholar of American state legislatures, said "that is a legislature that has been emasculated" (Greenblat, 2006). And systematic interviews conducted with Florida executive branch officials over the time period 1960 to 2005 by Professor Deil Wright at the University of North Carolina confirmed the governor's rise in importance. As shown in Figure 1, these respondents thought that the influence of the governor versus the legislature grew markedly during the Bush administration, and for the first time the influence of the governor of Florida exceeded the influence of the average governor in the United States.

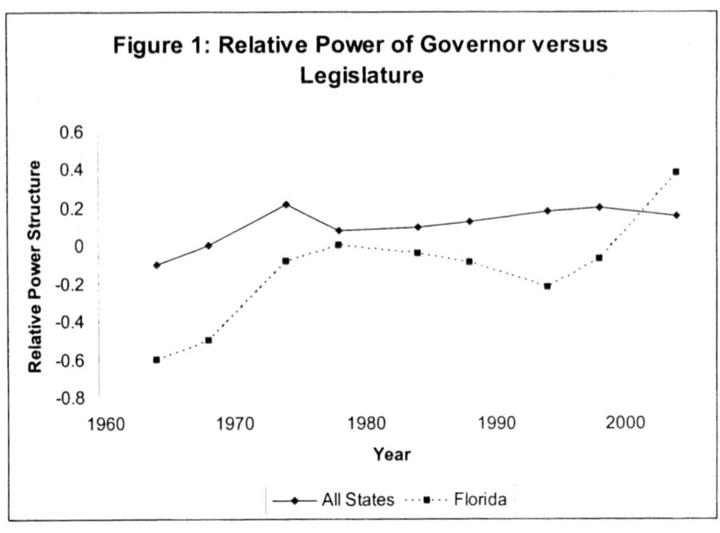

Summary

Jeb Bush was elected to the office of governor at a time when political and economic conditions could have hardly been more supportive of his party and his agenda. But he also inherited a governor's office that had comparatively limited formal power and that was widely viewed as less important in policy-making than was the state legislature. Recognizing that "the formal powers of the governorship constitute a foundation upon which a governor can build his or her political influence" (Sigelman and Dometrius, 1988, 158), Bush capitalized on constitutional revisions and the help of compliant legislative leaders to realize many of the objectives of mid-twentieth-century governmental reformers. He increased the formal power of this office and consolidated political control in Florida within the Executive Office of the Governor (EOG). He then used the EOG as a focal point for pursuing his conservative policy agenda in Florida.

Notes

1. Most of this description is taken from Richard S. Conley and Richard K. Scher, "I Did It My Way: Governor Jeb Bush and the Line-Item Veto in Florida," *Florida Political Chronicle* 15, no. 1 (spring 2004): 1–17.

2. Although legal experts disagree on the interpretation of the state constitution, this strategy may have allowed the governor to appoint Brogan's successor rather than force a special election to fill the vacancy.

Chapter 5

Governing to Build Core Constituencies

Introduction

Dick Morris, former advisor to President Bill Clinton, has written that "once upon a time, elections settled things for the term of office. Now, they are mere punctuation marks in an ongoing search for public support and a functioning majority. Each day is election day in modern America…A politician needs a permanent campaign to keep a permanent majority" (Morris 1999, 72, 75).

As governor, Jeb Bush clearly recognized and appreciated this feature of contemporary American politics and worked continuously to build and sustain support for his reform agenda among selected political constituencies. He self-consciously organized the office of governor to help promote his policy positions and to control presentation of his image. He was strategic and systematic in promoting this image and in developing and sustaining support among particular segments of Florida's electorate. He adopted a sophisticated and disciplined approach to these tasks, targeting specific constituencies and promoting public policies designed to solidify their allegiance.

Articulating the Message

The Bush political staff claimed that "the governor ushered in a new era of media relations in Florida through centralization of information and message discipline" (Baxter, 2005: 1). He accomplished this in several ways.

First, in contrast to previous governors who typically employed former journalists or other media figures as press secretaries and communications directors, Bush selected political operatives who were loyal to him personally and sympathetic to his conservative political ideology. A veteran journalist said that these individuals "saw their job as making the governor look good—not informing the public" (Morgan, 2003). This personnel strategy greatly reduced the chances that a message or an image other than the one the governor wished to portray would be presented.

Further, whereas previous administrations had permitted media access to (at least) the budget office and the legal counsel, Bush required that all media contacts with the Executive Office of the Governor come through his Office of Communications. The result of this strategy was described by one of the longest serving and most highly regarded journalists in the state: "Once upon a time a reporter could call the governor's lawyer or budget director or his expert on tourism and get an informed answer. These days a call to the governor's general counsel will produce a response from his press office, kindly offering to help us get an answer to the question. The answer will be slightly scripted and very pretty, but it may tell us nothing we really wanted to know and doesn't allow a follow-up" (Morgan, 2003).

Third, the Bush communications staff prided itself on the discipline it claimed it was able to exert when portraying the governor and his message to the people of Florida and on the consistency and focus of his message. Guided by conservative political philosophy, the Bush administration selected a small number of messages and focused on them throughout his administration. Education and the economy were the focal points and were highlighted at every opportunity. The campaign for these and other priorities unfolded as a marketing campaign, not a discussion, and was conducted as a sales exercise; the intention was to promote, not to explain. The governor was relentless in portraying his actions in a positive light, ignoring shortcomings in policy and in programmatic performance. This characteristic was perhaps most obvious in his support for his educational initiative where he routinely cited only the most favorable test scores when discussing the outcome of his A+ plan. But he also utilized this strategy when defending his privatization reforms and when promoting his economic development initiatives.

Governor Bush made determined efforts to control the message that emanated from executive branch agencies under his control as well as from his own office. The press offices for state agencies were required each day to submit a list of media requests to the governor's press office for clearance, "to ensure that the agencies reflected the overall message of the Governor" (Baxter 7). Adopting this same strategy, Bush administrative agencies also began to centralize their own media contacts in their central press offices.

Finally, in an effort to "go outside the truck route" (the Florida equivalent of "outside the beltway" in Washington) and to reach around the coverage of the capital press (one of the largest in any state), Bush employed a variety of alternative communications techniques. These efforts were not designed to completely exclude the Tallahassee media, simply to enlarge and diversify the number of individuals who carried his message to the people in Florida. In fact, Bush focused heavily on the Florida media during his administration and seldom responded to requests from the national press.

The "alternative" technique of which he was most proud (he proclaimed himself the first e-governor) was a weekly "In the News" e-mail to a list of over forty-two thousand subscribers (as of May 2005) who requested that their names be included. This communication permitted him to present his views about Florida government and politics in a completely unmediated manner.

Bush also used satellite feeds from the capital to conduct interviews with local television stations, employed public service announcements to portray his views about issues and problems affecting Floridians, and provided "talking points" to specific groups that were supportive of his positions. Each of these techniques reduced the influence that the Tallahassee media exerted in controlling the portrayal of the governor.

The Bush communications strategy received mixed reviews from the news media in Florida. Reporters respected and appreciated the governor's willingness to respond to them by e-mail. However, in his efforts to portray his agenda in a positive manner, the governor was often accused of making it difficult for critics and even citizens to gain access to public records that might show his initiatives in a different light than the one he portrayed. He tightened controls over public records requests and created time-consuming and costly processes for obtaining these records. Actions such as these prompted Barbara Peterson, president of the First Amendment Foundation in Tallahassee, to say "there's just been a tone—more than a tone, actually—with the Bush administration, where access to government information seems more like a problem than a constitutional right" (Begos, 2006).

This perception was so widely shared that the Republican governor who replaced Bush in 2006 took it up as his first order of business and his first act was to establish, in the Executive Office of the Governor, the Office of Open Government. This office was given responsibility for ensuring "full and expeditious compliance with Florida's open government and public records laws." The executive order also directed each state agency head to designate a person at his or her agency to serve as the agency's public records/open government contact person.

Peter Wallsten, who covered Florida politics for the *Miami Herald* and the *St. Petersburg Times* before moving on to the *Los Angeles Times,* said that Jeb's attempts to control the news created suspicion and distrust within the media and ultimately the public. This impression was confirmed by Lucy Morgan, the doyenne of Florida political writers, and by Gary Fineout of the *Miami Herald.* According to them, Bush's efforts gave the impression that bad things were happening behind closed doors (Baxter 11). Further, the efforts to "stay on message," which the Bush staff cited positively, was seen by reporters as an effort to "spin" the news in the favor of the administration and Wallsted saw Jeb's administration as the best in state history at this art (Baxter 12).

The Political Strategy: Appealing to the Base

Presidential scholar Grant McConnell argues that the essence of political leadership is "the ability to appeal publicly to large and widely different constituencies at the same time" (McConnell, 1967). Governor Bush adopted an alternative approach to leadership, one employed throughout the 1990s by conservative Republicans around the nation and explicitly designed to build core constituencies for the Republican Party. As described by Thomas Frank (2004: 5) this strategy focused on a narrow "base" constituency of business elites, advocates for smaller government and social conservatives. It channeled the conservative impulses of these constituencies into a few "red-meat" issues that did not threaten the corporate interests that provided the financial support for the Republican Party. The smaller government constituency wanted to reduce the hold of government over their lives, their finances, their schools and businesses, and their guns. The social conservatives fought to regain moral values they saw as disappearing in an increasingly secular world. And business interests hoped to avoid any action that threatened their bottom lines. The conservative political approach mobilized these constituencies with "aggressive polarizing strategies" (Edsal, 2006: 6) that brought attention to explosive social issues and married that to pro-business economic policy. "Thus cultural anger and discontent was marshaled to achieve economic ends" (Frank 5).

The groups to which Governor Bush appealed were courted in a variety of ways by conservatives throughout the nation. John Micklethwait and Adrian Wooldridge argue that Jeb's brother the president did this by "sometimes throwing them red meat to gnaw on, but more often by hinting that he is just about to" (Micklethwait and Wooldridge, 2004: 175). Governor Bush did less hinting about and more throwing of red meat. That is, he chose sides and took an aggressive role in controversial issues of public policy that were signature items for one or the other of his target audiences. He became a national spokesman for these audiences on some of these issues.

Cultivating the Social Conservatives

The role of political advocate for social conservatism came easily to Jeb Bush. His closest political allies in his early years in Florida, the Cuban Americans, were extremely conservative on most social issues and he adapted to their family values and "tough on crime" culture in his foray into Florida business and politics. Further, while he grew up as the prototypical American WASP, he had a religious conversion to Catholicism in 1994 after his defeat by Lawton Chiles and swiftly took to heart selected canons of that faith which appealed to the broader movement of social conservatives. He opposed abortion, for example, but supported capitol punishment. Like many converts Bush held his religious views strongly and he was prepared to articulate them and to interject government into resolution of disputes involving them. Thus over his years in office he was called upon repeatedly to take sides in the nation's "culture war." He did so with the enthusiasm of a true believer (Gailey, 2005).

Bush's appeal to social conservatives came primarily through efforts related to three issues: crime, affirmative action, and right to life.

Crime Fighter

As discussed in chapter 1 of this book, Bush's first campaign against Lawton Chiles was dominated by his efforts to appeal to the "tough on crime" constituency and to portray his opponent as "soft" by insisting that the death penalty laws in Florida were not being utilized effectively. According to Bush, Chiles was not executing prisoners as quickly as he might have.

As Governor Bush continued to focus on these issues and made much of his support for "get tough on crime" laws. These include a variety of mandatory sentencing laws such as the 10-20-Life Act, the Three Strike Violent Felony Offender Act, and the Habitual Offender Accountability Act, all passed in the glow of Bush's first-term victory. Despite evidence that the 10-20-Life law had no effect on the state's crime rate (Stoddard, 2006) Bush continued into his last year in office to cite these laws as some of the primary accomplishments of his administration.

Bush also took a tough stance on the death penalty and, contrary to the Catholic Church's position on this issue, was willing to impose the sentence each time he was presented an opportunity. Indeed, an advocacy group accused him of speeding up execution dates to coincide with elections (Floridians for Alternatives to the Death Penalty, 2002).

In other actions designed to appeal to the advocates of the death penalty, the governor dismantled the state offices that provided legal representation to death-row inmates and replaced it with attorneys in private practice willing to take such cases. He also threatened to reduce the supreme court's budget and staff in 1999 after it invalidated laws that would have accelerated death penalty executions in the state (Lanier and Handberg, 2002).

His rationale for privatizing death penalty appeals was that it would save the state money, because it would limit the amount of time that attorneys could bill for their services. Critics suggested that turning these complicated cases over to the low bidder would "dumb down" the appellate process, speed up the movement of cases through the criminal justice system, and produce increased numbers of executions. If this last objective was indeed the intent, it achieved only modest success, and in the end just three more criminals were executed during Bush's administration than during that of Governor Chiles.

Affirmative Action

Like social conservatives around the nation, Jeb expressed grave reservations regarding the idea of affirmative action and within months of his inauguration he took advantage of an external attempt to pass a constitutional amendment eliminating it in Florida. The effort was initiated by Californian Ward Connerly, an African American, Republican businessman, and the leading spokesman for the American Civil Rights Coalition, which campaigned for the elimination of affirmative action throughout the nation. When Connerly brought his campaign to Florida, Bush claimed that it would "divide and make it harder to get things done" (Neal and Broder, 1999: A1). Then, in a preemptive move that signaled the style that was to characterize his administration, he bypassed what was likely to have been a heated legislative proposal to change affirmative action laws and instead issued an executive order, labeled One Florida, outlawing the use of race and gender in university admissions decisions and in the award of state contracts. This action generated heavy criticism from African Americans in Florida and a very public demonstration at the capitol, but whites in the state were widely supportive of his stance. When asked directly if they supported affirmative action, only 16 percent of whites did so and 80 percent opposed it (Bennett, 2000).

In a political sense, Bush resolved the affirmative action issue. His decision has been publicly accepted and has not been a focus of serious political debate since the governor took action. Furthermore, there is a good argument to be made that the policy he implemented was superior to any that might have come out of a public referendum.

On the ground, the policy had mixed effects. State contracts with minority-owned businesses increased by almost $500 million over the time of the Bush administration, but university enrollment of minority students did not follow suit. At the same time that the governor announced that "we eliminated race as a criteria for admission to universities...and we've increased the number of minorities going to our universities" (AP, 2006), admissions data from the eleven state universities over the time from initiation of One Florida through the fall semester of 2006 showed a 4.2 percent decrease in the percentage of black students enrolled (Fineout, 2006). Also in 2006, a report from the Education Trust gave the state's premier university, the University of Florida, a "D" for its efforts to attract minority students (Education Trust, 2006).

Right to Life

Governor Bush entered energetically into the "culture war" surrounding issues related to the right to life and over the course of his administration consistently and aggressively supported the neoconservative position on this issue by "confusing a policy position that ought to be open for debate and alteration with a moral absolute that no true conservative should deviate from" (Douthat, 2008).

As governor, his entry into this arena came in his first year in office when he was called upon to support legislation permitting the state of Florida to offer a specialty license plate promoting the right-to-life side of the abortion controversy. The plate, containing the message "Choose Life," was available for twenty dollars and the proceeds went to organizations that provided counseling and support to pregnant women "who are committed to placing their children up for adoption" but not to "any agency that is involved in or associated with abortion activities including counseling." Not surprisingly the pro-choice advocates opposed the legislation. Bush's predecessor, Lawton Chiles, had vetoed the same measure on the grounds that it unnecessarily interjected religion into a public issue. Jeb sided publicly with the pro-life side of this debate and signed the bill into law when it came to his desk.

In that same year he also signed a bill requiring minors to notify parents prior to an abortion. The legislation was immediately suspended by the courts and in 2003, the Florida Supreme Court ruled it unconstitutional. In an action that was to be repeated over his term in office when he was defeated on an issue, the governor successfully introduced legislation to place the matter on the 2004 ballot as a constitutional amendment. The measure conveniently drew pro-life voters to the polls during the presidential campaign of 2004. The amendment was adopted, and most pro-life voters also presumably voted for the governor's brother in his reelection campaign.

In 2003, Bush again sided with pro-life advocates and entered into a more controversial battle in the culture war. In this case he ordered the appointment of a legal guardian to represent the interests of an unborn fetus being carried by a woman with severe learning disabilities who had been impregnated when she was raped. The woman, twenty-two years old, lived in a state facility, had no family, and could not speak. She was assigned an appointed guardian to represent her interests. The governor, who once instructed a reporter covering the case to refer to the woman's fetus as a baby, argued that the fetus was an unborn person who needed separate representation. Bush's intervention came after a Florida court ruling that appointing such a guardian would be improper.

Governor Bush also took the side of the right-to-life constituency in a battle to prevent the use of public funds in support of stem cell research. While this stance put him at odds with his economic development supporters, he argued that this technology "takes a life to give a life," and opposed a ballot initiative that would have amended the state's constitution to provide $200 million over ten years for this purpose. He also opposed actions to permit the Scripps Medical Institute to conduct research on this topic, even though he had committed $310 million of state-controlled federal funds to attract Scripps to Florida. At the same time he was attempting to lure the Burnham Institute of La Jolla, California, to build a lab in Florida, he also attached a condition that the Florida labs of this company, which was a leader in embryonic stem cell research, could work only on the noncontroversial stem cells from adults or umbilical cords.

Terri Schiavo

Undoubtedly the most visible example of the governor's willingness to engage in the "culture war" began in 2003 when he inserted himself directly into the explosive case of Terri Schiavo, a severely brain damaged woman in Florida whose husband and family engaged in a ten-year legal battle over whether she should be permitted to die without the use of extraordinary medical procedures. This story is told in some detail since it illustrates well the doggedness with which Governor Bush pursued his ideological priorities.

The war, which it became, over Terri Schiavo began prior to Jeb's election as governor, but as it came to its final resolve he coordinated his efforts with like-minded Republicans at the national level (Kam, 2005) and became the focal point of an effort that extended into the U.S. Congress and reached the U.S. Supreme Court on six separate occasions. His activities were designed to support the religious Right constituency in Florida by thwarting court-ordered efforts permitting Schiavo's husband to remove a feeding tube that was keeping her alive. In Bush's mind, Schiavo was "disabled" (Robinson, 2007), and he said that his actions were the product of his religious and social values and that he was "driven" by these values to intervene.

He began his efforts to override the judicial process in 2005 by proposing legislation to the Florida state legislature that prohibited the removal of her feeding tubes. This proposal was enacted into law but was declared unconstitutional by the Florida State Supreme Court on the grounds that it was a violation of due process since it was designed for Terri Schiavo only. When the Florida court struck this down, he introduced a second version, which even his Republican allies in the Florida state senate would not support. Simultaneously, he initiated a series of administrative and legal actions that so threatened the boundaries of the separation of powers that they prompted a Florida judge to remind him that "the executive branch and the legislative branch and the judicial branch are separate but equal...but neither the executive nor the legislative branch may go behind the final judgment rendered by this court" (Sommer and Silverstrini 2005). His actions included soliciting the opinion of a neurologist who was director of a biotech ethics center founded by leading Christian bioethicists and who was described by other neurologists as a "bogus, pro-life fanatic" (Goodnough and Liptak, 2005: A16; Sommer and Silverstrini, 2005). This doctor provided Bush a diagnosis different from that of the court-appointed doctors. Bush then brushed off a report from a highly regarded guardian ad litem that exonerated Schiavo's husband from charges that she was abused and reportedly sent representatives from the state's Department of Children and Families to seize control of Schiavo and reinsert her feeding tube (Kent Miller, 2005). This action led the presiding judge to issue a restraining order to stop DCF from bypassing the court and ordered the local sheriff to back up the city police should state agents show up at the hospice where Terri was being cared for. Concerned about Bush's fervor on this matter, the judge also took the unusual step of making "each and every singular sheriff of the state of Florida" personally responsible for protecting Schiavo, a fortuitous decision since the *Miami Herald* alleged that the governor dispatched agents of the Florida Department of Law Enforcement to take her to a hospital to resume her feeding. It was only when the local police told them that unless they had the judge with them when they came they would not be allowed to see Schiavo that FDLE backed down (Carol Miller, 2005).

In the end, Bush reluctantly conceded that he did not have the power to overturn court rulings and halted actions designed to interfere with them. However, in doing so, he could not help taking a last dig at the courts, When conceding the court's power, he said, "We are respectful of the judiciary and, you know, I think the defensiveness of the judiciary is a little over-blown, to be honest with you" (Cotterell, 2005: 3A).

Bush failed to achieve his immediate goal on this issue and Terri Schiavo subsequently passed away. But her death did not stop the controversy, nor did it stop Bush from pursuing his political objectives in the right-to-life "battle."

In the aftermath of Terri Schiavo's death, extremists who pushed Bush to intervene criticized him unmercifully for his failure to exert brute executive power and simply seize Schiavo, and Bush continued to search for ways to shore up support from this segment of his constituency. A new tact, focusing on allegations that Schiavo had not received appropriate care when she was stricken, was developed as a rationale for forcibly removing her from her medical facility. However, an autopsy conducted after her death undermined his efforts and those who pushed him to forcibly take possession of Terri when it validated the claims made by her husband that she had received appropriate care after her incident.

Still, Bush would not concede. Instead, implying that Terri Schiavo's husband had a nefarious connection to her collapse fifteen years earlier, he asked the state attorney from Pinellas County to investigate allegations made by Terri's family that her husband had delayed calling emergency medical personnel when he first found her unconscious in 1990 (Tisch and James, 2005). In a poll taken within days of his action, 58 percent of registered voters in the state expressed the belief that Bush was motivated by "politics" in this action as opposed to 32 percent who attributed it to "sincere convictions" (Clark, 2005: 7B). Further, the state's attorney in Pinellas County, a Republican, said, "When I conduct an investigation...I have some indication that a crime has occurred. In this circumstance, that does not exist" (Herbert, "Cruel and Unusual," 2005: A19). His subsequent investigation in the case confirmed this observation, but still Jeb stubbornly refused to accept that decision as final.

During the run-up to the 2006 legislative session, the governor developed a policy that would have allowed individuals who had a terminal condition to withdraw a feeding tube only if they had outlined that preference in a living will or if they had specifically authorized a representative to make that decision (Bell, 2006). Doctors and medical ethics professionals claimed that such a law would have forced feeding tubes down the throats of tens of thousands of Floridians and even the governor's Republican allies saw the futility of continuing the battle. When Bush could find no legislative sponsor for the bill he was forced, finally, to surrender.

But he was given one last opportunity to solidify his support in the pro-life community, and he took it. In the summer of 2006 he intervened in a probe by the State Board of Nursing into the actions of one of Terri Schiavo's nurses. The nurse was accused of violating state and federal privacy laws by talking about Schiavo's condition on national television. Responding to a complaint by another nurse, the Board of Nursing found there was probable cause that the nurse violated patient confidentiality and recommended her license be revoked. The State Department of Health, which oversees the board, initially said that divulging confidential patient information violated state administrative code and federal law. At this point, the governor met with department officials, who then changed their position and asked the Board of Nursing to dismiss the complaint. The board did so in August 2006.

Motivating the Smaller Government Constituency
Hostility to government has long motivated right-wing activists across the nation and is a driving force in Florida politics. The hostility takes many forms: from well-off retirees who have come to Florida to avoid a variety of taxes, to businesses attracted with subtle suggestions that environmental protection laws will not burden their operations. Groups such as these, and others, were targets of Bush mobilization efforts.

Freeing the Schools from Government Control
Homeschoolers and school-choice activists were identified specifically as political allies in the highly successful voter mobilization strategy called the "Victory 2004, 72 Hour Plan" that was used in George Bush's reelection campaign in Florida. They represent a segment of the electorate that accepts the economist Milton Friedman's argument that government monopolies are incapable of producing high-quality public education. Thus, they are a primary segment of the small government group that Bush and Republicans in general have targeted directly.

Governor Bush appealed directly to this group by adopting a variety of strategies designed to reduce the involvement of the government in public education. His actions include proposing more educational voucher programs than perhaps any governor in American history and by supporting the creation of hundreds of charter schools in the state. He maintained the support of school-choice supporters over the years by opposing legislation that would have held both the voucher and the charter school programs accountable to the same standards as were regular public schools. For example, he did not require schools that accepted students who left public schools with vouchers to make public their student's outcomes on the state's academic testing program, thereby avoiding a comparison with non-voucher students. He continued to support charter schools in the face of substantial evidence that the schools were highly segregated, that their students were not doing as well as were students in regular public schools, and that they experienced significant shortcomings in managing their finances. Ultimately he signed into law a bill that removed oversight of charter schools from local school boards and placed it with the Florida School of Excellence Commission.

Governor Bush also permitted the use of public funds to proselytize for charter schools. With money from the No Child Left Behind Act, the governor established two university-based centers to provide technical assistance to start-up schools. Both were, in essence, inside lobbies for charter schools. One of these, at Florida State University's College of Education, was listed on the college Web page as a component of its Center for Educational Research and Policy Studies. However, the only research listed at this site was from the Heritage Center, the Manhattan Institute, and other conservative "think tanks" that were advocates for charter schools. The center was described by the *Palm Beach Post* as a "Charter School Propaganda Center" designed to "manufacture a smiley-faced version of charter schools and vouchers." The *Post* went on to compare the money awarded to this center *unfavorably* to the money paid by the U.S. Department of Education to the radio commentator Armstrong Williams to shill for the No Child Left Behind Act. In that case Armstrong never claimed to be unbiased, said the *Post,* but in Florida, "FSU claims to run a public college of education. But the commitment is not to public education when a university ignores facts and excludes valid viewpoints simply so it can rake in a federal grant" (*Palm Beach Post* 2008).

One product of Bush's efforts in the school-choice area is a substantial infrastructure in the state that allows critics of public schools to get their children into alternative schools that are not directly accountable to taxpayers. Not coincidently these people constitute a large base of potential political support for the governor and his party.

Gun Owners and Other Sportsmen

The gun lobby is a prime constituency for the Republican Party nationally and for Jeb Bush and Republicans in Florida. Governor Bush appreciated this and paid appropriate homage to the group, both in rhetoric and in actions. He worked with the NRA during his brother's campaigns in Florida, he sought out opportunities to articulate the organization's philosophy, he promoted gun owner legislative goals, and he took advantage of opportunities to recognize members of the NRA for special awards.

Bush was particularly cranked up with red-meat rhetoric when the NRA held its national convention in Florida in 2003. He began his keynote address by declaring that "the second amendment is the original homeland security act." He then went on to say that "the sound of our guns is the sound of freedom" (Bush, 2003).

Bush's policy on firearms mirrored that of the NRA in much the same way that his other policy agenda followed that of other conservatives. That is, his firearms agenda is essentially that of the association. During his administration, he introduced and lobbied effectively for multiple pieces of legislation advanced by the gun constituency.

In 2004, he supported legislation that gave gun range owners immunity from environmental cleanup lawsuits. The law made it illegal for government officials to bring a claim against a shooting range forcing it to clean up old sites strewn with lead ammunition that might contaminate groundwater (*St. Petersburg Times,* 2004).

In that same year, he also supported a bill aimed at preventing police and other agencies of government from keeping electronic listings of gun owners. This support came over the objections of law enforcement officials who claimed that the lists often help their agencies track down suspects in criminal cases. Indeed, one opponent of the bill argued that "half the cases punished under the state's '10-20-life' laws would not be prosecutable" without such laws (*Miami Herald,* 2004).

And in 2005, the governor signed into law another piece of NRA legislation on the topic of gun control. The bill was written by the NRA and expanded the rights of Floridians to use deadly force when threatened in public places. This proposal known as the "stand your ground bill" expanded the rights of people to use guns or other deadly force to defend themselves without first trying to escape even in places outside their homes. The law stipulated that a person "has no duty to retreat and has the right to stand his or her ground and meet force with force, including deadly force" (Ulferts, 2005; Caputo and Fineout, 2005: 8A).

The bill was opposed by police chiefs in high crime areas like Miami and Broward County who claimed it would lead "drivers with road rage or drunken sports fans who get into fights leaving ball games to assume that they had total immunity" (Goodnough, 2005: A14). The Brady Campaign to Prevent Gun Violence argued that it could be used to defend people who shoot in the emotional rage associated with domestic violence and other high-stress events (Klas, 2005). And others pointed out that advocates could cite no case in which a citizen would have been protected by the law and claimed it would make little difference to public safety. According to them the legislation was simply a symbolic gesture to the NRA (NPR, 2005).

In the end, the bill was successfully maneuvered through the legislature by Marion Hammer, a Floridian and first female president of the NRA (and the only female recipient of the Roy Rogers "Man of the Year Award") whom Bush had promoted for induction into the Florida Women's Hall of Fame. Bush called it a "common sense" bill and in a special ceremony with the NRA signed it into law on April 26, 2005. In its e-mail "Alert" posted on May 4, the NRA said the bill gave "rights back to law-abiding people and forced judges and prosecutors who are prone to coddling criminals to instead focus on protecting victims." Wayne LaPierre, NRA executive vice president, then said that the group would use the victory in Florida to push for similar measures elsewhere. "We will start with red and move to blue" states (Goodnough, 2005).

In 2006 the governor signed six more bills sponsored by the NRA, one of which, the so-called shooter voter law, required businesses that issued fishing, hunting, and trapping licenses to offer voter registration cards as well. This legislation was thought to be aimed at a constituency that heavily supported Republican candidates and Democrats offered an amendment that would have required voter registration cards to be offered to new teachers when they got their state teachers certificates. This amendment was defeated and the president of the state association of election supervisors called the NRA bill a mandate and said it was unnecessary because citizens could register at driver's license offices, city halls, libraries, banks, and even on-line.

No New Taxes
If Jeb Bush learned anything from his father's experience in public office it was that support by a Republican for any effort to generate new money for investments in public programs by raising taxes was likely to have serious negative consequences. This is particularly true in Florida, which has a long low-tax history and is one of only seven states that has no income tax. Speaking in his first campaign for governor, Jeb said that his father's decision in 1990 to compromise his "no new taxes" pledge was a mistake, one he would not make. "It accomplished a lot of tactical goals, but it was a huge strategic mistake."

Over the course of his administration, Bush adopted with enthusiasm the no-new-taxes position and went beyond it by initiating a series of tax cuts and by supporting a state constitutional amendment that would have required a citizen referendum in order to approve any tax increase. These efforts were described earlier in the book and their outcomes will be discussed in detail in a later chapter.

In supporting his no tax policy, Bush adopted explicitly the theory of supply side economics that was the basis for much of the conservative political theory promoted nationally. In 2001 Florida faced a budgetary shortfall stemming in part from three years of tax breaks. Jeb denied that the shortfall was a product of the tax breaks and argued instead that these breaks were responsible for generating $3.4 billion in new tax receipts. "Over $1.6 billion in tax cuts over three years has yielded a 4.1% average annual increase because it is better to collect a smaller percentage of a larger pie than a larger percentage of a smaller pie" (*St. Petersburg Times,* 2001). He advanced similar arguments throughout his administration and expressed happiness that he was the only governor in Florida's history to cut state taxes in each of the years in which he served.

Supporting Property Rights
Shortly after the U.S. Supreme Court allowed New London, Connecticut, to force the sale of private homes for an economic-development project, a similar case emerged in Florida. Over a period of years preceding the decision, the City of Riviera Beach had exercised eminent domain law to buy properties to help

clear the way for a $2.4 billion development project that included a condo-minium-hotel, a marina, and stores and restaurants. This was a tricky issue for the governor, pitting as it did his social conservative allies against those from the business community. The governor initially supported the town's efforts, but when his longtime conservative supporter the James Madison Institute complained, Bush changed his position and felt compelled to make public statements about the power of government to take property being perhaps the most severe of all government powers. He then joined with the speaker of the Florida House of Representatives in creating a statewide committee to develop guidelines on the topic, thus initially sidestepping the problem. In the following year, the issue blossomed and in 2006 the legislature passed overwhelmingly a bill restricting the use of eminent domain. The governor, now fully on the side of the property rights constituency, signed the bill.

During this course of events, the City of Riviera Beach had signed several documents committing it to the project and immediately after the passage of the bill, but before it had been signed by the governor, called an additional meeting to sign a final contract with the developers with whom they had been working. The governor, now on the opposite side of the issue, said that "to rush to expropriate people's property just seems unseemly to me." He then questioned the city's legal right to proceed, sought legal advice from the state's attorney general, and went about trying to determine what the state could do to force compliance with the new law. The town's mayor said that he was surprised by Bush's efforts to curtail the project. "He used to be one of our biggest sup-porters," he said (Associated Press, 2006).

Bolstering the Business Community

Florida's business community was a core component of Jeb Bush's political base and wielded enormous clout with a governor who called himself the CEO of Florida and who often referred to Florida state government as an enterprise. Bush's policy actions consistently reflected the business community attitude that what's good for Florida business must be good for the rest of the state.

Bush's very first public meeting as a new governor was with the Council of 100, an organization of key Florida business leaders who are invited into the group, who pay $3,000 dues, and who must be approved by the governor. The fall 1999 meeting of this organization took place less than twenty-four hours after Jeb won election as governor and Bush was in attendance. Both Bush and the organization understood why he was there, they shared agendas. Reflecting the integration of the state's business community and the Republican Party, the president of the organization, Al Hoffman, also a Florida homebuilder and finance chairman of the Republican National Committee, said, "I don't know whether they're his ideas or the ideas of our constituency" (Kam, 2000). Bush asked for the council's help and adopted its plans for a variety of changes in Florida government including civil service reform and changes in the state's education system.

Over the course of his administration, Jeb and his staff also worked in concert with the other major business organizations in Florida, the National Federation of Independent Business, and the Associated Industries of Florida to craft legislation that addressed their views of state needs. In the case of civil service reform a Council of 100 task force headed by its president "provided the research, wrote the white paper, hired outside consultants to develop the civil service reform plan and even helped form the strategy to get it through the legislature" (Kam, 2000). In this and other ways, Florida's business community came to structure the Bush agenda and to exert influence on virtually all of his policy positions; on tax cuts, education reform, reform of the process by which constitutional amendments were adopted, Medicaid reform, and changes in the state's system of civil litigation.

The governor's efforts to address most business community issues were discussed in the earlier section of this book under specific headings such as tax reform, and education reform, and it is clear that business concerns in these matters were addressed. But one of the business community's top issues, "tort reform," merits separate consideration.

For years, conservative activists at places such as the Manhattan Institute, the Cato Institute, and the Hudson Institute and politically motivated writers such as Peter Huber and Walter Olson had clamored for reform of the nation's civil law system, claiming that it had created an "explosion of litigation, boundless punitive damage awards, unjustified class actions...and increased costs for everything and everybody" (Krauss, 2005). Although a sizable body of research both in Florida and throughout the nation cast serious doubt on many of these claims (U.S. Department of Justice, 2000; Vidmar, Lee, MacKillop, McCarthy, and McGwin, 2005; Chimerine and Eisenbrey, 2005; Peck, Marshall, and Kranz, 2000; Viscusi and Moore, 1993), Governor Bush supported the conservative position. Using statements such as "law suit abuse is one of the greatest threats to Florida's robust business climate" (Shayon, 2005), he joined the Florida Justice Reform Institute, a coalition of business and medical advocates led by some of the state's top CEO's, in supporting a variety of the remedies proposed by his conservative business allies. They included setting caps on medical malpractice claims, limiting class-action lawsuits, elimination of joint and several liability, limiting venue shopping, "end the asbestos lawsuit free-for-all," reforming bad faith legislation, and reversing "zone-of-risk" liability involved in such activities as high-speed police pursuits (Bush, 2005).

Critics of the governor's actions regarding tort reform argued that the notion that the reform was based on economic principles was tenuous. Instead, they claimed, it was a key component of his strategy to weaken the trial lawyers, a central constituency of the Democratic Party who represented a main source of Democratic funding.

Bush's efforts to reform the state's tort system began in his first year in office when he signed into law a package of bills described by one of the state's largest business publications as "the centerpiece of a legislative session chock-full of triumph for the business community" (Hokan, 1999). He supported this legislation in spite of a provision in the tort reform segment of this package that exempted from liability commercial airlines that were more than twenty years old. The provision was inserted in the bill late in the legislative process and was referred to as the "Boeing amendment" since the majority of the affected airplanes were manufactured by that company. It was opposed by the National Air Disaster Alliance/Foundation a grassroots advocacy group working for aviation safety and by the families of individual victims of the crash of the 1996 TWA flight 800, a twenty-five-year-old Boeing 747. While Bush claimed that he was "troubled" by a statute that meant that "the victims' families in crashes involving older aircraft would no longer be able to sue manufacturers for design defects in the planes," he still sided with his business allies and signed the bill (*Air Safety Week* 1999).

Some parts of his initial proposal to reform the tort system failed to pass. Most prominently, the effort to eliminate joint and several liability was delayed with a requirement that research be completed about its effect. In 2006, the governor reintroduced the proposal even though no study had been conducted. Bush maintained that the effects were well known and no study was necessary. This time the legislation passed and the governor signed it, "with great joy," saying that repealing the law "removes a barrier for businesses considering relocating to Florida" (Royse, 2006).

Bush's support of efforts to reform medical malpractice law provided another high-profile example of his philosophy regarding tort reform and also revealed much about his legislative style. In 2003, Bush sided with the medical community and other business allies and introduced medical malpractice reforms that would have limited pain and suffering judgments to $250,000. This legislation came in response to complaints from the Florida medical community that it was being driven out of business by increased insurance costs that were the result of excessive jury awards in malpractice lawsuits. Many of these claims had been effectively refuted by law professors at both Duke and Florida State University (Vidmar, Lee, MacKillop, McCarthy, and McGwin, 2005; Peck, Marshall, and Kranz, 2000), but critics claimed that Bush was motivated by animosity toward the trial lawyers who opposed the legislation and whom he labeled the "number one enemy to the Republican Party in Florida" (St. John and Boey, 2003).

When the 2003 legislative session opened, the house of representatives moved quickly to pass the governor's bill, but the senate balked, questioning the veracity of the assertions made by supporters of the bill concerning the rise in frivolous lawsuits, the loss of physicians to other states, the closing of hospital emergency rooms and trauma centers, and the declining profits of medical malpractice insurers. When senators delayed action and sought confirmation of these allegations, Bush became incensed. He retaliated by sending an e-mail to twenty-two thousand registered Republicans throughout the state attacking the Republican senators for "standing with trial lawyers who seek to maintain a system that protects their own special interests," and for "placing their own ambitions above the values that got them elected as Republicans" (Hirth and Cotterell, 2003). He asked these party members to communicate their displeasure to the lawmakers. He also met with officials from the Florida Hospital Association and vowed to call on business leaders to shut off campaign contri-butions to senate Republicans who opposed him (St. John, 2003).

In response to these actions, senate Republicans, for one of the few times during the governor's tenure, fought back. They closed down negotiations with the governor's office and Bush was forced to call three special sessions to re-solve the issue. In the end, the senate recalled earlier witnesses, put them under oath, and swore them to tell the truth and nothing but the truth. The resulting testimony undermined the "myths" upon which Bush's plan was based and led the governor to reluctantly accept a compromise that set much higher limits on pain and suffering than he wanted and also permitted exceptions in the worst case of injury (St. John, 2003).

A New Governmental Philosophy Takes Root in Florida

The policies promoted by Governor Bush and his allies in the state legislature were designed to mobilize the conservative base of the Republican Party and to motivate and repay its core voters. Their enactment reflected new philosophical agreement among Florida's elected officials and a substantial change in government ideology in the state. As shown in Figure 2, this ideology moved sharply to the right in the early days of the Bush administration and began to diverge from that of the Florida electorate.

Figure 2: Citizens Governmental Ideology: Florida 1980-2005

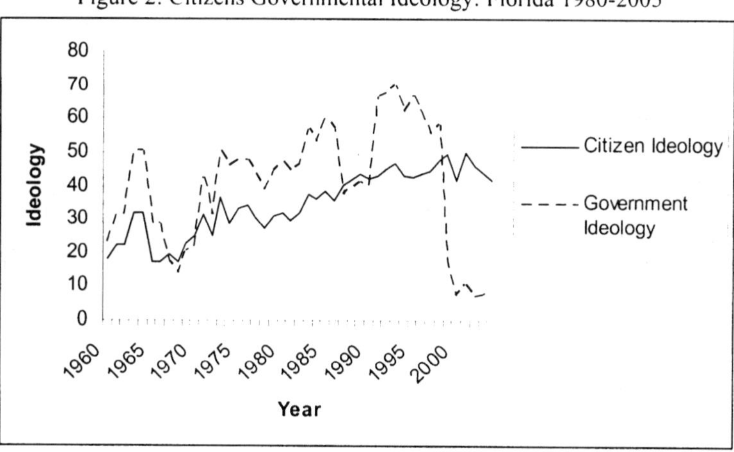

Between 1960 and 1998, the government's philosophy in Florida mirrored that of the Florida electorate; that is, they were closely aligned and reasonably conservative. During that time period the government philosophy had an average score of 33.7 on a 100 point scale, with 0 most conservative and 100 most liberal, and the electorate had an average of 32.9. By the time Bush came to office, both of these scores had risen and both the government and the electorate had become more liberal. At that point the government score was 58.2 and that of the electorate was 47.5, still relatively close to each other and moderate in tone.

Over the first two years of the Bush administration, the governor's efforts, and those of his fellow Republicans, to appeal to their conservative base brought about a huge change in governmental philosophy; government practice went one way, opinion another. During that time period, the government philosophy score plunged 40.3 points, and the Bush administration became the most conservative government in Florida since these data became available in 1960 and one of the most conservative in the nation (Coffey, 2005). At the same time, the ideology of the *electorate* stabilized within a 10 percent range. (Berry, Rinquist, Fording, and Hanson 1998; updated annually). Governor Bush expressed great pleasure in this ideological distance between himself and the Florida electorate, saying he "loved it because it made the liberal press go ballistic" (Robinson, 2007).

State senator Dan Gelber, a Miami Beach Democrat, said that the governor was able to pull the government to the right when the electorate was moving in the opposite direction through "sheer persistence" (Bousquet, 2006), but no elected official can accomplish such a feat without a base of public support. And it was here that the Bush message and his targeting strategy proved effective. In fact, the governor did not have widespread public support.

Instead, he generated overwhelming support from the conservative Republican segments of the population, thus providing Republican legislators justification for approving his policy proposals. The following section elaborates on this hypothesis.

Creating Division: Public Reaction to the Political Strategy

At one level, Governor Bush's political strategy was successful and his overall approval rating among all Floridians drifted in the mid-50 percent range over the course of his administration. Data from the Job Approval Ratings database maintained by the University of North Carolina at Chapel Hill show that his average job approval rating over his eight years in office was 56 percent, higher than that of his two predecessors, Lawton Chiles and Bob Martinez, but 16 percent lower than the average rating of Bob Graham, who served the eight years prior to Martinez.

The governor's ratings over the time of his administration were quite consistent, rarely falling below 50 percent and equally rarely rising above 60 percent. This consistency suggests that something other than job performance may have driven reaction to the governor.

Not surprisingly, the Bush strategy of appeal to narrow segments of the population found higher support among some Floridians than among others. Huge percentages of Republicans thought that Governor Bush did a good job, but very few Democrats agreed and he became the most polarizing governor since public opinion pollsters in Florida began asking questions about gubernatorial job performance. Although he did not create as much division between Democrats and Republicans as did his brother, the president (Jacobson, 2006). Jeb Bush did generate the largest political disagreement about performance in office of any of the three governors who were his immediate predecessors. He was also one of the three most divisive governors in the nation during the 2005–2006 time period (Jacobsen, 2006).

Data from Mason-Dixon opinion polls conducted over the course of Bush's term show that more than 80 percent of Republicans rated his job performance as either "excellent" or "good" while Democrats viewed him much less positively, with an average of just 33 percent giving him the same ratings, a 47 percent difference between the two parties.

Information from the *Florida Annual Policy Survey* at Florida State University shows that the average difference between Republicans and Democrats when rating Bob Graham was 6.2 percent, when rating Bob Martinez it was 10.1 percent, and when rating Lawton Chiles it was 20.8 percent. The first polls about the job performance of Charlie Crist, the Republican who succeeded Bush, showed virtually no difference in assessment of job performance between Democrats and Republicans (Quinnipiac University Polling Institute, 2007). Thus Governor Bush was more than twice as divisive as was the next most controversial Florida governor for whom information is available.

Partisan disagreement about the performance of the Florida legislature during the Bush administration was substantially lower than it was about the governor. This suggests that the disagreement about Bush's performance was not simply a product of the general increase in partisanship that has been observed throughout the United States in recent years, but rather that the governor himself was the cause. During the Bush administration, the average difference between Democrats and Republicans regarding the performance of the state legislature was 18.4 percent, nearly 30 percent lower than that regarding the governor (Florida State University, Florida Annual Policy Survey).

Summary

As was the case with many Republicans around the nation at the time, Jeb Bush adopted a governing strategy "explicitly in line with the purpose of building core constituencies for the Republican Party and undermining support for adversaries" (Edsal, 2006). He viewed himself as a spokesman for a relatively narrow set of policy, economic, and partisan interests and made a conscious effort to promote these groups in the political process at the expense of others. Not unexpectedly, his actions met intense opposition and led to historic levels of partisan polarization in Florida. Nevertheless, his strategy bought him the support among Republicans that he needed to put his conservative theory of government into place and to implement the policy prescriptions that the theory called for. The impact of these policies is discussed later in the book.

Chapter 6

Campaigning for the President, 2000 and 2004, and Reelection

Introduction

Over the course of his term as governor of Florida, Jeb Bush was a major participant in four statewide elections, two in which he was the candidate and two in which his brother George W. was the Republican nominee for president of the United States. In each of the presidential elections, Governor Bush utilized his official position to enhance his own political position and his brother's electoral prospects.

The candidacy of his brother George for the presidency of the United States created a unique and complicated environment for the sitting governor. The family relationship provided Governor Bush a substantial political ally, enhanced his visibility, and increased his political clout. But it also subjected him to pressures and criticisms that other governors do not face. The George Bush candidacy for president placed Jeb Bush in the middle of a highly partisan political battle that affected his leadership and policymaking priorities, hardened both his own and opposing constituencies, and led him to take positions that reinforced stereotypes that he had made some attempts to counter. This chapter describes the ways in which a governor of an important state and a national political campaign interacted in the presidential campaigns of 2000 and 2004. In particular it shows the constraints on both of the candidates involved as well as the advantages they gained from their relationship. It also discusses Bush's own reelection campaign in 2002.

The 2000 Presidential Election

At the outset of the 2000 presidential race, Governor Bush exhibited acute awareness of his visibility as the brother of the Republican presidential candidate and of the possible implications. Thus he began the campaign by trying to keep a low profile. He claimed that he wanted to downplay "the dynasty thing," he was sensitive to the fact that some thought he could over-shadow his brother and he was concerned about the potential charge that he was using the governor's office for partisan political advantage. "I'm a second year governor...I want people to know that I am committed to Florida" (Nickens, 2000: 1A). But there was also the suggestion that he "was miffed that George was going to get to be president" (Date, 2004: 25) Thus he contented himself initially with highly successful efforts to raise money for his brother from his own supporters and in one day in June, 1999, he helped George pick up more than $2 million by tapping into the same network of donors who helped put him into the governor's office (Nickens, 1999: 1B; March 1999, final ed.; Wilkie, 2000, 3rd ed., A1). His attempts to remain "above the fray" were made easier for him when, at least early in the campaign, the Republicans took Florida for granted and did not call upon the governor for much effort, although Jeb took a planeload of Floridians to New Hampshire where they handed out literature, made phone calls and knocked on doors on behalf of his brother (Becker, 2000).

However, as George began to lose ground to Al Gore, some disgruntled Republicans began to criticize Jeb for his subdued approach, complaining that his efforts have "been too low-key and unenthusiastic to mobilize a groundswell of support for his brother" (Tait, 2000: 15). This criticism and the narrowing gap in the campaign polls prompted Jeb to become more visible toward the end of the race, to make more time for campaigning, and to raise his national profile by agreeing to interviews with national news correspondents.

One of his actions during this period brought criticism from Democrats and a court injunction prohibiting them in the future. The action was a letter that the governor mailed to Florida Republicans. The letter, paid for by the Republican Party, was printed on stationary bearing the state seal and appeared to be an official communication from the office of the governor. It urged Republicans to vote in the upcoming presidential race and encouraged them to use the absentee ballot. At the time, Florida law required that voters certify that they faced circumstances preventing them from going to the polls as usual when requesting absentee ballots. The governor's letter suggested that voters could use the absentee ballot simply for the sake of convenience.

The African American Community in the 2000 Race

With one exception, it is unclear that Governor Bush's campaign efforts and his performance as governor had any effects on voting in the 2000 presidential race, since few people are likely to have made their presidential vote choice on the strength of how they felt about George Bush's brother. The exception was in the African American community.

Both during his first campaign for governor and later in his first year in office, Bush had made statements and had taken actions that had antagonized African American voters. When asked in his campaign against Lawton Chiles what he would do for the African American community if elected, Jeb had responded "probably nothing." He subsequently initiated action, through executive order, that dismantled the state's affirmative action program and again further focused the ire of the African American community on the Republican presidential campaign.

In 1999 California businessman Ward Connerly began a campaign in Florida to place on the 2000 ballot a constitutional amendment banning affirmative action. Although George, Jeb, and virtually all Republicans were opposed to affirmative action, they realized that the electorate was divided on the issue and that a campaign to eliminate it was likely to galvanize Democratic voters, particularly the African American community. Thus, they sought ways to derail the amendment initiative.

After discussions with Connerly failed to convince him to delay his initiative until 2002, Bush stepped in with an executive order banning racial and gender preferences in university admissions and state contracting. Called "One Florida" the governor's program guaranteed college admission to the top 20 percent of each high school graduating class, provided that students had taken college preparatory classes. It also required agencies of Florida state government to make special efforts to reach out to minority contractors and to increase state business with such companies without the use of set-asides and price preferences.

This action, and particularly the governor's failure to consult with leaders of the African American community when it was announced, led to a well-publicized sit-in in Bush's office. During this protest, the governor was caught on videotape saying to the protestors, "Your life's gonna be a living hell. Kick their asses out." Although the governor claimed he was addressing the reporters who were present, and not the African American legislators involved, his actions generated animosity toward both Bush brothers from African American voters and when George campaigned on the south side of St. Petersburg in 2000, he faced a skeptical audience. One voter said, "It wouldn't matter who was running against Bush. Just by the fact that his last name is Bush killed him in this community after what his brother has done in office" (Waddell, 2000: 3). After Governor Bush had won 14 percent of the African American vote against Buddy Mackay in 1998, his brother's support in that community fell to 8 percent, the lowest of any Republican presidential candidate in the state since 1964 (*Tallahassee Democrat,* 2004, 6A).

Nevertheless, the move was successful in forcing Connerly to drop his efforts in Florida, and for Governor Bush and George W. the larger political benefit associated with the policy was the favorable reaction among conservative white voters, both Democrat and Republican, who had long harbored resentment against affirmative action policies.

Governor Bush and the Resolution of the 2000 Electoral Dispute

As the 2000 presidential election in Florida drew to a close, it became apparent that the decision in that state would determine the national outcome and it was also apparent that the result in Florida was to be extraordinarily close.

As the first statewide vote totals were reported to the Office of the Secretary of State on November 8, Governor Bush left Texas where he had gone to view the outcome of the election and flew back to Florida by private jet. Although the governor officially recused himself from the recount, his return to Florida "had symbolic value and he would work behind the scenes to mobilize his political infrastructure and legal connections within the state" (Kaplan, 2001: 43). In the next few days, he coordinated the activities involved in the state's efforts to resolve the monumental dispute that ensued and "it is known that he was prepared to defy the Florida Supreme Court, if necessary, to ensure his brother's election" (Dean, 2004: 54). There is also evidence that Katherine Harris and the governor had exchanged e-mail messages throughout the recount, something that both denied (Bardach, 2004; Milbank, 2000).

Although the charges surrounding the 2000 presidential election are highly partisan and likely will never be satisfactorily resolved to the satisfaction of the Democrats, most objective observers suggest that the governor's activities, and those of Secretary of State Katherine Harris, who co-chaired with Jeb the Bush election campaign, provided George W. Bush an enormous advantage in the counting and recounting process. Harris certified Bush the winner before all the votes had been counted and "with Jeb Bush as governor, the Republicans controlled the machinery of state government and with it the power to set deadlines, enforce election laws in ways that were beneficial to the then-Texas governor and put obstacles in Gore's path. Secretary of State Harris also relied on advice from one of the leading Republican strategists in the state—J. M. "Mac" Stipanovich, a well-connected Republican lobbyist who was an ally of Jeb Bush" (*Washington Post*).

These activities led some to charge that George Bush "fixed the election of November 2000 . . . and got away with it" (Palast, 2003: 72). It also led to an investigation by the U.S. Commission on Civil Rights, which concluded that Jeb Bush and Secretary of State Katherine Harris "failed to fulfill their responsibilities and were subsequently unwilling to take responsibility" for the problems regarding management of the state's election system (U.S. Commission on Civil Rights, 2001: 1).

Governor Bush and the Purge of Florida's Electoral Rolls

Florida was one of only a few states that require persons who have been convicted of a crime but have served their sentence to formally petition to have their civil rights restored. In the aftermath of a suspicious mayoral race in Miami in 1997, the Florida legislature passed legislation to eliminate registration of ineligible voters, those who had changed their residence, those who had died, and felons without voting rights. If not officially restored by the Clemency Board, composed of the governor and the cabinet, then felon names had to be purged from the voter rolls. Between 1999 and 2004, Bush and the Clemency Board moved slowly to restore civil rights and an estimated 500,000 people were barred from voting in the state because of the felon ban. The board also rejected the highest percentage of applicants of any board in the preceding sixteen years. It was not until 2005 that the governor made a serious effort to clear up the backlog of applications for restoration of civil rights.

Governor Bush's administration did, however, make a serious effort to purge the voters list of felons. The implementation of the purge, which began in the years leading up to the 2000 presidential election, brought serious charges that the Bush administration in Florida deliberately targeted felons and African American voters for removal from the voting rolls, on the grounds that they were much more likely to vote Democrat than Republican. (The most complete descriptions of this episode are Stuart 2004; Palast, 2003; deHaven-Smith, 2007.) The leading participants in this purge, which continued over a four-year period, were a highly partisan group of public officials in the Florida Office of the Secretary of State and in the Office of Executive Clemency, which reports directly to the governor and the cabinet. The secretaries of state involved were Sandra Mortham, Governor Bush's initial running mate in 1998; Katherine Harris, who served simultaneously as secretary of state and as co-chair of George Bush's 2000 presidential campaign in Florida; and Glenda Hood, former Republican mayor of Orlando who was appointed secretary of state by Bush after the state's constitution was changed to permit appointment of this position.

The purge began in November 1998 when Florida election officials paid $2.3 million to "Accenture," a private technology firm with Republican ties to compile a "scrub list" of approximately 65,000 persons thought to be former felons and began the process of removing them from the voter rolls. This process was conducted "with a zeal and carelessness that worried local election professionals" (*The Nation*, 2001) and the Association of Florida Supervisors of Elections warned the secretary of state, at that time Sandra Mortham, that it had wrongly removed eligible voters from rolls. This warning was ignored and in May 2000, the new secretary of state, Katherine Harris, ordered counties to purge 8,000 Florida voters who she claimed had committed felonies in Texas. A review of the list showed that not one of these individuals was charged with felonies, and Harris recalled it and sent out a "corrected" list of voters who had committed felonies. However, this list also was in error, since a law enacted in Texas in 1997 allowed felons who had completed their sentence to vote. No attempt was made to re-register these voters. The secretary of state then authorized the removal of 714 voters from Illinois, 990 from Ohio, and another 1,400 from at least eight states that automatically restore voting rights and who therefore arrived in Florida with full citizenship.

These later actions came after two court cases, one in 1998 and another in 1999, had made it clear that these citizens had full citizenship in Florida and were to be permitted to vote. Governor Bush simply ignored these court cases and then issued a written order to the Hillsborough County supervisor of elections, who had questioned his actions, demanding that ex-felons trying to register, even if they came to Florida from another state that had restored their rights, make application for restoration of civil rights through the Florida Clemency Board that he chaired. He subsequently issued the same response to the Florida State Association of Supervisors of Elections.

The most sophisticated analysis of the outcome of Florida's efforts to purge its voter rolls showed that Governor Bush's activities in the purge produced three results: (1) it created a list which had an error rate of between 20 percent and 30 percent; (2) those errors were racially biased, such that more African Americans were on the list in error than either whites or Latinos; and (3) and the decentralized process by which the list was used to purge the rolls resulted in a sometimes judicious and sometimes partisan purging process (Stuart, 2004).

The effect of these activities on the 2000 election appear to have been substantial. According to calculations made by *The Nation*, Governor Bush and his allies in the Office of the Secretary of State denied over fifty thousand citizens their right to vote in the campaign between George W. Bush and Al Gore. Since about 80 percent of registered voters cast ballots in the 2000 presidential election, this denial cost the state about forty thousand votes. Given that about 90 percent of these voters were likely to have voted Democratic, "the voter purge cost Al Gore a good 30,000 votes" (Palast, 2001; Lantigua, 2001).

The 2002 Gubernatorial Reelection Campaign

For the governor's supporters, the gubernatorial election of 2002 came too soon after the presidential election and there were fears that animosity generated by that election might have a negative effect on Jeb Bush's reelection prospects. Thus, facing no primary, he concentrated on raising a huge campaign war chest and by the end of March 2002 had generated more than double the *combined* totals of his two major challengers, former U.S. attorney general Janet Reno and attorney Bill McBride. Not surprisingly more than half of this came from outside Florida, with the two biggest sources being Texas, his father's home, and Washington, D.C., where his brother was president (Smith, April 22, 2002).

Bush and his campaign handlers initially calculated that Reno would be a divisive candidate and would be an easier opponent than McBride. They also assumed that her base of supporters in south Florida was more intense than were supporters of either McBride or the other Democrat in the race, state senator Daryl Jones, and that the Reno voters would turn out at a higher level than would the more centrist voters likely to support McBride. Thus Bush asked the legislature to change the rules determining victory in a primary from a majority of voters to a plurality, hoping Reno would be able to motivate her base and win. He then spent the summer running ads against McBride attempting to knock him out of the race.

Despite the Bush attacks, McBride was able to narrowly defeat Reno through appeal to the more centralist Democrats. In the general election, McBride's campaign focused almost exclusively on the poor condition of Florida's systems of education and child welfare and argued that Bush had not done enough to address the issues involved. In the early part of the campaign these issues and McBride's down-to-earth style brought him to within three points of Bush in campaign polls.

However, once again, personal connections and conservative ideology came into play to Bush's advantage. The governor's brother, George W., "threw his weight behind Jeb, making more than a dozen campaign visits and tailoring a number of White House policies, on issues like Cuba and the Florida Ever-glades" to help (Padgett 2004; Grunwald and Pianin, 2002). In addition, the *New Republic* concluded after an investigation that "Florida seems to be getting a disproportionate share" of federal dollars in areas helpful to Jeb (Lizza, 2002). And, during the first three months of 2002, the Florida GOP raised seven times what the Democrats were able to raise during the same time period, with half of it coming from out of state. In the end the Bush campaign raised $30 million and was able to outspend McBride by four to one.

Bush countered his opponent's attack on his educational policy by arguing that McBride's proposals for improvement could not be implemented in the ab-sence of a tax increase. In Florida (one of only seven states that does not have an income tax), the suggestion that a tax increase might be possible is likely to doom a candidate's chances, and it did so to McBride when he was unable to articulate how he would pay for the improved schooling he promoted. In an election with an increased voter turnout over 1998, Bush won 56 percent of the vote and became the first Republican governor, and only the second Republican statewide candidate, to be reelected in Florida. The Republicans also won all the seats on a smaller cabinet (attorney general, chief financial officer, and commis-sioner of agriculture) that had been approved by the electorate in 1999 and were completely in control of the executive branch of government.

The 2004 Presidential Campaign

People who were close to Governor Bush say that he was shaken by the margin of his brother's victory in 2000 and by the fallout over the disputed elec-tion. Thus, he was much less reticent about campaigning actively in 2004 than he had been in 2000, using his own popularity and visibility as well as his offi-cial position to advance George's cause. Since his policies were virtually iden-tical to those of his brother, reinforcing George's policy position required no rhetorical gymnastics. He also continued his efforts in Florida to raise money for the national campaign (16 percent of the money contributed by individuals to George Bush in the 2004 campaign came from Florida) and traveled the nation raising money and talking to supporters. As part of this later effort, he wrote a letter, on state letterhead, to the originators of the malicious Swift Boat Veterans for Truth campaign, saying, "I simply cannot express in words how much I val-ue their willingness to stand up to John Kerry" (Zernike, 2006).

Other Republican officials followed the governor's lead and engaged actively in the political battle. One such person was Secretary of State Glenda Hood. In the after-math of a change in the Florida constitution, this office had been converted to an ap-pointive position and Hood, former Republican mayor of Orlando, had been chosen by Governor Bush to replace outgoing Katherine Harris, who had been elected to Congress. One of Hood's first actions on behalf of the Bush presidential campaign was to order Ralph Nadar's name to be included on absentee ballots. This order came after a state court had ruled against Nadar's claim that he met the requirements to be on the ballot and before the state supreme court had completed an appeal on this issue. This move was viewed by Democrats as a direct effort to draw off votes from their party's candidate, since two-thirds of his votes in the previous election came at the expense of Al Gore.

Bush also took advantage of his official position as governor of Florida to tailor policy actions to coincide with presidential policy stances, to time announcements to bolster the campaign of his brother, and to attack George's opponents publicly. And "the Bush campaign considered (Jeb) to be the spiritual leader in Florida, offering advice and direction and serving as a cheerleader" (Associated Press, 2004).

The Voters List Controversy Continues

Governor Bush and his allies in the state legislature and in the Office of the Secretary of State also continued throughout 2004 their efforts to purge the "felons list" of ineligible voters. Both the secretary of state and the governor dismissed complaints from the media and the public about the felons list and refused to open it to public scrutiny. In addition, in what many perceived as another effort to depress minority voting, Hood insisted that thousands of registration forms on which a citizenship box was not checked were invalid even though the applicant had sworn on another part of the same form that he or she was a citizen.

Dispute over the voters list continued and the Bush administration refused to release it for verification by external sources. Ultimately, a lawsuit was filed by Florida newspapers and a Florida judge forced the state to reveal the voters list. The contents created even more controversy.

First, the secretary of state acknowledged that she had "held out two months before scrapping the database…despite knowing about problems with the list and the vendor responsible for compiling it" (Associated Press, 2004: A6). Second, in reviewing the list, news organizations discovered that only sixty-one Hispanic voters were listed, but over twenty thousand African American names were present. Hispanics in Florida, particularly Cubans, are more likely to vote Republican than Democratic and African Americans are heavily Democratic. Critics argued that this was proof that the governor and his allies had intentionally used the list for partisan purposes. The governor and his secretary of state claimed that the small number of Hispanic voters on the list was a function of a computer problem that they had been unaware of. But the private company that had been retained to compile the original list testified that it had discussed the difficulties involving Hispanics felons with officials in the secretary of state's office in late 1997 or early 1998. Further, the *Sarasota Herald-Tribune* reported in October 2004 that an e-mail written by a state computer expert said that Bush knew as late as May 2004 that there were serious problems with this database, but denied the Department of State's request to "pull the plug" on the project (Davis and Doig, 2004).

Given George W. Bush's margin of victory in Florida in 2004, the effects of Governor Bush's efforts to purge the voters list of felons were arguably less important to the outcome than they were in 2000. Nevertheless, the controversy surrounding these actions reinforced stereotypes about both Governor Bush and President Bush regarding their support for minority rights. It also forced the Bush presidential campaign to devote increased effort to attracting the black vote in 2004 (which it was more successful in doing than in 2000) and left Governor Bush with a legacy of hostility among African American residents of Florida. Over his term in office an average of fewer than 25 percent (24.6 percent) of African American voters expressed positive views about the manner in which the governor performed his job and support for him within this community fell by 7.6 percent from 1999 to 2004 (Florida State University, 1999–2003). In 2004, African American approval lagged 25 percent behind that of white residents and 35 percent behind that of Hispanics (*Washington Post Florida Statewide Election* Poll, 2004).

Gubernatorial Policymaking and Presidential Politics

Governor Bush's policy priorities were so similar to those of his brother he had little need to tell voters why the president's policies were good for the state. He could simply talk about his own policies since "they sound so similar when Jeb speaks they often hear what the president is saying" (Susan MacManus, "Bush an Asset for Brother's Run"). Thus he used his two mandated official statements—the State of the State Address and the Budget Message—to highlight the issues he shared with his brother, but he also took pains in these statements to steer clear of controversial subjects that might have had an effect on George's campaign.

In 2004 a proposed repeal of an amendment to the state's constitution to mandate limits on class size in public schools and a plan to require doctors to notify parents before performing an abortion on a minor threatened to raise controversy. The class-size amendment, in particular, was thought to have a major impact on the state's economy and on its well-being. But Governor Bush, foregoing his usually aggressive style, did not raise either of these issues in his State of the State Address. Instead, in contrast to previous such messages, the 2004 version was "more of a rallying cry to fellow Republicans than an ambitious policy blueprint" (Bousquet, James, and Liberto, 2004). Others saw it as a "self-serving political speech, pointing out his administration's achievements in sweeping but debatable terms" (*Tallahassee Democrat,* March 3, 2004).

Conclusion

Governor Bush could well have thought that he was a member of the U.S. House of Representatives given the number of elections he participated in over his two terms in office. Almost every two years from 1998 to 2004, he was a central figure in a statewide political campaign. These campaigns demonstrated that he was a magnificent fund-raiser and a good, but not great, vote getter. There were nine gubernatorial elections in Florida between 1970 and 2002 and Jeb Bush was a candidate in three of these. The largest percentage of the vote he received ranked fifth among those who won these races. Over 40 percent (42 percent) of Floridians felt that even this performance had been helped by the fact that his brother was the president during his term (Quinnipiac University Polling Institute, November 2005).

The election also demonstrated that Florida's electoral machinery could be put to use to advance partisan purposes, and many people believe that were it not for this ability to manage the state's electoral process George Bush would not have been elected president of the United States.

Part III
The Effect of New Conservatism in Florida

Chapter 7

The Consequences of the Bush Reforms:
Economic Policy and Governmental Reorganization

Introduction

As governor, Jeb Bush proposed both a new theory of government for Florida and a series of policy proposals that stemmed from the theory, and he was successful in persuading his Republican allies in the Florida state legislature to enact legislation to put much of this theory and his policy agenda into place. Indeed, when evaluated by one commonly used standard of gubernatorial attainment—achievement of legislative goals—Governor Bush was the most successful of the recent Florida governors. As a consequence of his leadership, the Republican domination of Florida politics and the ideological cohesion within his legislative party, a larger percentage of Bush's legislative proposals were enacted in some form than were the proposals of any of the other Florida governors who served after 1966 (Crew and Lewis, 2007). He was successful with his efforts to change the fundamental assumptions underlying the state's social service system, to create a form of accountability and choice in the state's public school system, to restrain the growth of state government, and to turn over to private organizations responsibility for many of the state's activities. He pointed to these accomplishments as evidence that his reform of Florida government had been successful and that "our conservative approach to govern-ment" worked.

Achievement of legislative goals is an important measure of gubernatorial success, but it is not the only one and does not necessarily constitute a successful reformation. Another indicator of success is whether or not the proposals enacted into law had their intended effect or achieved their goals; that is, whether or not the theory that guided the governor was valid. The changes made by the new laws enacted by Governor Bush were not neutral. They altered public priorities, affected citizens in a variety of positive and negative ways, and had a greater impact on some citizens than others. A complete assessment of a governmental theory or the administration of a particular governor must take these effects, referred to in the literature on policy analysis as "intermediate" or "ultimate outcomes," into account.

Traditionally, evaluation of intermediate and ultimate outcomes is guided by posing and answering questions related to the intent of the policy involved. For example, Governor Bush argued that privatizing large components of Florida's government would improve the effectiveness and efficiency of service delivery to the citizens of Florida, and he persuaded the state legislature to adopt this strategy widely throughout Florida state government. An assessment of the soundness of the governor's strategy and of the validity of the underlying theory can be made by answering two questions related to the legislation's intent: "Is Florida's government more efficient or effective now than when Bush first took office? Is it more accountable?"

The governor also argued that elimination of the intangibles and other taxes would both spur the state's economy and provide economic benefits to the elderly and those who had modest incomes. Assessment of the outcome of passage of these laws—and the efficacy of the underlying theory—can be made by answering questions related to (1) the jobs created after abolition of the taxes and (2) the economic status of the individuals who were no longer required to pay the taxes when it was abolished. Other questions used in an outcomes assessment include: Is the state's current school system superior to that in place when Governor Bush came to office? Do the citizens of Florida think that the state is a "better" place to live as a result of Bush's actions? And, which group of citizens benefited from and which bore the burden of the governor's policies?

This chapter and the one that follows utilize such questions to evaluate the merits of the governmental theories that guided Governor Bush's actions and the policies he promoted. I begin with a look at the impact of the governor's efforts to change the state's system of public finance and to reduce the size and scope of government. I utilize both empirical and qualitative data in the analysis.

Changes in Tax and Spending Policy

Governor Bush's reliance on the governmental theory of economic conservatism led him to focus on reducing the burden of taxes in Florida and on restraining state government spending. To achieve these goals, the governor proposed tax cuts in every legislative session during his term in office. This legislative agenda was supported enthusiastically by his Republican allies in the Florida state legislature, and over the course of his administration Bush legislation produced $19.1 billion in tax cuts, clearly a success when measured against the standard of achieving legislative goals.

The centerpiece of Bush's tax-reform effort was the abolition of the state's Intangible Personal Property Tax, but school property taxes were also reduced, sales tax holidays for school clothing and for hurricane preparedness were provided, vehicle inspection fees were reduced, corporate income tax credits for school vouchers were put into place, and taxes were cut on equipment and supplies necessary to a variety of business enterprises. The following paragraphs describe more fully the nature of the governor's tax-reduction proposals and speak to some of the ultimate outcomes.

Abolishing the Intangibles Tax

When Governor Bush came to office, Florida was one of only a handful of states that utilized some form of an intangibles tax. This tax was levied on stocks, bonds, mutual funds, money market funds, and other such investments. "By design, the tax is aimed at the state's wealthier residents" (Holcombe 2003, 6) and in the absence of an income tax was initiated to derive at least some revenue from the personal income of wealthy citizens and corporations. While it was the most progressive of the taxes employed by the state, it was described by the governor as "evil and insidious," "counterproductive and unfair." Governor Bush worked to reduce it in every legislative session between 1999 and 2006, when it was finally abolished. Its elimination accounted for nearly 30 percent of the tax cuts he initiated.

Other Tax Cuts

Somewhat defensive about the criticism that his elimination of the intangibles tax benefited only the wealthy, Governor Bush touted several other tax cuts as beneficial to working- and middle-class Floridians, or as he once called them "Joe bag of donuts" (Follick, 2005). These included sales tax holidays for back-to-school and hurricane-preparedness items and two property-tax roll-backs. The tax holidays which were short periods just prior to the beginning of the school year and to hurricane season allowed parents to purchase back to school items without paying taxes on them and allowed Floridians to purchase hurricane-preparedness items without the accompanying taxes. These tax holidays made up about 2 percent of the total tax cuts that Bush initiated.

Combining the elimination of the intangibles tax with the other permanent tax cuts adopted during his term, Governor Bush and the Republicans cut recurring revenues by nearly $1.8 billion a year (Date, 2008).

The Immediate Impact of the Bush Tax Cuts

As a result of enactment of his tax-cutting legislation Governor Bush achieved two of his immediate goals; both state tax effort and per-capita revenue collection were diminished during his administration. In the first three years of the Bush administration, Florida's ratio of tax effort to tax capacity declined by 3 percent and in the first five years of his term Florida collected, on average, 30.1 percent less revenue per capita than did other states (Denslow and Weissert, 2005: 20).

These changes did not, however, accomplish the ultimate goals that the governor set for them. For example, when compared to other gubernatorial administrations in Florida, these changes in state tax law had minimal impact on the governor's primary goal of stimulating the state's economy. While there was job growth during the Bush administration, data collected by the state's Department of Workforce Innovation showed that its rate was lower than that in any administration since the 1970s and that Governor Bob Graham had actually created more jobs during a comparable time period than had Bush (Florida Agency for Workforce Innovation, various years; Date 2005). Further, since some of the governor's predecessors—particularly Askew and Graham—had *increased* taxes and job growth had also gone up, the argument that the Bush tax cuts were the driving force behind economic prosperity was undermined.

In addition to the argument regarding stimulation of the state's economy, the public rationale offered by Bush for the elimination of the intangibles tax was that it would reduce the tax burden on the "elderly...and those depending on a modest life savings to support them in their later years" (Bush 2005, *Governor's Priority: Creating a Climate for Job Growth*).

This argument also proved to be flawed. Instead, economists in Florida argue that the cut in the intangibles tax "doesn't do much for the middle-income household" (Follick, 2005). The tax was a 50-cents-per-$1,000 levy on stock and bond holdings that affected about 2 percent of Florida's population, those who as individuals owned $370,000 or more in intangible assets and who as couples owned $620,000 or more in these assets. The taxes are also applied to businesses that owned such assets in excess of $310,000. In 2004, the tax was paid by fewer than 237,409 people (90,493 individuals and 73,458 couples) or about 1.4 percent of the state's population. Also only 51,945 out of more than 1 million businesses paid the tax (ibid.).

The real winners in this change in tax policy were the millionaires in the top 4.5 percent of Floridians. According to an analysis of data from the Florida Department of Revenue, the average individual taxpayer helped by this measure had $1.6 million in assets and faced a tax bill of $700. The couples paying the tax, on average, owned $2.7 million and had a $1,107 liability.

By comparison, the savings to the average person from the sales tax holidays was $16.00. The small savings accruing to each of the wealthy individuals from the intangibles tax cut took $131 million from the state treasury in 2006 and $161 million in 2007 (Kennedy, 2006) and over the time of the Bush administration, Florida ranked fourth among the nineteen states in the nation where the income of the top fifth of the population grew faster than the income of the bottom fifth (Center on Budget and Policy Priorities, 2008: 32).

Other Bush tax cuts had a similar redistributional effect and, in addition, helped shift the burden of taxes away from the state onto local governments. The 1999 property-tax rollback lowered the millage rate by .42 mills, producing a savings of about $42 for the owner of a $125,000 home who also utilized the homestead exemption (Center on Budget Policy Priorities, 2008: 32). In 2006, the governor proposed another $570 million increment to this cut that saved most homeowners less than $100 a year but meant millions in reductions to large landowners such as the Disney Company and the St. Joe Development Company. The bulk of the property tax breaks went to businesses, and local property taxes *increased* as local governments were pushed to utilize them to pay for local services. By 2007, Florida TaxWatch reported that Florida relied more heavily than most states on local governments to fund all state needs (Calabro, 2007). When Bush came to office the state paid 72 percent of the schools budget. By 2006, the state's share had declined to 53 percent. At the time that the governor recommended the 2006 tax cut, he also proposed a surcharge to homeowner's insurance rates to refill the coffers of the state's insurer of last resort that were depleted by the four hurricanes in 2005. The surcharge wiped out the effects of the 2006 tax cut and went primarily (97 percent) for high-cost homes on the state's coasts.

Bush Tax Policy and Ultimate Outcomes

Changes in public policy are rarely neutral and this is particularly true for changes in tax policy. In achieving his immediate tax-reform goals, Governor Bush provided relief to the state's wealthiest citizens while increasing the tax burden on the average Floridian. One result of this policy was to further undermine the state's already "feeble" system of public schools, medical care, and other social services. But, the more general result of the Bush strategy was to make the state's tax system more regressive.

The elimination of the intangibles tax, the one source of state funds based on ability to pay, helped pushed the majority of the burden of state taxes onto transaction taxes (general and selective sales taxes), which are regressive. Over the course of the Bush administration, the percentage of total state revenue generated from the sales tax increased and the per-capita sales tax ranking rose from sixth in the nation in 2000 to third in 2004. By 2005, transaction taxes accounted for 77 percent of all Florida's state tax collections. The national average was 49 percent (Calabro, 2007). By 2003 (the latest year for which comparable information is available) these changes made Florida's state tax system the second most regressive in the nation. Floridians in the lowest income group paid five times the effective tax rate as did the wealthiest Florida families (McIntyre, 2003; Ettlinger, 1996). Two years later, an economist at Florida International University in Miami showed that "Florida placed the highest tax burden on the poorest 20 percent of its residents of any state in the South...and well above the national average. But it placed the absolute lowest burden on its richest 1 percent...almost 50% below the national average" (Nissen, 2005). This downward redistribution of the tax burden is an ultimate outcome of the conservative revolution in the United States and has been described as one of the "movement's greatest monuments" (Frank, 2005: 5).

Governor Bush was immensely proud of his tax-cutting efforts, telling a reporter for the state's top business publication that "I'm the first governor to have cut taxes every year and I'm proud of it. I just love it. I just think it's fantastic, and I like it when people get mad that I do it" (Howard, 2006).

Floridians in general thought that taxes were not among the most important problems facing the state. Neither did they share the governor's enthusiasm for tax cuts. In a poll taken in May 2006 after eight years in which the governor had relentlessly promoted the value of and the need for tax cuts, only 1 percent of Floridians thought that taxes in general were a serious problem (Quinnipiac University Polling Institute, 2006). Furthermore by a 60–33 percent margin, citizens wanted to use surplus funds in the state budget to address state needs, rather than for the additional tax cuts that Jeb proposed in 2005 (Quinnipiac University Polling Institute, December 2005). At the end of the Bush administration, only 9 percent of the population thought that the situation with taxes in Florida was better than when Governor Bush took office in 1999. Thirty-three percent thought it was worse and the remainder saw no change (Quinnipiac University Polling Institute, 2006).

Slowing Budget Growth

As a proponent of small government, Governor Bush advocated slow growth in spending and smaller state budgets and his tax policy was designed to produce low levels of revenue per capita. An analysis of state spending over the time period 1999 through 2005 shows that the governor achieved his goal of restraining growth in that spending. (Data for the analysis described below came from official State of Florida budgetary documents and are provided in Appendices 1–3.)

Over the eight years of the Bush administration, state expenditures for all government activities increased by an average of 3.8 percent per year in 2000 dollars. Further, there was virtually no change in the level of state spending as a percentage of Florida's gross state product, or GSP, between 1998 and 2006. In addition, the governor was able (barely) to redeem his pledge to keep spending growth below growth in the personal income of the state's residents. In June 2006, the state had 43.6 percent more spending than when Bush took office and 46.5 percent more personal income. In absolute terms, then, the governor's spending growth goals were realized.

Despite these efforts, the state's total budget grew by more than 27 percent in constant dollars between 1999 when Bush took office and 2005, and the size of this growth was only 3 percent less than that which had taken place under the administration of his predecessor, Lawton Chiles, whom Bush had roundly criticized for allowing too much spending growth. Ironically, this performance disappointed the governor's small government constituency and led some to call him a "big-government Republican." At the end of his term in 2006, the conservative Cato Institute criticized him for having overseen "explosive growth" and gave him a grade of "D" for controlling spending (Slivinski, 2006: 13).

Spending Policy

The Bush tax strategies facilitated his "starve the beast" spending policy and gave him an opportunity to make the kinds of choices in funding state government that he desired. In the end, these choices benefited what scholars of American state politics call "distributive" activities at the expense of "redistributive" and "regulatory" activities.

Redistributive policies "reallocate societal resources from the 'haves' to the 'have-nots'" (Peterson 1995, 43), are structured by class rather than geography (Wong 1989), and have benefits and costs that are geographically diffuse (Peterson, 1995). Distributive policies provide physical and social infrastructure and are generally perceived to be a concentrated benefit (Peterson, 1995:, 17). Expenditures for highways are an example. And regulatory policies impose governmental limits on individual choice in order to restrict "unacceptable" behavior. The administration of environmental protection laws is an example (Meier, 1993: 81).

Bush's lowest spending priorities were for Florida's agencies dealing with its most vulnerable citizens. Over the course of his administration, expenditures for redistributive agencies—Children and Families, Juvenile Justice, Elder Affairs, Health, and others that provide services to the disadvantaged—increased at a very slow rate and were lower (an average of 1.7 percent per year) than were expenditures for distributive agencies such as Transportation, Law Enforcement, Highway Safety, and the like (6.3 percent per year), or for regulatory agencies (see Appendix 2). Between 2005 and 2006, the decline in spending per poor person in Florida was fourteenth highest in the nation (Gais and Dadayan, 2008, 27).

One embarrassing consequence of his lack of attention to social services agencies emerged in the days just before Bush left office when his secretary of the Department of Children and Families was fined and threatened with jail time for failure to provide enough beds to treat county jail inmates with severe mental illness. Records from the department showed that it had called repeatedly for funds for adult mental health and that Bush had slashed every request—in one year by 95 percent (Hunt, 2006; Rushing, 2006). To avoid court sanctions, the governor was forced to ask the Legislative Budget Commission, an organization that authorizes appropriations when the legislature itself is not in session, for an additional $16.6 million for hundreds of new beds for these individuals.

Somewhat surprisingly given his rhetoric about small government and his promise that he would work to reduce the burden of government on the state's citizens, "regulatory" agencies such as Business and Professional Regulation, Management Services, the Public Service Commission, and other agencies charged with regulating the activities of organizations whose actions can affect the economic or social well-being of Floridians also grew, by 5.1 percent.

Education Spending

State spending for public education is examined separately because Governor Bush made education his top policy priority. It is also considered separately because there is disagreement about whether to place educational expenditures in the "distributive" or the "redistributive" categories. Some scholars classify education expenditures as redistributive in nature, arguing that money is taken in the form of taxes from everyone and redistributed disproportionately to the less fortunate in the state in order to provide an education they could not secure for themselves (Meier, 1992). Others point out that the distribution of education money is not equal and that wealthy districts often benefit much more than do poorer ones (Morehouse, 1977: 335). And Paul Peterson argues that education spending is more "developmental" than "redistributive" because investments in education are routinely shown to be among the best predictors of economic productivity (Peterson, 1995: 65). Governor Bush routinely promoted his education reforms in terms of their economic impact on the state.

Governor Bush's strategy for education reform focused predominantly on the nonrevenue solutions discussed in an earlier chapter of this book; the use of educational vouchers, a requirement that schools be graded on standardized tests, and the use of charter schools. But he was also required to provide funds for education, and he often complained that his education policies were judged on the amount of money spent in this area, the "inputs," rather than on educational performance, the "outputs."

There was, however, legitimate concern about the level of inputs and a university-based research institute claimed that the concerns were substantial. In 2005, researchers at the LeRoy Collins Institute at Florida State University concluded that the state would need to increase its commitment to educational funding by 10 percent annually in order to reach an adequate level by 2009–2010 (Denslow and Weissert, 2005: 170). This level of increase was never achieved during the Bush administration.

The governor made education his second-highest spending priority and, in constant dollars, this portion of the state budget increased at an annual rate of about 6 percent over the full course of his term (see Appendix 3). The 2006–2007 budget included a 9 percent increase but came over the objections of the governor. While Bush wanted to cut property taxes charged for school districts, the Republican-controlled senate insisted on using that money for schools. Over the course of the Bush administration, per-pupil expenditures increased by an average of 1.7 percent per year when calculated in inflation-adjusted dollars.

The tension between the governor's commitment to cutting state taxes and the need for additional funds for education led Bush to promote policies that shifted the burden of support for educational programs onto local government. When the governor took office in 1999, the state provided 72 percent of the funds expended on public education in the Florida. In his last year in office, this percentage had dropped to 53 percent and local support had risen from 38 percent to 45 percent. The governor argued that this change in the source of funds for education didn't matter, but critics pointed out that the shift forced school districts to increase local property taxes and Democrats were quick to complain that this shift simply allowed the governor and the legislature to justify political claims about reducing state taxes.

The percentage of the state's budget devoted to education increased by a modest 3 percent throughout the time that Bush was governor, and in the last year during the Bush administration for which comparable data are available for all states, Florida ranked forty-fifth in the nation on this dimension *(Education Week*, 2003). The state also fell into the lowest quartile of states in terms of expenditures for education as a share of gross state product (National Science Foundation 2006). Finally, the state's per-pupil funding ranked forty-sixth among the states (Denslow and Weissert, 2005), and *Education Week* showed that Florida remained below the national average in starting teacher pay and in average teacher pay.

There is disagreement in the education policy community about whether or not expenditures for public education affect educational performance, but the level of financial resources that Governor Bush devoted to education could not have been expected to change in any substantial degree the quality of education in the state. Former governor Bob Graham, who also made education a top priority and who had been willing to increase taxes to support his position, suggested that Bush's budgetary stance indicated that the state had "chosen to be in the middle of the pack or less" (Matus, 2005). And a report released by a bipartisan commission in 2005 noted that playing on a national educational stage required the state to provide comparable funds to other states; something Florida did not do. "We are down to a minimally acceptable effort already," and "in order to keep the gap between Florida and the rest of the country from growing, state funds must increase at nearly double their rate of increase in the recent past" (Denslow and Weissert, 2005: 11: 170).

Growing the State's Economy

Like governors around the nation, Bush argued that his tax and spending policies and his more direct economic development actions drove the state's economy. As his administration drew to a close, Governor Bush claimed success in leading the state to "unparalleled economic growth and fiscal responsibility." In his 2006–2007 Budget Message he said that the "state's economy is one of the strongest in the nation, with rapid job growth and income growth providing its citizens with a wealth of economic opportunities." He cited the lowest unemployment rate in the nation, an "unprecedented" job creation rate, the highest bond rating in state history and the largest ever state general fund reserve balance as evidence that his policies were having the desired effect (Bush, 2006).

A closer look at data on the Florida economy between 1999 and 2006 supports an alternative interpretation from that offered by the governor.

Job Growth and Economic Impact

As shown earlier in this chapter, the job growth in Florida during the Bush administration was, when compared to historical data, less significant than the governor claimed. In no sense was it unprecedented.

While there *was* job growth during the Bush term of office, it was smaller than that in any gubernatorial administration since 1978 (Date, 2005). In addition, much of the job growth was the product of a growing population rather than the tax cuts the governor generated. Adjusted for population growth, Florida's job growth rate was thirteenth best in the nation in the years 2001–2005 (Nissen, 2005: 6).

Further, while per-capita income in Florida increased between 1999 and 2004 (13.2 percent), it did so at a much lower rate than it did between 1990 and 1998 (42.9 percent) when Lawton Chiles was governor. It also increased at a slower rate between 1999 and 2004 than did the rate in the nation as a whole during that time period (U.S. Department of Commerce, 2005).

Most of the jobs created during the Bush administration were in the low-paying sectors of the economy. The state's 2004 median hourly wage ($13.10 per hour) was below the national average and the state had an unusually high percentage of *very* low-wage workers who earned wages at or below the federal minimum wage (ibid. 2005). Jobs such as these usually do not carry generous benefit packages and Florida had the second-lowest rate of private-sector pension coverage in the nation in 2005, it ranked forty-eighth in percentage of people who had no health-care coverage and only 27.9 percent of the unemployed collected unemployment compensation, a figure that was tied for forty-first in the nation (ibid.). The governor's major program designed to offset the low-wage job circumstances, development of a biotechnology industry in Florida, is in its infancy and, in the governor's own words, is a risky endeavor. As pointed out by *Florida Trend,* the state's leading business journal, "investing economic development dollars in a bio-tech is a dice-roll because the industry has huge startup costs and a tiny success rate" (Barnett, 2006).

Employment Conditions

Employment conditions in Florida in 2005 were ranked forty-second in the nation on a "decent work environment index," by researchers at the University of Massachusetts. The ranking was based on measures of job opportunities, job quality, and workplace fairness (Heintz, Wicks-Lim, and Pollin, 2005). In addition, data released by the Federal Deposit Insurance Corporation in January 2006 showed a large drop over the course of the Bush administration in the number of Florida households able to afford a median-priced home. In the first year of the Bush administration (1999) 69 percent of all state households could afford a median-priced home under normal mortgage guidelines. By 2005, that number had dropped to 33 percent (Federal Deposit Insurance Corporation, 2005). In 2006 in Palm Beach County, *90 percent* of the workforce could not afford to buy the median-priced home in that county and there was a $209,471 difference between what homes in the county cost and what the typical household could afford to pay (Economic Council of Palm Beach, 2006). Later in that same year the state's agency for labor development, the Agency for Workforce Innovation, pointed out that the housing price increase was hurting the state's ability to compete against other states for more jobs (Bruce, 2006, E1). And in September 2006, the Florida Chamber Foundation convened a conference at which major employers of technical workers complained that even professional people with above-average salaries were priced out of the rental and entry-level housing market and that the state was facing a "long-term systemic problem" (Stacy, 2006).

In spite of these conditions, the governor asked the 2006 legislature to cap the amount of money dedicated to affordable housing at $243 million—less than half of the amount that would have otherwise gone to remediate the problems (Deslatte, 2006, 1A). Monies for this program were not appropriated but came from a documentary stamp paid on the transfer of all real estate in Florida and this decision made it appear that the governor was more interested in his spending reduction goal than in resolving a serious problem facing average Floridians.

State Fiscal Condition

Governor Bush's claims about the state's overall fiscal condition presented one view of that condition, but a broader analysis of the relevant data presented a more subdued picture than the one he described. As the governor said, the three major credit rating agencies did upgrade Florida's bond rating in 2005 to their highest levels in history. At the same time, overall state debt increased by 33.5 percent over the 1999–2005 time period and the state's debt ratio also increased during the Bush term, leaving Florida with the third-highest ratio among the ten most populous states in 2005 (State of Florida, State Board of Administration 2005) and with a $22 billion debt that must be repaid at some time in the future. In the last year of Bush's term, these conditions, and others, led the Kennedy School of Government at Harvard to give the state a grade of C+ for its efforts to manage its money. Thirty-four states ranked higher (King, Zechhauser, and Kim, 2005: 48).

The data described in this section of this book speak to the outcome of particular policies promoted by Governor Bush, but they also raise questions about the validity of the conservative approach to economic stimulation adopted by the governor. The data suggest that the approach did not have the impact on the state's economy that was theorized.

Changing the Size of Florida Government: The Downsizing Movement

Reflecting the politically conservative view that government "is part of the problem," Governor Bush promoted an aggressive agenda to reduce the size of Florida state government, to restrict its scope, and to turn over to the private sector responsibility for providing public services to citizens. He was extremely successful in persuading the Florida legislature to adopt this agenda and achieved virtually all of his legislative goals in this area. In the following paragraphs, I discuss the ultimate outcome of these governmental reduction efforts on the governing of the state.

Modernizing the State's Personnel System

The first large-scale effort on the part of Governor Bush to reduce the influence of government in Florida was initiated in the second legislative session in which he was governor, and took the form of "modernizing" the state's personnel system. Like many of his reforms, this one—the Service First initiative—found its genesis in the business community and incorporated recommendations from the reports of two important business-oriented organizations in Florida, the Florida Council of 100 and Florida TaxWatch. Both of the reports were based on strict conservative principles. They asserted the superiority of private-sector employment practices over public civil service merit systems and saw the abolishment of civil service job tenure as a key step in making government more businesslike and more productive.

When Bush proposed his Service First reform, he argued that the existing civil service merit system had over the years changed from a system that protected the public to one that protected employees without regard for performance. His remedy was to relieve managers of "cumbersome personnel processes" and give agencies more flexibility to compensate high performers. The changes he proposed, putting hiring and firing procedures in the hands of agency political managers rather than in civil service rules, "better reflect the realities of the new millennium and better compete for the most talented public servants" (Bush 2001). Critics complained that these fire-at-will personnel practices were made a key element of this initiative because they were a component of conservative political philosophy, because research had shown that they did not automatically produce positive economic performance (Werhane, 1999). Thus, the governor's "Service First" initiative looked to some as if it were an ideologically driven "solution" unrelated to the problem involved.

The major provisions in the governor's modernization plan were to move 16,300 employees from the protected Career Service into the at-will Selected Exempt Service, to expand the definition of "cause" for employee suspension or dismissal to include poor performance, and to eliminate "bumping" in most instances when layoffs occurred so that supervisors could decide who stayed and who did not, without regard to seniority. Critics of this portion of the modernization initiative pointed out that bumping privileges were retained in professions, such as health-care providers, police and correctional officers, and firefighters, whose unions had supported the governor while those represented by the American Federation of State, County and Municipal Employees Union, an opponent of the governor, were eliminated. Subsequent reforms also implemented "broadband" job classifications that collapsed 3,500 job classes and 475 pay grades into 250 occupations and 25 pay grades and began a procedure for reducing per-employee office space.

Programs of governmental reform are inherently difficult to evaluate and the governor himself made no effort to assess the outcomes of his reforms of state personnel practices and their effects on performance. Thus their effects remain unclear, and the theory upon which they were based untested. Nevertheless, one external assessment conducted by scholars at Florida State University and at the University of Miami cast doubt on the governor's claims about its merit. Using a survey of persons assigned to the state's Senior Executive Service and interviews with officials in three of the largest state agencies, these researchers found that the reform was of little consequence at best and harmful at worse (Bowman, Gertz, Gertz, and Williams, 2003; Bowman, Gertz, and West, 2006).

Downsizing and Its Immediate Impact

Florida has long been a state with a "feeble public sector that extends from universities to environmental protection to criminal justice" (Barone 1993, 53), and when Governor Bush took office in 1998, the state had comparatively few state employees for its size and spent relatively little money on the state workforce. In that year, the Sunshine State ranked forty-eighth among the states in the number of state employees per 1,000 population and fiftieth in the amount of money spent per resident on state government salaries (State of Florida, Department of Management Services, 1999). Driven by conservative governmental philosophy, Governor Bush discounted these conditions and took steps to further reduce the size and importance of government in Florida. This effort was made easier by the Service First initiative and was to continue throughout his administration.

The governor began his downsizing effort in 2000 by asking state agency heads to develop plans to shrink their workforce by 25 percent over a five-year period. He rationalized his policy by saying, "I do believe that state government does too many things, and some things we don't do well" (*St. Petersburg Times,* 2000). Employing this rationale broadly over the course of his administration and utilizing a variety of strategies, Bush met his goal of reducing the state workforce (Florida Department of Management Services, 1999–2005). Information from the state's *Annual Workforce Report* shows that the state of Florida employed 172,069 people when Governor Bush took office and 165,198 at the end of 2005. Some state agencies suffered particularly large reductions; for example, the Department of Children and Families, a special target of the governor, suffered a 45 percent drop in authorized positions over the time period 2002–2007 (Cotterell, 2008). Others, like the Department of Corrections, increased in size.

Bush strategies for governmental reform also altered the nature of the public workforce in Florida. Although women and minority state employees made gains in salary and in status over the course of the Bush administration, the size of the state workforce, job security of employees, and buying power of their paychecks eroded. By 2005, the average salary dropped, and the pay of the typical Career Service worker fell from $92 above the Southeast regional average under Lawton Chiles to at least $536 below it. The average salary for all non-Career-Service level workers dropped from $61,186 under Chiles to $48,076 under Bush (Cotterell, 2005: 1).

While Governor Bush was successful in reducing the size of the state's official workforce, public administration scholars argued that the total number of individuals employed with state funds likely did not decline since private contractors employed by the state increased their own staffs in order to perform additional duties originally carried out by state employees (Bowman, Gertz, and West, 2006). Furthermore, many of the state employees who had been terminated were replaced with individuals hired through the "Other Personnel Services" or OPS, category. OPS employees are, theoretically at least, temporary workers who receive no health-care, retirement, or other benefits and their numbers are not counted as official state employees. Critics claim that the governor made these positions a permanent and growing part of a shadow government workforce, thus inflating his claims about reducing the size of state government. These criticisms find some support in official data from the state's annual workforce report. The ratio of OPS to permanent positions in state government rose by 17.5 percent over the course of Bush's term, from 9.7:1 in 1999 to 11.4:1 in 2005 (Florida Department of Management Services, 1999–2005).

Emergency Management: An Exception to the Downsizing Rule

Despite the governor's focus on governmental reduction, Bush's downsizing strategy was not applied universally. One exception was forced upon him by nature. In 1992, Hurricane Andrew wreaked havoc on Florida and pushed then-governor Lawton Chiles to initiate a series of efforts to ensure that the chaos that ensued would not occur again. One of his first moves was to bring into state government an exceptional team of leaders for the Division of Emergency Management. To his credit, when Bush took over he kept this team in place, kept building what he calls a "culture of preparedness," and made it clear that disaster preparedness was important (Skene, 2006: 126–128). When Hurricanes Charley, Frances, Ivan, and Jeanne slammed into Florida in 2004 and when four others made their way ashore in 2005, this culture served the state well. Over the course of his administration, the governor initiated a series of efforts to improve the state's capacity to manage such crises and his hands-on, micromanagerial style worked to his advantage. He stayed at home from the Republican National Convention when his brother was nominated for reelection in order to take control of the state's emergency response; he personally took charge of moving special-needs patients from a powerless hospital in one part of the state to one in another part of the state that had power; and throughout he exhibited the kind of stoicism and empathy that public relations experts claim are necessary to reassure citizens facing an emergency. And, with one exception, he avoided the "blame game" so common in the aftermath of such events.

This exception took place in 2005. After first defending FEMA and accepting the blame for a slow state response to Hurricane Wilma, a frustrated Bush could not bring himself to take all the responsibility, and said, "People had ample time to prepare, and it isn't that hard to get 72 hours' worth of food and water, to do the simple things we ask people to do" (Nolin, Kleindienst, and Wallman, 2005; Skene, 2006).

Despite these comments, he did not let his frustration hinder his concern about the state's ability to deal with these events and in the 2006 legislative session asked for $565 million to prepare for additional hurricanes, to strengthen the state's ability to respond to disasters, and to recover from the effects of those that did hit the state. By all accounts, Governor Bush left this component of Florida government stronger than it had been when he was elected and even Democrats gave him credit for a job well done.

The Ultimate Outcomes of Downsizing

In proposing his reductions in the size of state government, Bush said, "My hope is that we'll have a smaller government in terms of work force, but a better government." Unfortunately, as was the case with most of the governmental reforms initiated during the Bush tenure, no formal effort was undertaken by the governor to assess the extent to which his downsizing initiatives produced the desired outcomes, and there is no evidence that the quality of the state workforce improved as a function of this change in size. Despite Bush's assertion that "in the real world we are compelled to evaluate everything we do" (Andelman, 1992), no baseline data were collected by the state that would permit a comparison of actual job performance under the prior system to that in the reformed system. However, an analysis of overall management performance during the Bush administration showed no change while he was in office. Conducted by the Kennedy School of Government at Harvard and *Governing* magazine, the analysis gave Florida a grade of B- in 2000 when Bush first came to office and the same grade in 2005, the next to last year of his term (King, Zechhauser, and Kim, 2005: 48).

In the absence of empirical data that speak directly to the performance of Florida state government in the aftermath of Bush's governmental reforms, citizens were left with *impressions* of this performance and information from public opinion polls show that Floridians began to lose confidence in Florida state government during the Bush administration.

Citizen trust in state government suffered an 11 percent decline over the time period that Jeb Bush held office. The percentage of persons answering "always" or "most of the time" to the question, "How much of the time do you think you can trust the state government in Tallahassee to do what is right?"

dropped from 45.4 percent when he took office in 1999 to 34.0 percent in 2004 (Florida State University, 1996–2005). In another poll in 2006, 61 percent of Floridians rated state government performance as either fair or poor and only 39 percent as good or excellent (Mason-Dixon Poll, Released November 15, 2006).

Research about the relationship between political trust and the behavior of public officials at the national level shows that trust is most strongly a function of presidential actions and the president's personal characteristics (Citrin, 1974; Citrin and Green, 1986), and it is hard to believe that the views of Floridians about Florida state government were not spurred in part by the governor's relentless criticism of Florida government and its workforce.

In the end, Bush's pursuit of his governmental downsizing agenda was so aggressive and persistent that even members of his own party suggested that his real intent was "to starve state agencies to warrant privatization" (*Tallahassee Democrat,* 2004). The following section discusses the governor's efforts with regard to privatization.

Privatization/Contracting for Services

In the search for the seeds of governmental change in Florida, or any state, it is easy to miss important threads of continuity. This is particularly true with regard to the privatization "revolution" that took place during the Bush administration. Many Floridians have forgotten that Governor Bush's predecessor as governor, Lawton Chiles, had initially campaigned on a theme of "rightsizing" state government and over the course of his administration had brought substantial elements of privatization and kindred strategies into Florida government (Crew, 1992). Thus, when Bush became governor in 1999, the state was ranked first in the nation on a scale of government reinvention (Brudney, Herbert, and Wright 1999) and on a scale of privatization (Council of State Governments, 1997).

Despite these rankings, the governor sought to extend the use of privatization and moved quickly to adopt the theory as the fundamental philosophical principle of his administration, even though he initially disavowed any intent to rush implementation. Just prior to his election in 1998, Jeb Bush was campaigning in Tallahassee and was asked what his administration might mean for state employment, the underpinning of the capital city's economy. He said, "I don't have any master plan to privatize everything that walks and breathes up here. To the contrary, should I be privileged to serve, I'd go slow on a lot of things. There's time; no reason to keep turning the world upside down" (Cotterell, 2006).

Few of the governor's campaign statements faded faster than this one and in a word association game in Florida, the name Jeb Bush could very well be linked to the term "privatization." While there are various estimates of the number and value of the projects involved, there is little question that he made at least as great an effort to privatize government as any other public official in the nation and declared, "I would look at any outsource opportunity if we could extract monies from the delivery of the service."

The governor was extraordinarily successful in achieving his legislative goals regarding privatization. In the Bush administration, Florida hired private companies to administer programs that other states had also privatized; managing state prisons, collecting fees on the state's tollways, checking elevators in public buildings for safety, and cleaning state buildings. But Bush expanded privatization into uncharted territory and contracted out state personnel services (payroll, benefits, training, recruitment, etc.), the management of Medicaid billing, vocational rehabilitation activities, management of state computer services, the management of the Statewide Law Enforcement Radio System, the administration of a consolidated purchasing system for state agencies known as *MyFloridaMarketPlace,* enrollment of families into the state's children's health insurance program, the processing of applications for various kinds of licensing, and legal defense for death-row inmates. Many of these contracts extended over long periods of time and, according to one longtime state legislator, tied the hands of the succeeding governor through his two terms (Cotterell, 2006, December 9).

Like other public officials throughout the nation, Bush argued that he was privatizing Florida state government in order to bring about cost savings and efficiency. However, the speed and manner in which he initiated and carried out his plans led some to suggest that political philosophy was the driving force. This hypothesis found support both in the very earliest stages of the effort to privatize as well as later when privatization projects did not live up to their promise.

In January 2001, Governor Bush hired a former marine officer as an "efficiency czar" to oversee his movement to privatization. When appointed, Bush said, "She will help guide our efforts toward achieving a more limited government that spends our taxpayer's hard-earned money in the wisest and most efficient manner." The efficiency czar resigned within three months, saying that the administration was moving so fast that it wasn't even bothering to evaluate whether private contracts would save money or whether public employees could perform the services more cheaply and efficiently (Cotterell, 2001). Subsequent research shows that she "was unable to slow down the headlong rush to privatize, computerize and downsize state jobs, a reckless process that lacked analysis and data" (Williams and Bowman, 2007). A multitude of problems that emerged in projects begun at this time, and that showed up later, verified this claim and an analysis by a highly regarded observer of government in the American states, *Governing* magazine, said the administration "moved far too quickly for its own good" ("Grading the States: Florida," *Governing,* 2005) in its privatization strategy.

Privatizing State Technology

Declaring himself the state's first e-governor, Governor Bush took great pride in his knowledge of modern communications and data management technology and pushed its introduction widely throughout state government, claiming it would "serve as an enabler to achieve the state's business goals and challenges, including a smaller, more effective, more efficient government." Despite Bush's expressed support for IT, its actual use in Florida state government declined over the course of his administration and by 2005 the state ranked thirty-first in the nation in on-line government services (Brown University, 2005). Nevertheless, several of Bush's largest privatization efforts focused on technology-related projects. The three most prominent were privatization of efforts to unify the state's computer technology, a contract to create a universal accounting system for all state agencies, and the award of funds to a private company to manage the state personnel system. Each of these projects emanated from the governor's office and were adopted with little objection and input from the legislature. Unfortunately, they became the poster children for the problems associated with privatization and ultimately led even some Republicans in the legislature to question the concept.

The State Technology Office

The governor's rationale for the creation of a unified computer system was sound: state agencies had sole responsibility for their own information technology and in the absence of a unified strategy created "silos" of IT assets that multiplied across state government. Services to citizens were handicapped by agencies unable to share information or link processes and redundant resources drove up costs. However, his proposed remedies to these problems—consolidation of control over these activities into the State Technology Office (STO), and privatization of initiatives related to IT security, the state Web portal, help-desk services, data center consolidation, and equipment purchasing—proved problematic.

In its six years of existence the State Technology Office was plagued with virtually all of the problems typically warned about in the academic and professional literature about the privatization of public services; poor control over procedures used to let bids and to outsource jobs, questionable relations between agency personnel and the private vendors involved, and inability to demonstrate cost savings to the state. In the face of these problems, the governor held fast to his faith in privatization and refused to consider alternatives.

The governor attracted immediate attention to the STO when he appointed as its original director an inexperienced political aide whose personal legal problems quickly led to his resignation. This problem was followed shortly by a scathing comptroller general's report that alleged that the agency illegally solicited money from businesses with state contracts, failed to adequately account for expenditures, and may have paid for services that were not received (Florida Department of Financial Services, 2003). A subsequent auditor general report found that the agency had awarded a $126 million contract to a private technology company without documenting the need for the outsourcing and without making any real attempt to determine whether it would save money. The report also said that the contract was awarded with open-ended costs and with little protection for the state (Florida Auditor General, 2004). Finally, just before the legislature stepped in to deal with these problems, the agency head who had signed off on the questionable $126 million contract with the private contractor resigned to "pursue opportunities in the private sector." The opportunity proved to be a job with one of the primary contractors involved, Bearing Point. The individual appointed to fill the vacated job subsequently canceled $259 million in contracts and sent one to the Florida Department of Law Enforcement for investigation regarding criminal behavior.

By the time of the 2005 session, the legislature had become so disenchanted with the privatization effort in the State Technology Office that it moved to abolish the agency as a separate entity. Resisting until the end, Bush vetoed the bill. At this point, even the Republicans had grown weary of defending the initiative and refused to include funding for the agency in the governor's budget, thus finally putting it out of its misery.

Convergys and "People First"

The second major privatization effort mounted by Mr. Bush was designed to support Florida's 189,000 employees and elected officials by outsourcing the provision of personnel services such as recruitment and training, benefits and payroll administration, and retirement. Labeled "People First," this was a seven-year project, valued at $278.6 million, in which Convergys Corporation was to take over the management of the state's personnel system, replace that system with a more efficient one, and improve service delivery to state employees through upgrades in technology and consolidated management. The project was made possible by Bush's "Service First" initiative which removed job security for personnel management staff and eliminated 900 career service positions. It was the largest of the governor's privatization projects and the first-ever government contract for the private company involved. It was projected to save the state $93 million over the seven-year period.

In the abstract, there was a compelling rationale for making this shift and businesses around the nation had been moving in this direction. However, the company's inexperience, combined with that of the governor as a manager of complex administrative systems, created a disastrous environment. Conflict over this project and the attendant publicity raged throughout the Bush administration and contributed more than any other project to the impression that the governor's privatization strategy was unsuccessful. The story involved is told below in some detail.

Questions were raised about this massive project even as the initial planning began. In a letter dated March 5, 2001, Kathleen Kearney, Bush's appointee as secretary of the state's Department of Children and Families, told the governor that the procurement process for the potential contract was riddled with flaws. In particular, she said, it failed to "articulate a clear vision of what the state is seeking the vendor to provide" and the "evaluation criteria and point scale used will not ensure the vendor is competent as well as effective" (Hirth ,2005). The governor not only ignored the comments of his secretary but his chief of staff chastised her for putting them into an e-mail that was part of the public record.

Convergys was awarded the project in 2002 and almost immediately encountered problems. First, the company simply underestimated the technical complexity of the job involved and allowed only nine months from the day the contract was signed until implementation. Its naiveté proved disastrous for a project that involved multiple agencies using separate personnel systems. Some agencies operated on a biweekly payroll, others on a monthly. Some started the workweek on Friday and others on Thursday. There were sixty-five or seventy types of leave. All of these differences were to be incorporated into a new centralized system to be implemented using a "big bang" approach, turning the switch on at the same time for all agencies and employees. It didn't work, and even after the state gave up on the nine-month deadline, problems abounded. Employees, including elected officials, lost health insurance, payroll deductions were omitted, payroll checks were miscalculated, and calls about these problems were put on hold for long periods of time. The state's universities said that the average wait when their employees called was forty-five minutes to an hour. The company missed "go-live" dates for three of the four primary functions it was to perform and by 2008, the contract had been amended nine times and extended to nine years in efforts to allow the company to complete the required work. At that time, the contract costs had risen to $349 million, total employee pay errors had *increased,* and problems with payroll production (e.g., electronic fund transfer cancellations) exceeded the levels prior to implementation of People First (Florida OPPAGA, May 2008).

As Convergys assumed control over Florida's personnel data, concerns also began to arise about the extent to which the company was protecting the privacy of state personnel. In December 2005, the inspector general in the Department of Management Services, the responsible state agency, said that Convergys employees were able to leaf through personnel files for their own amusement, download data to disks, e-mail it or print it out—often without leaving a computer trail. Further, Convergys subcontracted a part of the work involved to GDXdata which, according to two of its own employees, tried to cut costs for data-scanning from six cents per page to a penny by sending the work to India, Barbados, and possibly China. The attorney for the American Federation of State, County and Municipal Employees (AFSCME) claimed that this procedure violated state law requiring companies holding confidential personal data to notify affected people of "unauthorized release" of data and asked the attorney general to force Convergys to warn tens of thousand of state workers of the possible breech of personal information in their personnel files. Convergys ultimately admitted that files had indeed been sent to India; the Department of Management Services sent a letter of apology to affected state employees and levied a $5 million fine against the company. The state also paid $500,000 to Navigant Consulting, Inc., to conduct a special investigation into the procedures used at the contractor site in India. The investigation concluded that no employee data had been stolen but that "significant deficiencies" were present in system security and personnel hiring practices (Florida Department of Management Services, 2007).

Compounding its technical problems, Convergys also miscalculated the project's political complexity. Large public projects such as this require input and support from multiple political constituencies; state employee unions, legislators, and the varied end users of the services spread throughout state government. Convergys, conducting its first government contract, was naïve about these groups and failed to create a management structure capable of dealing directly with their constituencies. And the governor, with implicit faith in the efficacy of the private sector, added no pressure to do so. This failure led to significant difficulties, not the least of which was the design of a system to be run from a Windows 2000 platform when thousands of state desktop computers operated on Windows 95 or 98 systems.

Oversight of the project's implementation began with only two state employees, both from the oversight agency, the Department of Management Services. As problems arose this number was expanded to eight people and finally, three years after the project began, to twenty-two with a full-time oversight boss who reported directly to the secretary of management services. This group was "mirrored" one-to-one by Convergys employees. Only at this point was a "leadership council" of agency heads and other top administrators created and an advisory team of agency personnel officers added to provide regular contact with the relevant stakeholders. At approximately the same time the state university system felt forced to approach Convergys with an offer to help the company solve the personnel problems faced by university faculty that had been created by the transition from the state to the private personnel system (Simmons, 2005).

Shortly after this management upgrade, in August 2005, Bush declared People First a success, because "the state avoided a $80 million plus capital investment" (Cotterell, August 2005) A member of the staff in the governor's own Office of Policy and Budget said, "I wish he hadn't said that [about the project's success]. I've seen the data and the numbers [to support Bush's claim] aren't there." In letters to the editor of Florida's capitol city newspaper, state agency personnel complained that Convergys really wasn't running the project at all, that the company provided only a skeleton crew of technicians to manage the system and had to be supported by a "tremendous expenditure of [state] employee and new management time," creating "mini-personnel offices all over the state" (Meyers, 2005).

In the end, the state could not determine whether or not People First had achieved its projected cost-saving benefits. The auditor general's report concerning Convergys released in 2005 said that no cost-benefit analysis was completed prior to releasing an Invitation to Negotiate with the company and "at no time did the Department of Management Services ever demonstrate that viable alternatives, potential hazards, and costs of outsourcing had been fully considered prior to launching the procurement process" (Florida Office of the Auditor General 2005, 3). The legislature's research staff said that "the net cost impact of People First cannot be reliably determined, as DMS has not established a methodology to capture project savings" (Florida OPPAGA 2006). By 2008 projected cost savings had been reduced from $93 to $12.3 million with the expectation that these figures would be further reduced as additional staffing and training needs were met (Florida OPPAGA 2008, 6). Furthermore, the manner in which the huge Convergys contract was drawn made cancellation problematic since, according to the chair of the relevant senate oversight committee, it lacked protections for the state's interest (Kam, March 2006).

Reflecting conservative political ideology about privatization, the governor's spokesman said that "if we saved one dollar, if it was a wash, it was the right thing to do" (Cotterell, April 2006). The secretary of the Department of Management Services appointed by Bush's successor had a different view, calling it "an ugly pig" that she would have to make the most of since there was no prospect of returning state personnel services back to government. "I can put lipstick on it, but it remains an ugly pig" (Cotterell, January 2007).

Project Aspire

In Bush's first year in office, the governor determined that the state was not maximizing available information technology to make its financial operations more efficient. At his prodding, the legislature commissioned an analysis by KMPG, the giant financial consulting firm, about how to achieve this goal. The firm recommended a universal management system that required every state agency to participate in a standardized accounting system. Bush budgeted $100 million for the project, contracted it out to the Bearing Point firm that was also the contractor on the State Technology Office project, and set a target date of February 2006 for completion.

Over the course of the Bush administration, the managers of Project Aspire ignored the KMPG recommendations and instead continued to develop individual management systems within each agency's arena. Rather than replacing the existing mosaic with a modern system, the project began to harden that system. And it did so slowly and at great expense. By late 2006, the state had spent $89 million, the project was seriously behind schedule, and Florida's newly elected chief financial officer commissioned a study of the progress. The report concluded that Project Aspire had not utilized conventional industry practices in its work and that it was poorly planned, poorly managed, and poorly implemented. It went on to say that "there is a strong possibility that the state will not succeed in replacing the current financial system and transforming its business to effectively process and analyze financial information in the future" (Cotterell, May 2007). On the basis of the report, the CFO ordered the work stopped and the newly elected Republican governor concurred.

Other Privatization Programs

Privatization problems were not limited to those in the technology area, and the Reason Foundation, a conservative public policy think tank that promotes choice and competition in government, suggested that systematic flaws in the state's privatization effort "threatened to derail current initiatives and call into question existing contracts" (Segal, 2005). Two kinds of problems emerged; some associated with oversight of the contracting process and some associated with the quality of the product provided by the contractors.

Many privatization projects failed to establish systems through which their activities could be monitored and with which the state could hold contractors accountable. The MyFloridaMarketplace contract did not include a process to track associated costs and therefore could not be evaluated (Florida Office of the Auditor General 2005). It also had such poor controls that vendors could have been paid more than once for the same work (Florida Office of the Auditor General, 2006). The system created by the Department of Children and Families to monitor the activities of contractors hired to provide services to welfare beneficiaries was insufficient, and accountability for oversight of community providers of care for at-risk children was poor (Florida OPPAGA, December 2005; Florida OPPAGA, February 2006; Florida OPPAGA, June 2006). Privatization projects in Florida were also hounded by reports that they were used to meet political objectives. A Republican state senator said that the "governor has a history of reflecting accommodation of special interests as evidenced by his agencies' contracts" (Cotterell, August 2006) and that "companies can't lose in privatization deals with the state. When something doesn't work, the state either adapts to less service or companies fix it and pass the cost back to the public" (Cotterell, January 2005). At the end of Bush's term in office the state's new chief financial officer—a Democrat—said there were oversight problems associated with the contracting process in almost every arena of privatization that led to millions of dollars of waste (Rushing 2007).

Additional privatization problems were related to the quality of the work of the private contractors employed. A prime example was the program Bush initiated to privatize the representation offered by the state for death-row inmates. Designed to save the state money and to speed up the appeals process, the program did neither, resulting instead in delays because of inexperienced private lawyers and a lack of oversight. A judge appointed to the state supreme court by Governor Bush claimed that privatizing the appeals process led to "some of the worst lawyering I have seen" (Berlow, 2005, 5E), and the State Employee Attorney Guild said that the cost of outside counsel quadrupled after Bush took office as the numbers of private attorneys increased (Cotterell, January 2006). At the same time, the state legal aid agency that pays private lawyers to represent indigent clients ran out of money, leaving the private attorneys waiting for their checks or working for free (Waller 2006), and some Broward County court-reporting agencies refused to transcribe depositions without pay and cases backed up in court. Finally, in 2007, the chief justice of the state supreme court asked the Senate Criminal Justice Appropriations Committee to reinstate the public agency that had been replaced by Bush. He said, "This Court is unanimously and firmly of the view that the [public agency] is far superior to the private attorney registry approach" (Kam, 2007).

While Convergys and People First became the most visible example of privatization projects gone awry, the state's Department of Corrections also faced nearly constant controversy with its contracts, ranging from problems with food services to a sudden end of a contract to separate and distribute prescription drugs to inmates. The private company that ran the states' maximum security prison for girls gave up its contract after the state threatened to yank it for continually failing to control violence and keep the girls and the guards safe (Gruskin, 2003). Two companies running Florida prisons for profit were allowed to overbill the state nearly $13 million and "put profits for the politically well-connected companies ahead of the public interest" (Florida Department of Management Services, July 2005). This company was ultimately permitted to settle their account by paying the state an amount that represented about 42 cents on the disputed dollar (Cotterell, 2007). The head of the state's Correctional Privatization Commission was sentenced to thirty-three months in prison for dipping into prison maintenance and repair funds. The private company employed, over protests about the adequacy of its bid, to provide health care to inmates in south Florida's state prisons abruptly ended its state contract in November 2006 because it was not making enough money (Hollis, 2006). The same company was permitted to re-bid and was again awarded the contract, at an increased amount. The department justified its decision by claiming it would save taxpayers $20 million. Less than a month later, however, the DOC reneged on this contract and decided to take on the task of providing health care itself, using what it called a hybrid form of privatization that involved issuing 145 smaller contracts and purchasing orders. The DOC secretary said that this would add an additional $12 million in costs to the project in the first year but that the department would save money in the long run. In 2009, the state also took back the prison food service contract that had been awarded to Aramark. This came in the aftermath of "seven years marked by numerous irregularities, fines for sloppy service and a state report that flagged the vendor's 'windfall' profits" (Bousquet, 2009).

As the Bush administration came to a close in 2006, a large-scale state and federal investigation into the DOC found major contracting problems with the private vendors that provided commissary items to inmates and their families. The investigation led to the resignation of the agency's secretary and one of his regional directors and their subsequent conviction for accepting kickbacks from the providers who had been awarded no-bid contracts. The person appointed by Bush to replace the secretary subsequently voiced skepticism about prison privatization. Commenting that "I actually think the state is better at running prisons," he went on to say that he didn't see privatization as a "growth industry" (Cotterell, August 2006).

In still other areas, research about the privatization of the state's welfare program indicated that private providers were less effective than were public or nonprofit organizations in finding employment for welfare beneficiaries (Crew and Lamothe, 2003).

Throughout the first five years of his privatization initiative the governor brushed off criticisms of the projects from whatever sources, including the legislature's own research staff. This response seemed to confirm the thinking of those who argued that Governor Bush had not engaged in privatization to test a hypothesis about its value, but rather as an article of conservative political and philosophical faith.

Then, in 2003 the governor's own inspector general issued a report that found "controls over contracting to be in a state of disrepair" (Florida Governor's Office of the Chief Inspector General, 2003). And the problems associated with the multi-million-dollar contracts to privatize the state's technology system and its personnel system spurred even the Republicans who had supported Bush's efforts to privatize to begin to speak in terms of "accountability" in contracting out state services. Bush responded by admitting that he had made mistakes in negotiating big-ticket deals, by budgeting $1 million for creation of an office of procurement to help state agencies drive a better bargain when they contracted out for services and, finally, by directing the state's Department of Management Services to create a "Center for Efficient Government" authorized to conduct a statewide evaluation of Florida's outsourcing and privatizing efforts. The center was to develop statewide outsourcing standards and "a business case template applicable to any proposed outsourcing project." In creating this center, Bush also called for continuing efforts to "identify opportunities for additional outsourcing initiatives."

The Center for Efficient Government struggled to get off the ground. When created by the governor, it was composed of Bush-appointed heads of five large state agencies and a small staff. The center was to use new standards and guidelines to manage outsourcing projects through a five-stage review process and was to focus on agency projects worth more than $10 million. In order to increase the project's reach, and to give the legislature a greater role in oversight of privatization initiatives, the 2005 legislature moved to codify the center into law, to create a commission to oversee its operation, to approve state contracts, and to adopt rules setting standards for state agencies that contract out work.

Governor Bush saw this as going beyond oversight and into "meddling" in executive branch affairs and vetoed the bill. This veto prompted the chair of the senate committee which crafted the bill to say "the Legislature should not be left out of the policy making and procurement process to the point where we have no accountability and we just stand there and write a check" (Cotterell, June 2005: 1–2A). In the aftermath of the veto, the governor created by executive order the "Governor's Center for Efficient Government" designed to evaluate outsourcing opportunities for the state. Finally, in the Florida Efficient Government Act of 2006, the legislature formalized this center as the Council of Efficient Government. This legislation was a turning point in the state's attempt to assess the implications of the governor's privatization agenda. Six years into its massive privatization experiment, Florida finally created a mechanism through which its value could be assessed.

Ultimate Privatization Outcomes

The Bush administration credits his privatizing efforts with saving the state millions of dollars, for increasing service quality, and for expediting customer service. In almost all cases, there is simply no way to determine the effect of these initiatives since very few efforts were made at the beginning of these programs to identify a base line of costs and performance against which to measure progress. A number of audit reports on individual projects made this point, as did the 2007 Annual Report of the Council of Efficient Government. The state's chief financial officer who was elected in the administration that succeeded that of Governor Bush reiterated this concern in 2007. The 2003 inspector general's report cited above said that the state's privatization efforts exhibited a "lack of follow-through and performance evaluation after implementation." The OPPAGA report on another privatization project, People First, made the same point.

In 2007, the first annual report of the Council of Efficient Government provided the most complete picture of privatization outcomes in the state. The report showed that 92 percent of the 226 privatization projects initiated during the Bush administration had not completed cost-benefit analyses of the activities that they engaged in. The report went on to say that "a project cost-benefit exercise is…essential to a sound financial evaluation of an outsourced project. Without a complete cost-benefit analysis, it is difficult for the Council to assess the feasibility of an outsourced project and the benefit provided to the agency and the public" (State of Florida, Council on Efficient Government, 2007).

By the end of the Bush administration, it was too late to take effective action in some areas of privatization. In the election to select Jeb's successor, the person chosen as Florida's chief financial officer in the state office responsible for overseeing state contracting, said that Convergys was so mismanaged that it might have been too late to repair the damage and recover the lost tax dollars (Rushing, 2007). And in its widely respected "Government Performance Project," the Pew Charitable Trust called the privatization effort in Florida "an insidious problem [that] threatens to undermine the efforts to deliver services effectively to citizens" (Pew Charitable Trust, 2005).

Summary and Conclusions

With the cooperation of his Republican political allies in the Florida state legislature, Governor Bush made substantial changes in the way in which Florida state government was financed, organized, and managed. Together the Republicans adopted much, if not all, of the government reduction/reorganization agenda outlined by the conservative movement in the United States. Their actions reflected a view of the role of government that was fundamentally different from that shared by Bush's predecessors.

The assumption that drove these policies was that the private sector was a more efficient provider of necessary public services than was the government. Thus Governor Bush moved to dismantle public functions in favor of privatization and to reduce the ability of government to finance its activities. He eliminated taxes, limited state spending, reduced the size of state government, and made state employees more responsible to political influence. He turned over to nongovernmental organizations responsibility for a large number of the activities traditionally provided by agencies of state government. And he created new instruments through which private-sector organizations could compete against government in providing public services.

The governor argued that these changes created a more efficient and effective state. Although the governor's administration made very little effort to evaluate the extent to which his downsizing and privatization activities achieved their goals, evidence from a variety of official analyses of these efforts cast serious doubt on their effectiveness and cost saving. Therefore his theory that a smaller, privatized government is a more efficient, "better," government than was the state government in place when he took office cannot be substantiated.

Governor Bush also touted the reforms he made to the state's tax system. Data from official sources show that these changes had comparatively little positive effect on the state's economy and that the burden of paying for state activities was shifted onto citizens with fewer economic resources. Job growth during the Bush term did not expand at a greater rate than it had in earlier administrations, and overall economic circumstances—availability of affordable housing, distribution of wealth, and public debt—deteriorated. The elimination of the intangibles tax lightened the tax load on only the state's wealthiest citizens.

Chapter 8

Outcomes for Social Policy and the Environment

Introduction

In addition to its theories about governmental structure and finance, the governmental philosophy that guided the actions of Governor Bush also had specific prescriptions for what were viewed by political conservatives as serious ills in several major areas of public policy for which the American states are responsible. These include public education, social welfare, and protection of the natural environment. The governor made many of the policy initiatives recommended by conservative theorists the focus of his efforts in these areas and was able to persuade the state legislature to enact many of these prescriptions into law. This chapter discusses the impact of the adoption of these policies.

Education Reform

Governor Bush saw his efforts to reform public education in the state as his primary accomplishment. Putting into place the theories and instruments of educational choice promoted nationwide by conservative think tanks, he argued that he had "reformed education in a way that no other state can claim." His commitment to these reforms carried on after his term ended, and he created two organizations to promote his policy proposals and to fight efforts to undermine what he saw as his achievements in this arena. Calling on one of these organizations even before he left office, Bush used the Foundation for Florida's Future to raise $250,000 to fund research about his educational policies by a conservative think tank in California. The Hoover Institution at Stanford University conducted the research, pronounced his educational initiatives successful, and called for their continuation (Peterson, 2006).

The Hoover Institution and the individual scholars involved in this research were well-known advocates of the educational choice strategies that Bush had initiated—vouchers, charter schools, and educational accountability—and their analysis came as no surprise to political observers. Here, a broader perspective is employed to examine the outcomes of the governor's educational policies.

School Choice

School choice theorists argue that public schools perform poorly because their students, particularly those with limited incomes, have no options when selecting where they will get their educations and therefore there are no incentives for their schools to exert themselves to improve educational outcomes. By providing an option for students to attend a different and better school than the one they are required to attend, the state can ensure that students will get a better education and the school that the student abandoned will be forced to improve or will suffer decline. In short, so goes the theory, competition among a number of school choices will create a better education for all students.

Chapter 2 of this book described how Governor Bush adopted this theory as the basis for his reforms for Florida's school system and implemented it through legislation that (1) provided a variety of educational vouchers that could be used by students who wished to attend a school other than the one to which they were assigned; (2) expanded an established system of charter schools; and (3) put into place a system of grading public schools in order to hold them accountable for student performance. The following sections of this chapter examine the issues that arose in putting these reforms into place as well as their educational outcomes.

Vouchers and Charter Schools: Management and Accountability
School choice theory devotes little attention to issues associated with creating and managing charter schools or with potential problems in the administration of voucher programs. The underlying assumption of the theory is that alternatives to the regular public schools will enjoy high-quality management that will not affect the nature of the education involved. The Bush administration discovered that this assumption was too optimistic and that such issues can affect substantially the performance of these schools. Journalitic reports and governmental analyses released throughout the Bush term showed that his voucher and charter school reforms generated many questions about management and accountability, questions remarkably like those that were raised about his other efforts to turn over public services to private organizations.

The research arm of the state legislature, the Office of Program Policy and Governmental Accountability, issued four reports on charter schools during the Bush administration. Each of these cited weaknesses in management and accountability that affected performance. The problems ranged from limited experience in financial management (Florida OPPAGA, March 2005) to the absence of information needed to hold schools fully accountable for performance (Florida OPPAGA, April 2005; see also Florida OPPAGA, March 2002; Florida OPPAGA, April 2000).

A series of articles published by the *Orlando Sentinel* showed that nearly one-half of the charter schools that had been audited in 2005 had operating deficits; more than 140 schools had "intertwined business relationships that would raise questions at traditional schools or at charters in several other states";

and that "basically they live paycheck to paycheck, and when you look at it, there's no money left for students" (Shanklin and McClure, March 26, 2007).

As could be expected, lax oversight of charter schools led to some serious problems. One example was in Escambia County where the Escambia Charter School hired out a group of students to cut grass and weeds along county and state roads during class time and paid them less than state law required. This activity earned the school about $200,000 at the same time it was taking tax money to teach the children. To satisfy the local school board, Escambia Charter School sent false attendance records to the school district showing that the students were in class and false report cards showing that the students had completed their courses. The school subsequently pled no contest to grand theft, but remained open (McClure and Shanklin, March 27, 2007).

A second example was in Palm Beach County where the Survivors Charter School had a ten-year, $10,000 contract for eight season tickets to Miami Dolphins games, which it distributed to the principals and others (Shanklin and McClure, March 26, 2007). In addition, over seventy charter schools had to be closed over the time period 1996–2006 because of poor fiscal management, lack of leadership, and governance issues (Florida Department of Education 2006, 4).

Many charter schools, which were to have been laboratories of innovation that competed with public schools in order to force improvement in the entire public school system, were said to have degenerated into vehicles "for private companies to team with developers to offer home buyers an upscale amenity—tuition-free taxpayer-supported schools for their developments" (Fischer, 2002). The companies involved no longer focused on educational innovation. Instead, the schools, referred to as "McCharters," offered the standard curriculums provided in regular public schools. Further, and perhaps most ominously, the use of charter schools by developers of up-scale residential neighborhoods and by individuals who simply wanted their children out of the public schools contributed to a racially segregated public school system. Scholars at Florida State University showed that 82 percent of charter schools in place in Florida in the 1999–2000 school year were racially segregated, compared to 51 percent of public schools (Crew and Anderson, 2001: 208).

It was not until Governor Bush left office that the state legislature proposed legislation to provide greater academic scrutiny over charter schools and to tighten supervision over their fiscal arrangements.

Governor Bush's voucher programs also encountered the kinds of accountability problems other privatization projects faced, but he would take no action to correct them even when the Florida Catholic Conference, a major beneficiary of vouchers, pushed for accountability standards (Date 2004, January 4) and the Florida Senate and the state auditor general specifically criticized the McKay Voucher Program for failure to screen and monitor the types of schools being awarded the funds involved and for allowing operators who did not have the capability to provide proper educational services to enroll students in their schools.

In addition, a member of the staff in the Department of Education who complained publicly about the absence of accountability in voucher programs was fired. Despite a personnel file that contained only positive evaluations, the staffer was given no written explanation for the firing. His own view was that it was "political payback" for the public relations embarrassment involved (Date and Miller 2004, March 6). Not surprisingly, given this inattention to oversight, a number of embarrassing incidents ensued.

One Boynton Beach homeschool consultant received McKay voucher money even though she provided no direct services to special-needs children and a school in Jacksonville accepted McKay funds for fourteen special-needs children who had returned to public school. In addition, students were permitted to qualify for the program when classified as hospitalized or homebound for any number of physical or psychological problems, including temporary illnesses such as broken legs. Once accepted into the voucher program, students were allowed to receive vouchers until they graduated from high school or became twenty-two years of age, regardless of whether they still needed to be kept at home. The authors of a major report on the McKay Voucher Program released in 2007 said that "for decades, parents and advocates for students with special needs have been fighting to ensure that schools are held accountable...and that children with special needs are included in state education accountability programs. The lack of accountability in the McKay program is a giant step backward" (Mead, 2007: 4).

The Corporate Tax Credit Voucher was briefly suspended after two years because of inability on the part of the state even to identify all the schools involved. An employee of the Office of School Choice in the State Department of Education said, "There's $50 million out there, and I don't know where it's gone. I can't name a student. I can't name a school. I can't name a student in a school" (Date, 2003). The program caused particular embarrassment in 2003 when the Florida Department of Education learned that the Islamic Academy of Florida, which received $350,000 in tax credit voucher money, was named in a federal government indictment for alleged terrorist connections. The cofounder and director was convicted of being the U.S. leader of a Palestinian Islamic Jihad group and sent to prison and the school's treasurer allegedly encouraged people who wanted to support the movement to write checks to the school (Date, and Miller 2003; Kiimberly Miller 2003). In other incidents, an Ocala man was convicted of grand theft for collecting $268,000 in voucher money and failing to give out a single voucher, seven people associated with the Faith Christian Academy in Bartow, Florida, were arrested for allegedly embezzling more than $250,000 of voucher money (Lauer 2005, B1) and the principal of the Community Christian School took female students on field trips to Disney World, calling the students "princesses," and dressed them in his personal collection of swimsuits (Troxler, 2003). The Ocala conviction was subsequently overturned on appeal when Florida's Fifth District Court of Appeals ruled that the law creating the program had been so loosely written that the state could not prove that a crime had been committed (Date, 2007, April 13).

Despite these problems and the Republican senate president's complaint that "voucher accountability has got to happen; frankly, we ought to be ashamed that we already don't have it" (Date, 2005, November 16), Governor Bush would not support additional regulations on vouchers that were introduced in both the 2004 and 2005 legislative sessions (Johnson and James 2005). Instead, he continued to suggest vouchers as a solution to the educational problems he identified. He introduced legislation that would have allowed school districts to give students a $3,500 voucher to be used at a private school, create a $3,500 voucher program for private kindergarten programs, and expand the corporate voucher program so that more children would be eligible. The bill failed, but Bush kept pushing voucher programs as a solution to the overcrowding problem. In 2005 he introduced a new version, dubbed A++. The A++ plan called for "reading compact vouchers" to be available to students who for three years in a row could not achieve scores beyond Level 1 (out of five levels) on the Florida Comprehensive Assessment Test. The vouchers could be used to buy access to any private school—religious or nonsectarian—in the state. Once again, success in this venture was presumed since no mechanism was included in the implementing legislation that would allow the state to determine whether or not the private schools to which voucher recipients went were effective in helping the students who utilized them to enroll. This voucher proposal was also rejected by the Florida legislature, but separate legislation putting into place a voucher program for pre-kindergarten education was passed in that session.

The Florida Pre-K Voucher Program was authorized in a 2002 amendment to the state's constitution and was funded at $2,500 per student. By 2006, the program hovered near the bottom of a national ranking for such programs, suffering both on measures of quality and funding (National Institute for Early Education Research 2006). Public schools were required to participate in the program only if they first met the class-size reduction requirement of the state's constitution, a major challenge for most schools in the state. Thus almost all of the schools involved were private preschools and child-care centers run by religious institutions. The program had no mandated curriculum and faith-based schools were not restricted from teaching religion. Like the other voucher programs, oversight of the schools involved was virtually nonexistent and "quality and equity were sacrificed in favor of the principles of freedom of choice and efficiency" (Kennedy-Salchow, 2005).

Educational Performance with Vouchers

The theory underlying school choice is that alternatives to the public school system provide "better" education than do regular public schools and that providing educational vouchers that make it possible for students to attend these schools will benefit both the individuals involved and the entire public school system, as regular schools compete to retain their students and to maintain their academic reputations. Validating this theory requires that the alternative schools provide evidence of the academic performance of their students. However, while Governor Bush publicly accepted the need for accountability in his voucher programs, for reasons that were never adequately explained, his administration successfully avoided attempts to include evaluative components in any of them, arguing that parents would know if the schools were performing well and would remove their children if they were not achieving success. Thus the validity of the theory as implemented in Florida cannot be determined.

Students attending private schools with the use of the Opportunity Vouchers and the Corporate Credit Voucher Program were required to take the tests measuring academic progress that were required of those who attended regular public schools, but were not required to disclose the results of tests. As an alternative, Bush supported the suggestion of the executive director of the Florida Council of Independent Schools that private schools that received public money not be graded but instead be required to submit the results of tests of their own choosing to a private entity to evaluate (Brown, 2005).

In the case of the McKay Voucher Program for students with disabilities, the students were not even required to *take* such assessments, leaving both advocates and critics to speculate about the educational performance of the children involved. In an effort to gain some insight into the academic outcome produced with these vouchers, the *Palm Beach Post* examined the curriculums of the 641 private schools taking McKay vouchers in December 2001 and the qualifications of their teachers. The investigation found that 496 of the schools did not have classes "specifically designed to meet the needs of children with exceptionalities" and most of the teachers involved were not certified in Florida to teach special education. The law creating this program did not require that teachers have a college degree—only that they have "special skills, knowledge or expertise."

In the last year of the Bush administration, the Florida legislature did pass legislation that increased oversight of the state's educational voucher programs, but still protected participating schools and students from the accountability standards required of regular public schools. The law provided for better monitoring of voucher school finances, required that schools participating in the Corporate Tax Credit Voucher Program administer standardized tests to their students and required criminal background checks for teachers and other workers at voucher schools. The law did not, however, require academic standards for teachers, and the results from the required tests were to be given only to a third-party group and were explicitly not to be used to reflect how any particular school was performing, a key element in the governor's system of accountability for regular public schools.

By the end of the Bush administration, multiple millions of dollars of public money had been expended on the assumption that providing students a choice of moving from a "poor" school to a better one, whether the better one was public or private, would improve the quality of education in Florida. And in a November 2007 interview with Peter Robinson of the Hoover Institution, Governor Bush claimed that "public schools are better in Florida today because parents have more choices" (Robinson, 2007).

As was the case with most of the theories underlying Bush administration proposals, "school choice" was never subjected to direct test by the administration. But a number of preliminary research projects conducted in Florida schools suggest that the underlying theory was flawed and more systematic analyses of the outcome of long-running school-choice programs in Milwaukee, Wisconsin, and in San Diego, California, undermined the choice theory in more substantial ways.

A limited analysis of school choice conducted by the *Orlando Sentinel* showed that students who left Orlando's Jones High School, a four-time F school, improved their FACT reading scores by 3 percent, while those who stayed improved by 5 percent. Students who stayed at Ribault High, a four-time F school in Jacksonville, saw their reading scores climb by 2.5 percent while those who transferred gained 2 percent. A similar analysis conducted by the Broward County School District found that 842 students who transferred from "worse" to "better" schools within that district scored no higher than did the 46,291 students who stayed in their neighborhood schools (Shanklin, 2005). A more rigorous analysis of the Opportunity Voucher program conducted in 2009 by a Northwestern University economist reached similar conclusions (Matus, 2009). And the only refereed professional journal article to address the question of whether the threat of vouchers from the Opportunity Voucher Program provided an incentive for public schools to improve education showed that it did not (Figlio and Rouse, 2006).

The results from both Milwaukee and San Diego indicate that such results are part of a broader pattern. In San Diego the researchers concluded that "at a minimum, the results [of choice] raise doubts about the ability of choice programs alone to increase the achievement of participants" (Betts, Rice, Zau, Tang, and Koedel, 2006: iv). The Milwaukee experiment showed that school choice "is not a powerful tool for driving educational improvement," producing instead "bad schools" and "little change" and that "relying on public school choice and parental involvement to reclaim the Milwaukee Public Schools may be a distraction from the hard work of fixing the district's schools" (Dodenhoff, 2007: 2).

Educational Performance in Charter Schools

In contrast to voucher programs, some, but not all, charter school students *were* required to submit to the same testing and reporting requirements as were regular school students. (About 40 percent of charters routinely did not receive letter grades because of small class sizes or the composition of their student bodies.) As a consequence, limited information about the performance of these schools is available. The evidence, both from Florida and from around the nation, undermined the conservative theory that charter schools would outperform regular schools, drive these regular schools to higher levels of performance, and thereby improve the overall quality of education in the state (Braun, Jenkins, and Grigg, 2006).

Multiple studies in Florida, employing analytic techniques of varying sophistication, demonstrated that charter schools did not produce "better" educational outcomes than did regular schools. One of the most rigorous studies of charter schools in the nation was conducted in Florida by an economist at Florida State University. Employing longitudinal data on all students who attended public school (charter schools are public school) in Florida between 1996 and 2003, Professor Tim Sass found that "student achievement in the average charter school is 1.2 scale-score points lower in math and 0.5 points lower in reading than the average traditional public school." Further, charter school performance lagged behind that of regular schools for five years before it finally began to rival that of regular schools. Among charters, those targeting at-risk and special-education students demonstrated lower student achievement than students in regular public schools, and charter schools managed by for-profit entities performed no better than charters managed by nonprofit organizations, thus further undermining the privatization theory supported with such vigor by the governor. Professor Sass also demonstrated that competition from charter schools did not, unless there was a charter within two and a half miles of a regular school, produce improvement in the performance of the regular schools located in close proximity. In general, there was no correlation between the presence of charter schools and reading achievement test scores in regular schools and only a 0.4 higher scale-score in math (Sass, 2006).

Other research supported the findings of Professor Sass regarding academic performance and also showed that Florida charter schools had higher administrative costs than did regular public schools, that students got less teaching for their money than did regular school students, and that many schools ignored the requirements of the state's class-size amendment (Florida OPPAGA, April 2005; Crew and Anderson 2003; Florida Department of Education, 2006). In addition, a disproportionate number of charter schools were among the worst schools in the state, earning about 25 percent of failing grades, even though they taught about 3 percent of the state's students (McClure and Shanklin, 2007; Crew and Anderson, 2003). In one school in Escambia County, no more than 12 percent of the student body had *ever* been able to read at grade level.

Despite this evidence, charter schools were promoted relentlessly by the Bush administration, and questions about their viability were ignored. Jim Warford, who was chancellor of the public school system during a portion of the Bush administration, said that neither the governor nor the State Board of Education wanted to hear about problems. "It was symptomatic of their approach and style," he said. "From the top down, 'You are either for us or against us.' To even question means you are against us" (McClure and Shanklin, March 27,

2007). Sustained by conservative ideology, the governor ignored the premise of the original charter school theorists who argued that charter schools were to be experiments testing alternative educational programs and would be closed if they did not outperform regular schools. Instead, in his last year in office Bush promoted and signed into law legislation which his opponents characterized as an effort to ensure charter school continuation regardless of their performance. The bill removed oversight of charter schools from local boards and gave to the Florida Schools of Excellence Commission authority to approve or deny charter school applications, renew or cancel charters, and conduct reviews of facilities and curricula. The commission named as its director a former state representative who had been the sponsor of many of Bush's educational initiatives, including the commission, and paid him $140,000. Members of the commission were political appointees and charter supporters. Three years later, this law was overturned by Florida's First District Court of Appeals on the grounds that it was "facially unconstitutional" and the Department of Education, now under a new administration, notified districts that it would not appeal the decision. Then in 2009, when Florida faced a huge budget crisis, the state legislature cut all funds for the commission. Conservatives on the editorial page of the *Wall Street Journal* blamed Governor Charlie Crist, saying that he "had handed a victory to opponents of school choice" (Follick, 2009; *Wall Street Journal*, 2009).

The Legal Status of Vouchers
The initial Bush proposal to use vouchers supported by public funds to pay tuition in private religious schools—the Opportunity Voucher Program—instantly raised concerns about violations of the state constitution and prompted a lawsuit in 2001 that drug on throughout most of the Bush term. Ultimately, in December 2005, the Florida Supreme Court ruled this voucher program invalid on the grounds that it undermined the state constitution's requirement that Florida maintain a "uniform, efficient, safe, secure and high quality" public school system. In the eyes of the court, the diversion of money to private schools not only reduced money available to free schools but also funded private schools that were not "uniform" when compared with one another or to other public schools. The state chose not to ask whether they were efficient. While restricted to the Opportunity Voucher Program, the ruling also raised questions about the viability of the other voucher programs described above.

The supreme court ruling on vouchers challenged one of the fundamental elements of Bush's neoconservative governance theory: that policy positions are moral absolutes rather than options open to debate and alteration. And he was angry. In his subsequent State of the State Address he called school choice a "moral imperative" and labeled its demise an outcome that "defies decency and common sense." He immediately began efforts to overturn the decision by introducing legislation that would have amended the state's constitution to allow vouchers. And here he faced the most-embarrassing defeat of his administration.

The Florida House of Representatives easily passed a bill authorizing the change Bush proposed, but the legislation got caught in an internal dispute over leadership in the state senate and failed to gain support. Four Republican senators joined with all but one of the Democrats to defeat the amendment proposal. Despite frantic efforts to revive the proposal in the final three days of the legislative session, the governor could not persuade any of the four Republicans who had voted against the amendment to reconsider. In the end, he settled for a new law, rather than a constitutional amendment, that enhanced the trouble-prone Corporate Tax Credit Voucher Program and allowed corporations to pay for the vouchers of the students in the Opportunity Voucher Program as long as the children who received them qualified for free or reduced lunches. The corporations were to write the schools a check and the state would then give the corporation a dollar-for-dollar tax credit. While there were questions about the constitutionality of this measure also, it was the best the governor could do to sustain what some viewed as the signature feature of his administration.

In addition to failing to satisfy the Florida Supreme Court, Governor Bush was never able to persuade the citizens of Florida of the merit of vouchers. At the end of his term, in 2006, a poll conducted by the *St. Petersburg Times* found that 61 percent of those interviewed opposed the use of vouchers in pursuit of school improvement (Matus and Winchester, 2006).

Reflecting the stubbornness in pursuit of his objectives that had characterized his administration, Bush ignored this sentiment and never gave up on vouchers as a technique for improving educational performance in the Florida public schools. He continued his campaign for them even after he left office and in 2007 campaigned for a governor of South Carolina who was advocating vouchers in that state. In that same year, the director of Bush's Foundation for Florida's Future, who was also his top education aide while he was governor, and other Bush supporters were appointed to the state's Taxation and Budget Reform Commission, which is convened every twenty years to suggest constitutional amendments relating to the state's tax and budgetary conditions. While education issues appeared to be outside the jurisdiction of the commission, Bush's supporters used it to try to place two amendments on the November 2008 ballot that would have reversed the court decision that found vouchers unconstitutional (Date, 2007, December 17). In a suit brought by the state's educators, the state's supreme court found that the amendments were indeed outside the boundaries of the commission. As one justice said, it's "about as far afield as you can get" (Leary and Matus, 2008) and in a unanimous decision in September 2008 threw the amendments off the ballot. Reflecting the concern that Bush and his conservative adherents would not give up on the issue, the executive director of the ACLU of Florida said, "It's naïve to think this is the end of the battle" (Kaczor, 2008).

High-Stakes Testing and Accountability

The second component of Governor Bush's educational reform program focused on changing the way in which Florida's regular public schools delivered their product and reported on their performance. The policy contained two components: (1) grading public school reading, writing, and mathematics performance on an A–F scale; and (2) annual reporting of these grades to the public. The policy pushed teachers and school administrators to focus more intently, critics said exclusively, on reading and mathematics at the expense of other subjects.

There is no question that the publicity that the governor's rules brought to educational performance changed the behavior of the state's public school system and made teachers and school administrators more sensitive to the quality of their reading and mathematics products. One editorial writer suggested that these requirements were Jeb's greatest legacy and that his actions "put an end to complacency in Florida's public schools" (Berlow, 2006, 5E). Whether these efforts improved the quality of education in Florida is more debatable.

The public debate over the educational effect of these initiatives raged throughout the governor's tenure and Bush mounted an aggressive effort to defend his A+ Plan, citing the quality of the FCAT and improved student performance on the test as evidence that the plan worked. The governor's position was that the narrow focus on reading, writing, and mathematics that he advocated ensured that all students had similar experiences that prepared them for the future. His critics argued that the claims about increased performance were questionable and the focus on testing left out creativity and a broader curriculum, "led to a reduction in instruction in untested subjects and brought attention to test-wiseness rather than general student achievement" (Dorn, 2007). A researcher at Johns Hopkins University cited the focus on testing as an explanation for Florida's high dropout rate—the state was second in the nation in number of "dropout factories" (Associated Press, 2007). Within two years of Governor Bush's last year in office these, and other, complaints led the state legislature to reduce the importance of the tests in evaluating school performance and in student promotions.

Assessing the impact of a standardized test on student learning is problematic. While at least one national education organization (Achieve, Inc.) claimed that the FCAT is not "overly demanding" and reflects "modest expectation," many students and their parents complained that it was too difficult. In 2005, results from the test showed that 71 percent of fourth graders were proficient in reading when only 30 percent of these students achieved proficiency on the National Assessment of Educational Progress (NAEP) exam. And in 2006, 60 percent of the schools that scored either A or B on the state FCAT test failed to meet the standards for the federal No Child Left Behind Law.

Other data also suggested that educational achievement in Florida was not high. Florida was one of only two states in the union that showed a decline from 2004 to 2005 in the percentage of high school seniors demonstrating college-level mastery on at least one Advanced Placement Test (Associated Press, February 7, 2006), and the average composite score for Florida students who took the ACT college exam declined over the time period of the Bush administration (www.act.org). In 2006, the state ranked forty-eighth in the nation on the composite SAT test and forty-ninth on the essay portion. Finally, a 2005 study of high school students entering south Florida's community colleges showed that most lacked the basic skills they needed to take college-level classes and were required to take remedial courses after being admitted to college even though they had passed the FCAT. The dean of curriculum at Palm Beach County College said that "there's a disconnect between what is required for students in high school and what is required to be placed in college-level courses" (Travis, 2006).

When asked to justify his educational policies, Governor Bush asserted that "the A+ Plan has yielded rising student achievement," typically citing improvement in the skills of third or fourth graders. On this the governor was correct. There were improvements in student performance on the FCAT over its history, especially with regard to elementary school children. In fact, critics argued that the governor consciously focused on elementary students because they were easier to help. Jim Warford, who served as the state's chancellor for K–12 education from 2002 through 2005, told a reporter that "Bush knew middle and high school students would be much harder to fix and wanted to wait until the end of his term to try—too late for him to be held accountable if the plan failed" (Pinzur, 2006). Whether or not the improvements that did take place can be attributed to the A+ plan is questionable.

Efforts to raise educational expectations for students in Florida and to specify standards for meeting the goals began as early as 1972 and the FCAT itself was conceptualized and first administered during the administration of Bush's predecessor, Lawton Chiles (Florida Department of Education, 2005). In response to these efforts, educational attainment in the state had begun to improve prior to the passage of Bush's A+ Plan and therefore cannot be attributed solely to the Bush innovation of publicly assigning grades to schools. Other factors, "the concentration of Title I programs in elementary schools, the state support of elementary instruction through the Florida Center for Reading Research, the importance of non-tested subjects in secondary schools, the cumulative effects of grade retention, and a cohort effect of the Healthy Start program," may also have been responsible (Dorn, 2007: 10). Further, the change involved in educational attainment was not uniformly positive. For example, mean reading scores for tenth graders in 1998 were higher than in 2006, and these scores declined every year between 2001 and 2005.

Some educators felt that performance on a test like the FCAT, for which teachers primed their students throughout an entire school year, was not a valid measure of student learning and focused instead on information from the National Assessment of Educational Progress (NEAP) exam in order to evaluate the effect of the governor's reforms. These data also raised questions about the governor's argument that his A+ plan brought about positive change in public education in the state.

The NEAP data for Florida show performance both prior to and after the initiation of the Bush A+ plan and cover the years 1992 to 2005. After an initial decline from 1992 to 1994, *overall* reading scores for fourth graders began to improve in 1998, prior to the initiation of the Bush A+ plan, and continued to do so into 2005. At the same time, the numbers of these students who were deemed *proficient* in reading—meaning that they had mastered fundamental skills— declined from 2003 to 2005. Eighth-grade scores in reading, which were first reported in 1998, improved in 2002, *declined* in 2003, and declined again in 2005. The numbers of eighth graders who were proficient in reading also declined from 2003 to 2005.

Mathematics scores showed a pattern similar to that of the fourth-grade reading scores. Fourth-grade math scores, first reported in 1992, began to improve in 1996 before the A+ plan and continued to do so into 2005. Eighth-grade scores, which were first reported in 1990, improved in 1992 and in 1996, both prior to the initiation of the A+ plan, and continued to do so after the initiation of the plan into 2005. However, math *proficiency* scores declined between 2003 and 2005 (National Center for Education Statistics, 2005).

Despite the changes, which Governor Bush said were the results of his efforts, the state still hovered at just the national average on both mathematics and reading in both fourth and eighth grades. In 2005 Florida was slightly above this average in fourth-grade scores, but below the average in both reading and math in the eighth grade. "Furthermore, few changes in the achievement gaps among different population subgroups are statistically significant and for those grades with evidence of improvement, factors other than accountability may be responsible for the changes" (Dorn, 2007: 1). In addition, in 2005 the highest percentage of students on any test who were rated as "proficient" was only 37 percent. Even the governor's most loyal supporters, the business community's Council of 100, said that "the middle schools and high schools are still way below national average," as was the university system (Scott, 2006: 1E). At the end of the governor's term a leading newspaper suggested that "the tough truth is that Florida, the fourth-most populous state in the nation, consistently remains among the lowest states in most frequently cited measures of educational performance and quality."

The citizens of Florida also seemed to recognize the limitations of the A+ Plan. A Mason-Dixon Poll conducted in June 2002 found that only one-third of the respondents believed that the plan had actually improved public education, although more than two-thirds believed Bush genuinely wanted to do so (Bridges, 2002). And in Bush's last year in office in 2006, only 41 percent of Floridians said that Florida's public education was good or excellent while 58 percent deemed it fair or poor (Mason-Dixon Corporation, October 2006). Finally, the bipartisan Constitutional Accountability Commission faulted the state for its educational performance, saying that Florida was failing to meet a constitutional requirement to provide its children with a "high-quality" education (Florida School Boards Association, 2005).

In spite of evidence that most of his educational strategies had failed to achieve their goals, the governor continued to promote them and in 2008 after his term had ended, he announced the formation of the Foundation for Excellence in Education to carry out programs to demonstrate the value of vouchers, school accountability, and teacher merit pay. The FEE, as it is called, differed from the first foundation that he created to perpetuate his educational programs, the Foundation for Florida's Future, in that it qualified for tax-free contributions. The Foundation for Excellence in Education was backed by a handful of powerful corporations that had been supporters of Bush during his term in office and was staffed by "some of Bush's closest political advisors" (Matus, 2008).

Nevertheless, support for the governor's A+ reform continued to wan, and in 2009 the state legislature reduced the emphasis of the FCAT exam in determining high school grades. This bill made the FCAT only 50 percent of a high school's grade, reserving the remainder to graduation rates, student participation, and passage of the Advanced Placement and International Baccalaureate exams.

Reducing Class Size

One other education issue hovered over the Florida education policy agenda throughout the last half of Bush's administration, one that revealed much about the limits of the governor's thinking regarding solutions to educational issues.

During Bush's campaign for reelection in November 2002, Florida voters approved an amendment to the state's constitution setting restrictions on class size in the public schools. Although the governor had decried overcrowded schools and classrooms during his first run for office and had sent his own children to private schools that used their small classes as indicators of a quality education, he vigorously opposed the passage of this amendment, criticizing it almost as much as he criticized his opponent in the gubernatorial campaign. Reflecting his view that additional money was not the solution to the educational problem in Florida, he argued that reducing class size would be too expensive for the state. In order to support this position, he projected what proved to be inflated estimates of the costs involved (Date, January 2005) and claimed that the expense would "blot out the [budget] sun." Floridians ignored Bush's admonitions and passed the amendment, and the governor spent the remainder of his administration criticizing it and seeking ways to avoid allocating the money necessary to its implementation. The executive director of the Florida Association of School Administrators said that the governor missed multiple opportunities to get compromise on this issue during his term. "There was an arrogance, a hubris, a lack of collaboration, cooperation on every major issue" (Kaczor, 2006). In the end he avoided the mandate and refused to fund it at the appropriate level.

In the year in which the amendment was adopted, state economists estimated that Bush would need to set aside about $10.7 billion to fully implement the program by the 2010 deadline. This was an investment that the governor was unwilling to make. Between 2002 and 2006, in years of budget surpluses, the state spent only $3.7 billion to implement this amendment and the governor and Republican legislators made it the scapegoat for reductions in other arenas, particularly higher education.

By 2006, Florida schools were the largest in the nation (*Education Week*, 2006), and their size was being blamed for the state's second-place ranking on a list of "dropout factories" where no more than 60 percent of students who start as freshmen make it to their senior year (Associated Press, 2007). At this point Republicans were arguing that there was not now enough time to build the necessary schools, even though funds were available. Local school officials claimed that the state's reluctance to pay for new schools only increased the costs and forced the counties to expend local tax money that could have gone toward replacing portable classrooms and repairing older schools. Finally, facing the results of private polls which showed that voters did not want to repeal the amendment, the Republican leaders in the senate took action in the 2006 legislature, over the objections of the governor, to set aside $3 billion from a budget surplus in order to begin to pay down on the school construction needs mandated by the amendment.

The governor also attempted to limit the effect of the class-size amendment in other ways. In 2005, he proposed a constitutional amendment that would have raised some teacher salaries in exchange for scaling back the class-size requirement. Most observers of Florida politics viewed this as a blatant political ploy to peel off teachers' union support for class-size reduction, but it foundered when large county delegations in the Florida legislature realized that their own teachers were being paid more than the new minimums that Bush proposed and that their schools were the most overcrowded. Thus the proposal never reached the ballot.

In that same year the governor also abruptly ruled that school districts could no longer add extra teachers to crowded classrooms—a practice called co-teaching—in order to lower the student-teacher ratio. Under the original law, if schools were unable to meet the mandated class sizes, the Department of Education required them to use operating funds normally used for teacher salaries and materials to construct new classrooms. Facing this dilemma, some schools opted to put two full-time teachers in a large classroom in order to lower the student/teacher ratio while they arranged for new classrooms. The state prohibited this after one year, but its ruling came just a month before the August opening of school when many schools had already arranged for co-teachers. School super-intendents and others saw the decision as a "vindictive move" by a person who wanted to undermine the constitutional amendment (Kahn, 2005).

Displaying the resolve that characterized his actions regarding his privatization proposals, the governor would not give up on his opposition to the class-size amendment and in 2006 made one final attempt to rid himself of it. In his final legislative session Bush proposed another constitutional amendment that would have watered down the existing class-size requirements. But in a vote which, like that on vouchers, got entangled in the battle over leadership in the state senate, the Republicans were able to muster only twenty-one of their twenty-five members in support of the amendment and the governor failed to achieve one of his prized objectives.

Citizen Response to Educational Reform

The analysis provided above suggests that Governor Bush's educational reforms failed to achieve the goals he set for them. And, in the end, Governor Bush was unable to convince the citizens of Florida of their merits. In a poll conducted in his last year in office by the *St. Petersburg Times,* Floridians displayed opposition to virtually all of his educational initiatives. A minority of citizens (40 percent) liked the way he handled education in general, over 60 percent (61 percent) opposed using public money for private school vouchers and the use of the FCAT came in for heavy criticism. Sixty-eight percent said teacher bonuses should not be linked to the FCAT, 70 percent said that schools should not be penalized because of FCAT results, 57 percent said that they should not be rewarded because of these results and more respondents (42 percent) said that the test had hurt education in the state more than it had helped (37 percent). Finally, a majority of respondents continued to support the class-size amendment that Bush had fought throughout his career in office.

These poll results raised the obvious question: "What does it mean to have a reform that doesn't have popular support?" The governor did not respond to questions about the poll results and a spokesperson said that Bush "did not put stock in polls," but the former K–12 chancellor of education in Florida said that the "public is saying to the next governor: it's time for common-sense course corrections" (Matus and Winchester, 2006).

Reform in Social Services

As was the case in the arena of education policy, the Bush social services reform program focused heavily on organizational and managerial changes. These changes, outlined in chapter 2 of this book, were designed, in large part, to enable private companies, nonprofit organizations and faith-based organizations to provide services that had traditionally been provided by the state: economic benefits to low-income citizens, protective services to children at risk of harm, community services to people who suffered from developmental disabilities, and medical services to poor citizens. Here I describe the outcome of these efforts.

Research and data on these topics suggest that the theory that privatization of social welfare programs would produce more-efficient and higher-quality services at a lower cost cannot be substantiated. Nor were the organizations who took over management of the activities involved more accountable than were the public agencies they replaced.

The Faith-Based Organization Initiative

Governor Bush publicly promoted faith-based organizations as an alternative to government agencies in the provision of a variety of services in Florida. However, his actions in implementing his faith-based program left the governor open to criticism that his activities in this arena were primarily designed to appease a political constituency. (For a similar criticism of the effort at the national level, see Kuo, 2007.)

First, it was not clear what constituted a faith-based organization in Florida. The state provided no formal definition of the term and a wide range of organizations were included under the rubric. Thus some entities were included even though their funding came from multiple and diverse sources and when the activities they engaged in ranged from those that were religious or spiritual to those that were clearly secular. At least some of the organizations involved—Lutheran Social Services, for example—provided typical social services such as assistance with transportation or rent and clothing and offered no obvious faith-oriented activities.

Second, it is difficult to determine how much support, other than rhetorical, that the governor actually provided faith-based organizations in Florida. As the focal point for the faith-based initiative, Bush initially created a small unit within the Office of the Governor. He then cooperated with the director of the president's faith-based initiative to sponsor two conferences for faith leaders, ostensibly to provide help with federal grant procedures. One of these, in Miami, took place just ten days before the 2004 presidential election, and both were criticized by a member of President Bush's own staff as simply an effort to generate support for the president among evangelicals in battleground states (Kuo, 2007).

In 2006, the legislature established the Faith-Based and Community Advisory Council by statute and charged it with advising the legislature on this topic. This office provided a list of contacts within state government agencies to faith-based organizations seeking access to state government funding and technical assistance in preparing applications. But the coordinator of the faith-based initiative kept almost no information about the extent to which and the manner in which state agencies had committed state funds to these organizations. Thus it is impossible to determine whether or not Jeb Bush's administration actually provided these organizations with state tax dollars. In 2006, the coordinator of the faith-based initiative had only a list of *federal* grants to faith-based organizations in Florida that had been provided by the White House Office of Faith-Based Initiatives.

The larger issue regarding the faith-based initiative was that virtually no effort was made to evaluate the activities of the organizations that received public money or to compare their costs and quality of service with those of other service providers (Mears, Roman, Wolff, and Buck, 2006). In the absence of criteria that distinguished faith-based programs or activities from those that are secular, such analysis was impossible and as a consequence the state knows very little about the relative advantages and disadvantages of using faith-based organizations to deliver public services.

Reforming the Welfare Program

In a substantial break from traditional managerial practices in this arena, Governor Bush made fundamental changes in the mission of the state's welfare program and took Florida's primary social services agency, the Department of Children and Families, out of the business of providing welfare services to disadvantaged Floridians. As described by one official involved in the program, "we're about employment now, not solving social service problems" (Fording, Schram, and Soss, 2006: 7).

The high visibility of welfare programs, the partisan conflict that surrounded them in the United States, and Governor Bush's efforts to interject the private sector into Florida's system of managing them generated great interest among scholars in the field of social policy, and substantial research about the effect of these changes is available.

Three important findings emerge from this research: (1) oversight and management of the numerous private- and nonprofit-sector organizations brought in to replace state agency workers in this area was problematic; (2) the performance of these private organizations was not "better" than that of the public-sector organizations they had replaced; and (3) the ultimate outcomes of the changes were substantial, and sometimes, but not always, validated the conservative theory upon which they were predicated.

The management structure created to oversee the implementation of the privatized welfare program in Florida struggled to administer this system. As of 2006, DCF was spending over $118 million on 104 contracts to provide economic self-sufficiency programs to disadvantaged citizens. But a major report issued in that year indicated that "there have been long-standing concerns regarding the department's contract and monitoring system;" (Florida OPPAGA, 2006, February, Report # 06-16; 3) concerns great enough that legislation was enacted requiring that the department take specific steps to improve its contracting process. There was evidence that the department failed to safeguard its ability to make objective decisions with regard to the contracting actions involved, provided inadequate training to its staff in procurement and contract management, and provided insufficient monitoring of contracted community based lead agencies.

In addition, the state's efforts to streamline the front end of the welfare system, the application process, also encountered problems. The Bush administration effort to automate the process of seeking eligibility for welfare services was touted by agency officials for bringing substantial gains in efficiency, a reduction in error rates in the award of food stamps, and a large reduction in the staff assigned to the initial processing of these applications. There was a reduction in the eligibility determination staff, but the food stamp error rate increased to one of the highest in the nation in 2006, bringing threats of fines from the federal government (Ash, 2006).

As was the case in other states, the changes required by the federal welfare reform law had a significant effect on Florida's welfare program and, by two measures, validated the conservative governmental theory upon which they were based. The changes did reduce both the state's welfare caseload and the state's expenditures on welfare. Between 1995 and 2004, Florida's caseload declined by 78 percent, well above the national average (Lurie, 2007), and in 2003, Florida ranked forty-third in the nation in per-capita expenditures on public welfare (U.S. Census, 2003). Much of this change can be attributed to the stringency of the state's sanctions related to program participation. The Florida program adopted some of the strictest time limits and work requirements in the nation and these sanctions were applied at an extremely high rate. For example, while Illinois had a full-family sanction rate of 13 percent, New Jersey had 17 percent and South Carolina had 5 percent, the comparable rate in Florida was 47 percent (Pavetti, Derr, Kirby, Wood, and Clark, 2004).

Moving people off the welfare rolls was a major goal of the Personal Responsibility Act of 1996. A second was to ensure that recipients of welfare benefits worked in exchange for their benefits. Here conservatives argued that restrictions on welfare would lead to gainful employment and improved economic conditions for welfare recipients. In light of this goal, requirements were added to the welfare reform bill that made the states responsible for finding employment for the "leavers." These requirements created the basis for a second measure of the ultimate effectiveness of the reforms: the extent to which those who left the program found employment. Finally, given the Bush administration focus on privatizing the welfare system, a third measure was the relative effectiveness of private- and public-sector organizations in finding employment for those who left the welfare rolls. A series of analyses conducted by scholars at Florida State University and at other places over the period 2000 to 2004 addressed these issues.

The research found that individuals who left the Florida welfare program as a result of the new program requirements met a hostile employment environment. Fewer than one-third of them (31.1 percent) found employment in all four quarters of the year following their exit from the program, the wages of those who found employment were very low (average salary $11,155), and job benefits such as personal health insurance, health insurance for children, sick/personal days off, and others were rare. In 2002, OPPAGA reported that the average hourly wage of those who found work was just 68 percent of what officials estimated to be a financial self-sufficient wage (Florida OPPAGA, 2002). Not surprisingly, large percentages of those who left welfare, 24 percent to 58 percent, experienced incidents of economic hardship such as being unable to purchase food, getting behind on rent, or having their vehicle taken for inability to make payments (Crew, Eyerman, Graham, and McMillan, 2004). After five years, 43 percent of those who were required to leave welfare as a result of the reforms had still not found employment (Crew and Lamothe, 2003a).

Additional research conducted in the early years of the Bush reforms examined the state's effectiveness in finding employment for those who left the welfare system and tested the proposition that private-sector organizations were more effective than were public ones in this task. This research found that private organizations were less effective in finding full-time regular jobs for those required to work in exchange for welfare benefits than were both public and nonprofit organizations. And public-sector organizations were given higher rankings for how they treated citizens when assisting them than were private organizations. Finally, the costs associated with the use of private organizations increased at a proportionally greater rate than did those from public or nonprofit organizations (Crew and Lamothe, 2003b).

Subsequent analysis by other scholars revealed that the free-market principles upon which Florida's welfare reform program was based and the "chronic pressure" generated by the business model of management adopted to guide the implementation of the reform did not improve client performance in finding work and in advancing their careers, regardless of the kind of organization that provided the case management service. Further, the burden of this performance management system fell most heavily on disadvantaged clients such as racial minorities and those with less education (Fording, Schram, and Soss, 2006).

Revitalizing Child Protective Services

The implementation of the governor's shift to privatization of the program of child protective services was incremental and it was not until April 2005 that the last two counties, Miami-Dade and Monroe, were brought fully on line. At this point, the state's responsible agency on the matter, the Department of Children and Families, was providing $625 million to a group of private and nonprofit "Community Alliances" responsible for managing the program and to five hundred subcontractors employed to oversee family preservation, emergency shelter, foster care, and adoption services for forty-four thousand children. Both the department and other promoters of privatization such as Florida TaxWatch claimed that "it's [the privatization effort] working" (Florida TaxWatch, 2005). And as he left office the governor claimed that major improvements were made in a system that had been a complete disaster when he took office (Associated Press, December 14, 2006).

Alternative views were expressed by others who participated in this privatization effort. A longtime employee of the Department of Children and Families who had adopted special-needs children from foster care and had thus become a "client" in the new system claimed that it was no different than it had been ten years earlier: overworked and underpaid case managers and a paucity of families willing to take in abused and neglected children. "It's the same people doing the same jobs, just under different agency names" (Conner, 2006).

Systematic research about privatization of the state's program of child protective services was released both in Governor Bush's last year in office and in the following year. And the findings were similar to those in the welfare arena; privatization did not automatically bring about the improvement in program outcomes that the governor claimed it would. Further, as in other arenas, program accountability was problematic.

An investigation published in 2006 by the legislature's research unit, the Office of Program Policy Analysis and Government Accountability (Florida OPPAGA, June 2006), revealed that foster children were obtaining permanent placements more quickly than when the program was administered by the state, a major goal of the reform, but that high percentages of children experienced re-abuse and return to foster care. Further, the cost of privatizing the state's foster care system rose almost 70 percent over the time period 1998–1999 to 2004–2005. Another report showed that only 28 percent of potentially eligible former foster care youth received financial assistance through a program designed to assist them (Florida OPPAGA, December 2005), and the number of children missing from the child welfare system rose from 400 in 2002, the year of "crisis" in the child protection system, to 652 in 2005 (Carol Miller, 2006).

The 2006 OPPAGA report also found that accountability for the program was poor, a recurring problem with efforts to privatize government. The state had not required that private entities providing the services involved document administrative costs such as rent and upper-management salaries, and the Department of Children and Families struggled to identify or fix underlying factors that led to poor performance (Florida OPPAGA, January 2006: 3). The troubles encountered in the administration of the program in five southwest Florida counties and in Lake County provided insight into the nature of the problems involved when multiple private agencies were asked to cooperate in managing the welfare program.

The lead agency, or contractor, for the Community Alliance in Lee, Collier, Charlotte, Hendry, and Glades counties was the Children's Network, a locally based nonprofit company with a nearly $100 million contract. The Children's Network was owned by Camelot Community Care, a Clearwater-based organization, which, in turn, was controlled by Providence Service Corporation, a Tucson, Arizona, company traded on Nasdaq. The Children's Network had an $8.7 million five-year management agreement with Providence and had another $8 million contract with a wholly owned subsidiary of Providence, Family Preservation Services, to act as case managers. The multiplicity of organizations involved created confusion among foster parents, one of whom said, "I'm not sure who to call anymore. You can't even keep up with their names."

In an effort to bring all case management activities in-house and to resolve some of the attendant confusion, the board of directors of the Children's Network, made up of local child advocates, fired Family Preservation Services and two other case management companies. The parent company, Camelot, then disbanded the Children Network's board, violating the state requirement that lead agencies in this effort to privatize child protection services be locally controlled. The dispute was ultimately resolved when the Department of Children and Families stepped in and forced the creation of a locally controlled board, but the disruption at the top trickled down and concerns remained about the ability of DCF to manage the complicated interrelationships among the overlapping private companies involved.

In Lake County, the Sarasota Family YMCA, the Community-Based Care lead agency and Directions for Mental Health, Inc., the Y's subcontractor, "failed to adequately provide the care, safety, and protection" (State of Florida, Department of Children and Families, 2007) of a child entrusted to them who was taken to Wisconsin where she was discovered living in a home where a woman's body was buried in the back yard and where her brother had been tortured. This incident came on the heels of a poor performance report that cited the organization's management culture and style as "defensive, arrogant and retaliatory against anyone who criticizes or disagrees with the agency" (Ackerman, 2007) and led to threats to withdraw the contract from the YMCA.

Other reports on the implementation of the child protection program added to the concerns of those who had been leery of privatization. An August 2007 report conducted by the Chapin Hall Center for Children at the University of Chicago found that "South Florida children in foster care do not receive regular immunizations or preventive dental care, often do not get needed counseling or therapy, and get bounced from foster home to foster home because caregivers become frustrated over a lack of support from child-welfare agencies" (Carol Miller, 2007).

The problems documented in these reports reinforced the findings from a report from the legislature's Office of Program Policy Analysis and Governmental Accountability. This report described "critical weaknesses" in the oversight of community-based lead agencies and their subcontractors and documented a variety of problems, the most important of which was failure to install the computer system designed to provide the Department of Children and Families key information needed to monitor the services that were outsourced. This failure occurred despite the expenditure of $181 million and emasculated the department's ability to ensure that providers were fulfilling the terms of their contracts. Thus, some lead agencies were not monitored at all, seventeen of the twenty-two lead agencies were not monitoring their subcontractors adequately or at all and DCF took only "limited action" against poor performing companies (Florida OPPAGA, June 2006).

Perhaps the most ominous finding in the body of research described above was that Florida could go only so far in sanctioning poor performing contractors because DCF no longer had the staff to take over the functions involved and there were not always alternative providers. The academic and professional literature about privatization had long warned about this possibility (Rehfus, 1989) but in haste to implement conservative political ideology, the state had not required the posting of performance bonds or the purchase of interruption insurance and had no plan for contract interruption other than to have contractors from other regions take on additional responsibility for short periods of time.

Assisting Persons with Developmental Disabilities

The governor's attempt to remedy what had been serious problems in Florida's program of developmental disabilities was carried out with the use of two strategies, one—a substantial influx of tax dollars—which was unusual for Bush, and a second that was characteristic—reliance on private contractors to provide the community services involved. Taken together, these strategies had a mixed effect.

As might be expected, the addition of new money to the disabilities program enabled the state to serve a larger number of citizens with a greater variety of services and by 2006, 25,000 people were being assisted. In the five years prior to this time, the program more than doubled the number of clients served and it increased the level of services provided to clients. Not unexpectedly, program costs also more than doubled and the number of people waiting for services climbed (Florida OPPAGA, 2002, Report No. 02–09).

In research conducted to assess the impact of the increased commitment to the program, the state looked at both substantive outcomes and managerial performance. A series of reports from OPPAGA and the state auditor general spanning the time period 2000 to 2003 and legislative hearings throughout the Bush administration showed that the state's disabilities program experienced problems both in meeting performance standards and in managing the private providers given responsibility for providing services to the agency's clients.

An early assessment of the program that focused on program outcomes found that injury rates for residents at state institutions exceeded legislative performance standards and that the quality of life of clients living in the community also "had not met its legislative performance standards" (Florida OPPAGA, 2000). Three years later an OPPAGA report said that the "program has made limited progress in providing more cost-effective services that better meet client needs" (Florida OPPAGA, 2003).

Much of the explanation for the failure to meet performance standards was attributed to issues of management and the oversight of the private organizations employed to provide services to the agency's clients came under substantial criticism. In 2001 a state auditor general report found "significant deficiencies" in the monitoring of service providers (Florida Auditor General, 2001: 4). And in 2002, OPPAGA said that controlling the costs of the program would "require major structural reforms" (Florida OPPAGA, 2002: 10). By 2007, the problems had grown to the point that the new director of the Agency for Persons with Disabilities told the legislature that the program was "fundamentally flawed" and that the state had little control over program costs because many decisions about how to spend the money were being made by private contractors. The director said that "in some ways, it's like we're a spectator to our budget, but we're not a participant" (Saunders and Circelli, 2007).

Then, in a remarkable departure from the conservative doctrine that had driven decisions in the Bush administration, the director went on to recommend that six hundred state employees be hired to replace one group of the private contractors employed in the program (Saunders and Circelli, 2007). A reversal of a strategy so central to Bush's theory of government was unlikely from a legislature that had bought into the strategy in such a substantial way. Nevertheless, the argument that public employees be allowed to provide these services suggests that skepticism about the ability of private companies to provide the kind of service necessary to improve the lives of Florida citizens who suffer from developmental disabilities was manifest.

Medicaid Reform

The Bush plan for reform of Medicaid described in chapter 2 of this book fundamentally altered the underlying assumptions regarding the state's responsibility for helping disadvantaged citizens find medical care, and critics complained that Florida had abandoned its commitment as a social safety net for its most vulnerable citizens.

The governor proposed his plan as a way in which the state could more accurately predict and control its costs. Critics pointed out that no benefits were guaranteed, that access to care for all low-income families was questionable, and that there were no safeguards to make sure that private plans kept their promises. In particular, the AARP questioned whether or not service packages offered by the participants would be meaningful and cover the needs of persons with chronic conditions and special needs that the private market chose not to cover. It also wondered whether the premiums to be offered would be sufficient to purchase an adequate service package (Roy, 2005). As this book went to press, these and other questions regarding the program were unanswered, but early reports raised some concerns and expansion beyond the pilot counties was delayed.

Research by the Georgetown University Health Policy Institute found that the pilot program in Duval and Broward counties "appears to be reducing the number of physicians who accept Medicaid beneficiaries," and 51 percent of doctors interviewed said that the new program's rules "made it more difficult to provide medically necessary services to children" (Aker and Hoadley, 2007). Then, in September 2007 the inspector general for the Agency for Health Care Administration, the state department responsible for the program, found additional problems; some beneficiaries with complex illnesses used the maximum allowed-for drug coverage and were left uncovered; twelve of seventeen insurers made it difficult to determine which medications were covered and had errors on their doctors lists, and beneficiaries had problems picking the most appropriate plan; beneficiaries had trouble finding specialists who accepted the coverage, a common problem with regular Medicaid; and although participant complaints were down, it was partly due to the state having no system in place to receive complaints (State of Florida, Agency for Health Care Administration, 2007). Based on these findings, the inspector general recommended that "further expansion be delayed until such time as these improvements are made." In December 2007, the secretary of the Agency for Health Care Administration accepted this finding and announced that he would not make any recommendations during the 2008 legislative session to expand the program statewide. Instead he said, "We will continue to monitor the progress of the pilot" program. When asked about the reason for ACHA's reluctance to expand the program, the agency's spokesperson said that the issues raised in the December report needed addressing and that the results of University of Florida research on the program needed to be considered (Dolinski, 2007).

In the interim, newspaper reports said that "doctors are fleeing the insurance plans. Patients are complaining about difficulty getting expeditious care. And observers like the Jesse Ball DuPont fund have released report after report criticizing the program's implementation." (Cox, 2009). Then in March 2009, the Broward County Commission, the largest of the five participating in the program, adopted a resolution asking to be removed from the pilot program because their citizens were being delayed in getting medical care. A State Representative from the Broward area and one from another county involved, Duval, introduced legislation seeking to limit the state's authority to operate the experiment, saying "this is a program that not only should not be expanded but should be stopped because innocent people who need medical care are being injured." (Associated Press, 2009).

Protecting Florida's Environment

Motivated by conservative orthodoxy that had little to say about environmental protection, Jeb Bush paid little attention to issues related to the environment in his first run for governor, and some members of his own party thought it cost him the election. Allison DeFoor, II, who had founded the Theodore Roosevelt Society in order to promote environmental consciousness within the Republican Party, said that "if he had just mumbled a few platitudes, he'd have won" (Grunwald, 2006: 330). Bush responded to this criticism in his second campaign, promoted a series of environmental plans, and throughout his tenure declared protection of Florida's natural resources as one of his highest priorities. Here I discus the outcome of his efforts to leave this environment in better condition than when he came to office.

Policy efforts to protect and improve the natural environment in Florida have historically been framed by a long-running battle between conflicting views of how best to respond to demands that the state's most marketable resource, its climate and access to water, be utilized. In a sense, the state faces a "dilemma like that of Disney's sorcerer's apprentice—it must keep growing to avoid disaster" (Mormino, 2005: 149), and the dilemma produces a political battle between stronger environmental protection and more growth. Judgments about how well or how poorly a governor performed as a steward of Florida's environment are closely tied to the growth versus environmental protection positions, and analyses of Governor Bush's performance to mediate the dispute are necessarily somewhat normative. Bush supporters argue that he was a good steward of Florida's natural environment. His critics claim that he "talked the talk" on environmental issues, but did not "walk the walk."

Conservation of Natural Resources

Recognizing both the intrinsic and economic value of Florida's unparalled environment, Governor Bush committed himself in his first year in office to the continuation of Florida's long-term effort to protect its natural resources by setting aside funds to purchase environmentally sensitive lands, even though he had singled out this program for budget cuts in his first campaign (*St. Petersburg Times*, 1999).

Florida had begun acquiring land for conservation in the 1920s and in 1960 passed a "bathing suit tax" on recreational items to initiate a formal program for this purpose. In 1972 Governor Reubin Askew's "Lands for You" program, funded by a $240 million bond issue, inaugurated a bipartisan tradition of land buying for conservation purposes that every subsequent governor continued. In 1990, Republican governor Bob Martinez pushed the state legislature to establish Preservation 2000, a ten-year program that utilized revenue from the sale of bonds to raise $300 million per year to be used to acquire environmentally sensitive lands, to restore damaged environmental systems, to develop water resources, and to increase public access to Florida's natural resources. This quickly became the nation's premier program for saving environmentally sensitive lands and the monies expended in this program were greater than those expended by the federal government for this purpose. It was enormously popular in Florida and during the time of its existence, the state used the funds to purchase over 1.25 million acres of land to be preserved.

As Preservation 2000 came to its expiration, environmental leaders supported plans for a successor program and proposed a constitutional amendment requiring the legislature to make provision for the conservation and protection of natural resources. Seventy-two percent of Florida's voters supported this amendment in 1998, and in 1999 the Florida legislature created Florida Forever to implement its requirements. The new program produced about $300 million annually from the sale of bonds, with control over the available funds given jointly to the governor and the cabinet. As governor, Bush signed the legislation authorized by the constitutional amendment, publicly supported the program over the course of his administration, cooperated with the cabinet to expend over $1 billion in bond money on purchases of land of environmental importance to the state, and routinely used his support of this program in promoting his environmental legacy (Struhs, 2004). Nevertheless, only a year after the passage of Florida Forever, the governor undercut the program, and raised questions about his commitment to environmental conservation, by raiding its funds in the amount of $75 million in order to cover budgetary shortfalls that he was unwilling to raise taxes to cover.

As part of his environmental agenda, the governor also touted his efforts in preventing oil companies from drilling in the Gulf of Mexico, in purchasing privately owned mineral rights in the cypress swamps of the Everglades, and in supporting the demolition of a dam on the Ocklawaha River that would restore an important river ecosystem.

Conflict over the Ocklawaha Dam ran throughout most of Governor Bush's term, and he consistently supported the environmentalist position. These interests wanted to destroy the dam in order to release water from a reservoir that had flooded a large area of ecologically important land. Opposition was led by the sport fishing industry, which saw the reservoir as an important base for the bass fishing economy. Bush rebuffed entreaties from the sport fishermen, who went to the legislature and found success in getting a bill passed calling for preservation of the reservoir. The governor vetoed this legislation, and as the Bush administration ended the issue was still alive in Florida and the dam had not been destroyed.

With the oil drilling deal, Bush gained some credibility with the environmental community when he initially opposed the President's and the national Republican Party's position supporting oil exploration throughout the United States. He strongly lobbied his brother to scale back drilling in a gas-rich section of the eastern Gulf known as Lease Sale 181 and in July, 2001 secured an agreement with the U.S. Department of Interior for a moratorium on activity in this area until 2007, later extended until 2012. Triumphant, he released a statement saying "there will be no new drilling in the Lease Sale Area off the coast of Florida under my watch," and environmentalists applauded. Unknown at the time, Karl Rove had agreed to this deal in recognition of Florida's electoral importance (Hamburger and Wallsten. 107-109) and after his re-election, Bush began to backpedal on his commitment. In 2004, he announced that he would work with his brother's administration to negotiate a deal to permit oil exploration in Lease Sale 181. (Klas. July, 2005)

The first deal, announced in August 2005, was included in a proposal by Congressman Richard Pombo, R-California, that provided an inducement to states to exploit their oil and gas reserves by providing them a share of the lease revenues. It restricted oil exploration within 125 miles of Florida's coast unless Florida state government enacted legislation that reduced these limits. Environmentalists, skeptical that the Florida legislature could resist pressure from oil and gas industries that had pumped $695,000 in contributions into the Florida Republican Party between 1999 and 2004, reminded Bush of his previous commitment. Bush said that unless some accommodation was made, the entire eastern Gulf could be opened to drilling after the existing moratorium expired in 2012. He then made light of those who hoped to extend that moratorium, saying, "I'll talk to the fairy godmother about it" (Lytle and Kennedy, 2005). The provision in the federal legislation permitting the state to relax its rules governing oil drilling was subsequently dropped in negotiations between the U.S. House and the Senate, but reemerged in 2006 with the provision granting permission to drill within fifty miles but giving state legislatures the right to restrict it within one hundred miles. By this point, the governor had become a lobbyist for drilling and went to Washington to urge lawmakers to support this bill, providing more justification for the "talk the talk but not walk the walk" label among Florida environmentalists. The legislation that passed allowed drilling in approximately 8.3 million acres in the eastern Gulf of Mexico, including 2.5 million acres within Lease Area 181. As the governor's term ended, the Department of Interior was proceeding to open large portions of the Lease Sale Area to drilling, with public hearings scheduled one week after the 2006 election in Florida.

The governor's support for the purchase of mineral rights in the Big Cypress National Reserve in the Everglades also had political overtones. The rights had for decades been in the hands of an influential Florida company, which for economic reasons had not attempted their exploitation. Then, in the early months of 2000, the company filed multiple applications for oil exploration in these areas and was very public about its intentions to drill for oil. In response, the Bush administration in Washington offered to buy the 400,000 acres involved for $120 million, a deal that Governor Bush fully supported. Congress balked and ordered a review of the sale. The investigation found that the $120 million price tag was grossly inflated and strongly criticized the Department of the Interior for brokering such a deal. These actions raised charges that the governor and his brother had agreed to a huge political payoff to the owners of the property, who were major contributors to the Republican Party and to Governor Bush.

The governor was further criticized by environmentalists for bowing to the demands of campaign contributors in another conservation project, protection of the Ichetucknee River. Shortly after taking office in 1999, Governor Bush and the director of the Department of Environmental Protection (DEP) canoed down the Ichetucknee, a pristine spring-fed river in northcentral Florida, and vowed to preserve it by refusing to grant permits to a company with a checkered environmental record that wanted to build a cement kiln a few miles from the river's head spring. Five months after denying the permits, Bush changed his mind and permitted the plant building to proceed.

The governor argued that the company, Anderson-Columbia, would have been successful in a lawsuit it had threatened and sent his staff to negotiate a settlement. As a result, the state secured assurances that Anderson would resolve outstanding environmental complaints and institute new environmental protection procedures at its properties, and the director for the DEP claimed that "we will have more protection for Ichetucknee Springs...than we would ever have imagined just a few weeks ago" (Matus, 1999). Despite these assurances, critics used this flip-flop as another example for their claim that Bush "talks the talk" on environmental issues but does not "walk the walk." Their claim was bolstered when the *Miami Herald* disclosed that executives and lawyers representing the company involved in the project poured nearly $190,000 into state and national Republican Party coffers in the two days following resolution of a key part of the deal (McGee, Wallsten, and Grotto, 2002).

Saving the Everglades

The largest conservation project in which Governor Bush was involved was the effort to restore the Florida Everglades. The "unwavering commitment of Governor Bush and the Florida legislature" to saving the Everglades was cited by Bush's first secretary of Environmental Protection as the "crown jewel" in Florida's environmental legacy (Struhs, 2004). A mammoth undertaking, the project for restoration had its roots in the administration of former governor Bob Graham and his "Save Our Everglades" program. Graham continued this effort when elected to the U.S. Senate and his "Restoring the Everglades, An American Legacy Act" authorized the Comprehensive Everglades Restoration Plan (CERP), which passed during the Clinton administration.

This legislation involved both the state of Florida and the federal government and was just the kind of big-government spending plan that Bush had deplored throughout his campaigns for office and subsequently as governor. Nevertheless, when President Clinton signed the Water Resources Development Act in 2000 that included the Comprehensive Everglades Restoration Plan, Bush attended the ceremony in Washington and said, "the restoration of America's

Everglades has been one of my administration's top priorities" (Florida Department of Environmental Protection, 2000) and said later that it was *the* highest environmental priority (Florida Governor's Office, 2003). Subsequently, he pushed the Florida legislature to provide the funding for Florida's contribution to the restoration and to do so in advance of federal funding for the project. This legislation was widely supported by environmental groups even though it contained a controversial provision that allowed only those who could prove that they were personally affected by a project to file a challenge to environmentally risky development in the area. Bush's support earned the governor the "Steward of the Everglades" award from the Everglades Coalition.

Governor Bush also kept additional funding promises to the Everglades. In 2004, he unveiled a $1.5 billion plan called "Acceler8" to complete eight components of the restoration, most of them water-supply reservoirs that would restore water flows ten years ahead of schedule. The plan was financed with Wall Street bond money. And in 2005 he proposed a $200 million initiative to clean up Lake Okeechobee.

Actions such as these embellished his environmental bona fides, but the governor raised questions about this commitment with other actions. First, he disbanded the Governor's Commission for a Sustainable South Florida that had been created by his predecessor Lawton Chiles to represent major groups historically interested in the Everglades ecosystem. This commission, which represented a balanced set of interests, was replaced by the Governor's Commission for the Everglades, which was stacked with builders, farmers, and businessmen. Second, he discussed with a subsidiary of Enron, the Azurix Corporation, the possibility of privatizing the Everglades restoration. In exchange for helping Florida pay its $3.9 billion share of the restoration, Azurix would gain the right to sell the water captured by the project. While this deal dissolved with the implosion of Enron, it raised credibility problems for the governor among environmentalists (Grunwald, 2006: 331–332; Barnett, 2007: 159–160).

These credibility problems were exacerbated when the sugar industry, a major polluter of the "River of Grass" and a major contributor to Republican coffers, sought to delay the cleanup efforts involved and the governor took their side. In 2003, facing increased pressure to meet deadlines for reducing the amount of phosphorous it dumped into the Everglades, the sugar companies orchestrated a massive lobbying effort to extend the time period in which to meet the standards that had been specified in the 1994 Everglades Forever Act. They hired thirty-three lobbyists, carefully selected to reach different constitu-encies within the legislature, and succeeded in extending the deadline from 2006 to 2016. Bush supported this extension, arguing that 95 percent of the Everglades would meet the phosphorous standard by the original target date, that the remaining 5 percent could not but that it would achieve a "net improvement" standard within the established time frame. Although he claimed that the bill "strengthened" the original act, he was skittish enough about his position that he went behind closed doors to sign the measure and would not allow reporters into the governor's office to watch or to ask questions (Morgan 2003). David Guest, an attorney for a coalition of conservation groups in the Everglades case, was quoted as saying that this amendment amounted to an end-run around the 1992 settlement (Sokoloff, 2006), and former senator Bob Graham said it sent a signal to Congress that there was less than full commitment to restoration in the state where the Everglades is located (Goodnough, 2007).

The restoration of the Everglades is a long and complicated process and could not have been expected to be completed during the administration of a single governor. As Governor Bush left office, a report by the National Research Council indicated that some progress had been made in the restoration process: a project to restore the Kissimmee River had shown positive changes in the ecosystem; stormwater treatment areas have helped reduce harmful levels of phosphorus in agricultural runoff; and a process to monitor and assess changes in the ecosystem caused by the plan's initiatives had been set up (National Research Council, 2006).

At the same time, no CERP projects had been completed by the time Bush left office. All ten of the plan's components that had been scheduled for completion by 2005 were delayed, as were six pilot projects originally scheduled for completion in 2004. In a U.S. Senate hearing conducted in 2007, an inves-tigator from the Goverment Accounting Office said that only two of the benchmarks for the Everglades had been met. Four more should be completed in two to five years and four more should be finished in eight to twenty-five years (Morgan, 2007). Critics complained that these delays were tipping the scales in favor of reserving water for farms and urban developments rather than for use in reviving the dying Everglades, and when the governor initiated his "Acceler8" program, the president of the Everglades Foundation, a former Republican U.S. senator from New Hampshire, argued that Bush's plan placed too much emphasis on the wrong things—enough drinking water and flood control to accommodate rapid population growth—rather than the natural system (Cox, 2007; Goodnough, 2007). The environmental journalist Cynthia Barnett argues that this growth is the biggest threat to Everglades restoration, "the one that led to the marsh's decline in the first place: the force of growth and development as that net total 1,060 people continued to move to Florida every single day" (Barnett, 2007: 185). She also raised the question "whether the plan to restore the Florida Everglades was really as much about environmental protection as it was about increasing water supply for southeast Florida's booming population" (Barnett, 2007: 86). This leads to the growth management issue, which I discuss in the section that follows.

Growth Management

The public debate regarding Governor Bush's efforts to preserve Florida's environment reflected substantial disagreement about the merits of the governor's proposals, but few would accuse him of reluctance to take action to address the problems involved. This is less true with regard to the Bush strategy for moderating the effects of growth in Florida. Here the governor was caught in the ongoing Florida battle between the wishes of the development community to grow and the demands of the environmental community to moderate the growth that it believed was destroying the environment. As he became enmeshed in this conflict, Bush moved very slowly, made little effort until very late in his administration, and according to his critics missed opportunities to curb growth. With regard to growth management, the governor seemed to abandon the theory of aggressive gubernatorial leadership that had characterized his behavior in other areas of public policy and his behavior was uncharacteristically timid.

After his election in 1999, the governor moved cautiously to redeem what had been strong growth management campaign pledges. Raising immediate concern among environmentalists, the governor waited a full year before he took any action regarding growth management and then, rather than propose initiatives, he asked the Department of Community Affairs to survey Floridians about the issues involved. The results from the survey suggested broad public support for protection of identified state interests, for a state vision and a stronger state plan, for limiting urban sprawl, for establishing urban growth boundaries, and for a "strong, wide-ranging role for the state and expanded access for citizens" (Florida Department of Community Affairs, 2000). Governor Bush, allegedly under pressure from the development community, declined to accept these findings and appointed instead a Growth Management Study Commission to make appropriate recommendations. Another year passed before the commission completed its report and announced support for many of the findings from the 2000 survey, but in a crucial difference recommended limiting the role of state government in regulating the growth management process (Florida Department of Community Affairs, 2001).

This recommendation set the tone for the governor's growth management strategy and in the ensuing four years, Bush and the State Department of Community Affairs were accused of retreating from their support for a strong state role in growth management and embarked on a series of activities that critics saw as efforts to placate the state's powerful development interests (FSCC State News Services, 2000).

Some of these activities focused on ensuring that the agencies given the responsibility for overseeing the state's growth management program were "sensitive" to the concerns of the people and groups they regulated. Thus, in 2001 the secretary of the Department of Community Affairs initiated an internal, introspective exercise designed to respond to charges from developers that state growth management regulation was heavy-handed and "arrogant." This exercise included training sessions designed to sensitize departmental attitudes toward developers and other clients. In addition, the Department of Environmental Protection Agency's ombudsman, a highly regarded state employee who had received a special recognition/accomplishment award, was terminated by the same secretary who had given him the award. A former DEP attorney asserted that this firing "sends a chilling signal to DEP employees that dissent will not be tolerated, even if it is in the interest of the health and safety of Floridians" (Gallagher, 2000).

In other actions staff resources for the DCA were limited and the agency's oversight of local comprehensive plan amendments was curtailed. During most of the Bush administration, the governor and the legislature cut the DCA budget and staffing levels in drastic fashion and reduced substantially the number of proposed changes from local comprehensive plans that it disapproved. Through most of the 1990s the department struck down an annual average of 15 percent of such changes. This number dropped to less than 3 percent during Bush's first term (DeWitt, 2005). These actions generated substantial anxiety in the Florida environmental protection community and led to public comments of concern by the secretary of community affairs appointed by Bush's successor. At the press conference when newly elected governor Charlie Crist, a Republican, announced his appointment for secretary of the DCA, the new appointee questioned whether the agency at the time had the staffing and expertise to enforce the concurrency laws and said that "it's very important that this agency be adequately staffed to achieve its mission." The director of Audubon of Florida claimed that during the time of reduced state intervention in growth management issues, more than a million acres of farmland and natural areas were converted to housing developments.

In 2002 Governor Bush intensified criticism about his position on growth management by proposing an aggressive marketing effort designed to lure even more retirees to the Sunshine State. The idea for this program—"Destination Florida"—came from Al Hoffman, Florida's biggest homebuilder and the head of Jeb's fund-raising effort in both 1998 and 2002. Hoffman feared the reduction in revenue that came with the loss of retirees relocating in North and South Carolina instead of Florida and argued that "we must act before Florida loses untold billions in revenue and its sustained quality of life to other states" (Barnett, 2007: 100). "Floridians—many who had called the state home for generations, many who had just moved down—were furious. A torrent of letters to the governor's office questioned the need for another classic marketing campaign as they expressed concerns over pressures created by growth" (ibid. 102). In the face of such opposition, the legislature refused to allocate money for the project and the governor subsequently dropped his support for it. Destination Florida, however, raised more suspicion within the environmental community about Bush's commitment to growth management.

In 2005 Bush finally introduced legislation that would overhaul the state's growth management laws and pay for efforts to address the state's growth management problems. Described as the most important piece of growth management legislation adopted since the seminal 1985 legislation in this area, the proposal linked the approval of development with the ability of local governments and school boards to support the added demands of new growth. The plan required a "pay as you grow" system, where decisions about new development were to be based on the ability of the affected communities to provide adequate infrastructure. Under this system, local comprehensive plans were to require a budget and timeline to address the backlog of infrastructure—schools, roads, water, and so forth—as well as the increased demands on new development. It also gave local officials authority to deny permits for residential development that would cause nearby schools to become overcrowded. Bush's secretary of the Department of Environmental Protection described the legislation as a "bold proposal [that] allows Florida to effectively plan for growth in a way that expands our economy...the coordinated, collaborative funding plan ensures services and infrastructure for Florida's communities are available to meet the needs of our citizens" (Florida Department for Environmental Protection, 2005).

The bill's provisions were widely applauded, but were undercut by the funding mechanism. The plan called for local governments to meet the revenue requirements by raising their own taxes and tapping into what the governor estimated was a $5.3 billion pool of local funds available through local-option gas and sales taxes. However, local property taxes in the counties affected by new growth were at their maximum at the time and gasoline was selling at prices over $2.50 per gallon. Thus increasing local taxes was unlikely and the governor and the legislature made no effort to provide the necessary resources. Furthermore, the governor quietly vetoed a proposal for a state task force on concurrency that would have conducted research on new ways to support the effort. Without additional resources from the state, the concurrency requirement became a mandate that had little real impact, and the secretary of the Department of Community Affairs appointed by Jeb's Republican successor described the legislation as "an unmanageable statute...It's a mess" (Skene, 2007).

In the 2006 legislative session, the governor took what environmentalists said was another step back from his early strong growth management statements by signing a bill designed to weaken or kill some state reviews of new development in the state. Among the provisions included was one to exempt certain projects from a review called the Development of Regional Impact, used by the Department of Community Affairs to study big projects like shopping malls and planned communities that have a regional impact. A second was to make it easier for developers to expand hotels, condos, office parks, or phosphate mines without triggering a review by DCA. And a third permitted large projects in rural counties to get around the sprawl rule designed to restrict growth beyond the suburbs, the so-called exurban areas. By 2007, the state's newly appointed director of DCA was calling on the state "to *restore* the Department as an effective advocate and positive force for better planning for growth management and to replace the 1985 Growth Management Act." He also hoped to remedy "the Santa Claus-sized grab bag of changes the legislature has passed" since the passage of the act (Skene, 2007; emphasis added).

Judgments about whether Governor Bush did as much as other governors did or as much as he could have done to address the growth management issue will always be driven by the values of the observer, and he is not the first governor who has been forced to compromise on this issue. The policy director for Audubon of Florida captured the nature of the problem that Governor Bush faced in dealing with growth management when he said that "even if Bush had been a great environmentalist in the vein of Graham or Askew, the legislature and the development community would never let him get by with it" (Barnett, 2007: 96).

The fundamental question that remains about the Bush growth management policy is how the compromises that were made in promoting growth affect Florida's environmental quality of life. As Governor Bush left office, development was still wiping out wetlands and stressing the state's acquifers, and bulldozers were clearing an estimated five hundred acres of pasture and forest per day for new development. Environmentalists also argued that Florida had not done enough to create a buffer zone from development along the edge of the Everglades. As one student of Florida's environment said, "In coming decades, as sprawl marches east into the Everglades and west into the Everglades Agricultural Area, south Florida could become an uninterrupted asphalt megalopolis stretching from Naples to Palm Beach. Perhaps it could be called the Napalm Beach" (Grunwald, 365). And another environmental scholar said that these developments are "draining Florida's cultural identity and, it is no exaggeration to say, the spirit of its people" (Barnett, 2007: 189).

Comments such as these are individual expressions of frustration with the progress of development in Florida during the Bush administration. But a larger expression emerged in 2003 with a proposed amendment to the state's constitution that would have required public votes on any significant change to a community's comprehensive plan. Titled "Hometown Democracy," the amendment reflected broad public discontent over growth and the manner in which it was managed. The secretary of community affairs said, "Citizens watch this process. They lose confidence. They think the plans are changed willy-nilly. They think the commissions are in the pockets of the developers" (Deslatte, 2007). In 2009 supporters of the initiative were able to collect enough signatures to get the proposal on the ballot and its opponents were forced to admit that it represented a fundamental critique of the way in which growth in the state had been managed.

Summary

There is little question that Governor Bush made an effort to lead a revolution in public policy in Florida. Motivated by conservative governmental principles and an aggressive theory of gubernatorial leadership, the governor promoted a large agenda of proposals designed to address a variety of public policy problems in the state and to change the way in which Florida's government managed these problems. The governor achieved most of his legislative goals, and many of these proposals were put into statute.

Despite these efforts, little improvement has taken place in the areas in which Bush focused his attention, and the governmental theories of conservatism that motivated his actions cannot be validated. Substantial evidence suggests that despite Bush's assertions regarding its improvement, public education, a top priority of the administration, is not demonstrably better now than it was at the outset of the Bush term. Indeed, an editorial writer from the capitol's daily newspaper said, "No state that ranks near the bottom in high-school graduation rates and per-student funding for public education can sincerely lay claim to a world-class system of schools. So let's stop fooling ourselves" (*Tallahassee Democrat,* 2008). Further, the "most vulnerable" citizens, including children in protective care and those relying on the state's system of public assistance, are not better protected or cared for, efforts to manage Florida's constant population growth fight an uphill battle to slow the destruction of the state's fragile environment, and the Medicaid reform endeavor has been slowed by problems that emerged in the pilot counties. It appears that it will be years before the effect of the Medicaid policies enacted in the 2005 legislative session is known.

Given these conditions, the Bush administration was unable to convince Floridians that it had made a significant difference in the state, and most citizens feel that conditions in Florida did not change for the better during the Bush term. In polls conducted late in 2005 few voters thought that conditions in education and other specific areas had improved over the course of Jeb's two terms. Further in answer to the general question, "Since Jeb Bush became governor, do you think things have gotten better, gotten worse, or stayed the same?" 61 percent answered either "stayed the same" or got "worse" (Quinnipiac University Polling Institute, November 2005). In addition, a majority of the state's residents predicted that things would not get better over the *subsequent* five years (Mason-Dixon Corporation, November 2006).

Part IV
The Bush Legacy and His Future

Chapter 9

What Difference Did Bush Make?

Introduction

All governors have legacies. That is, they leave something durable that others will remember and will benefit from or will be required to deal with as time passes. Despite the inclination of historians and others to define a single legacy for a governor, assessments of the impact that a governor has had during his term more properly should focus on several dimensions: judgments about overall performance in office, impressions of the norms and values that guided a governor's behavior, assessments of the particular governmental arrangements, political circumstances and public policy effects left to succeeding administrations, and evaluations of the governing theories that guided the governor's actions. Legacies can be either positive or negative.

Definition and evaluation of legacies is, of course, influenced by the vantage point of the observer and a variety of people are led to these analyses. Some are obvious critics of the particular governor, others obvious supporters. While public officials generally take their legacies seriously, Governor Bush scoffed at the idea, saying, "This legacy thing is, really, it ain't me" (Kleindienst, 2006). Nevertheless, he created two organizations, the Foundation for Florida's Future and the Foundation for Excellence in Education, which were designed to promote it on his own terms.

While a complete picture of a legacy cannot emerge except in the passage of time, it is possible to describe some of its elements at earlier points. This chapter is an early word on the Jeb Bush legacy. It describes a view of the legacy at a very early point, beginning with the general impression that he left with Floridians as he left office.

Performance in Office: The People's View

As might be expected given Bush's attacks on some of the fundamental elements of Democratic Party philosophy, views of the Bush legacy among Democratic officials were not positive. Democratic congresswoman Debbie Wasserman Shultz called him "literally the most inflexible public official I've ever encountered in my 16 years in public office." Mitch Ceasar, chair of Florida's Broward County Democratic Party, said, "Jeb Bush was very often out of step with most Floridians and, I think, with most Americans" (Padgett, 2006). And State Senator Frederica Wilson, a Miami Democrat, called him an "arrogant monarch."

More surprising is the range of views among Republican activists. Former Florida Republican Party chairman Al Cardenas claims that "as a result of [Bush] leadership, we in essence accomplished a revolution" (Reinhard, 2006). A "revolution" seemed a little excessive to Republican state represen-tative David Rivera of Miami, who said Jeb "did more to consolidate the success of the Republican Party or Republican candidates across the state of Florida than any political figure previously" (ibid.). And another former Republican Party chair, Tom Slade, was reported to have said that "when Jeb Bush walked out of Tallahassee, it was the lifting of a ton off of everybody he'd been associated with in this town" (Date, 2007).

The average citizen in Florida came away from the Bush administration with a modest impression of the governor's performance in office. The results from two public opinion polls taken in the last year of his administration show that Bush was seen as a "good but not great governor who for the most part has not made things better in the state since he became governor" (Richards, 2006). Taken together, the two polls showed that 17 percent of Floridians thought of Bush as a "great" governor and 13 percent thought he was "bad." The remaining 70 percent saw him as either "good" or "so-so."

Over 60 percent of Floridians interviewed in the last year of Bush's administration said that "things in Florida" had either gotten worse or stayed the same over the time that Bush was in office. Further, the governor left citizens with little optimism about the future. In another poll conducted in late October 2006, 66 percent of those interviewed said the state would be either the same or a worse place to live in the next five years (Mason-Dixon Corporation Poll, Released November 15, 2006).

Polling results also show that a sizable majority of Floridians would not support Jeb Bush if he ran for president, certainly a sign of a modest legacy. Over the course of his administration Floridians were asked several times if Governor Bush should run for president or if they would vote for him if he did so. Nearly 70 percent said that he should not run (Quinnipiac University Polling Institute, December 7, 2004, and February 24, 2005) and nearly 60 percent said that they would not vote for him if he did (Quinnipiac University Polling Institute, November 16, 2005).

Explanations for Governor Bush's standing with the citizens of Florida are complex and attempts to link it to specific factors are highly speculative. Although he was widely praised for his actions during the hurricanes that hit Florida while he was in office, several high-visibility events in which the governor was involved during his term portrayed him in a less than positive light. Perhaps these events are the things for which Bush is remembered and are what drive his legacy with the public. They include his behavior in the disputed presidential election of 2000, his actions regarding Terri Schiavo, and his relentless efforts to enact policies that failed repeatedly to find favor among Floridians: school vouchers, elimination of school class-size requirements, and privatization of state government services. His personal style, which was viewed as aloof, arrogant, and combative, is likely to have contributed negatively to the public's judgment about his job performance.

The Political Legacy

One component of a legacy for an elected official is the extent to which he or she affects the political circumstances in which he or she serves. Some officials—FDR, John F. Kennedy, Ronald Reagan, and Barack Obama, for example—generate new interest in politics and public life and inspire new participants to involve themselves in electoral politics or in their political party, thereby laying the ground for subsequent success for their political parties or their ideas. Others simply ride existing waves of support or, like Herbert Hoover, contribute to a decline in the political fortunes of his party.

A variety of empirical measures permit an objective assessment of the political legacy left by a governor. These include the extent to which a political figure affects partisan attachments among citizens, the degree to which he or she improves the electoral fortunes of his or her party, and whether or not she increases the strength of that party as an organization. An examination of these measures in Florida reinforces the view that Governor Bush left a modest political legacy in the state.

Voter registration records and pubic opinion polls covering the time period of the governor's term in office show that few gains were added to those made in voter registration and in partisan identification by the Republican Party in Florida during the 1980s and early 1990s. Instead, these gains reached a plateau when Bush came to office.

Overall voter registration in Florida increased as people continued to migrate to the state throughout the 1980s and 1990s. However, the Republican gains in voter registration and in partisan identification did not accelerate in the aftermath of Bush's election. Official data from the Florida Department of State show that the percentage of all voters in Florida who were registered as Republicans declined by 2.4 percent between 1998 and 2006. And information about the partisan identification of Florida voters showed that the percentage of citizens who thought of themselves as Republicans declined from 39.4 percent in 1998 to 36.2 percent in 2005 (Florida State University, College of Social Sciences, 1999–2005).

While all of this change cannot be attributed to Governor Bush, he apparently did not serve as a catalyst for increased citizen attachment to the Republican Party in Florida. Durable political change requires that the party benefiting from large victories take measures to give voters a reason to convert their protest into new loyalties. This conversion did not take place in Florida while Bush was in office.

The governor's effect on the electoral fortunes of his party was modest and, if anything, solidified rather than added to previous gains. Republicans gained control of both houses of the Florida legislature in 1996, two years prior to the election of Jeb Bush. They increased this majority and also achieved parity with the Democrats on the Florida Cabinet in the election of 1998, the year in which Bush was first elected. These victories, however, should not be attributed to the governor's coattails, since he ran behind five of the six officials competing for statewide office that year. Indeed, much of the credit for the growth of the Republican Party's electoral fortunes can be tied to the organizing work of Al Cardenas, Tom Slade, and other Republican Party officials during the 1980s. Between 1998 and 2006, and after a 2000 reapportionment favorable to the party, the numbers of Republicans in the state house of representatives increased by six and the number of senators increased by one. Over this same time period, the party lost one cabinet seat.

The governor unquestionably made a substantial contribution to the overall health and well-being of the Republican Party *as an organization*; one that helped ensure that the once moribund party will be capable of competing into the foreseeable future for offices at all levels of government in Florida. He participated actively in the efforts of the GOP to recruit candidates for office and to raise funds for party activities and candidates, and his stature as brother of the president of the United States gave him access to money that was unavailable to others. He also appointed hundreds of Republicans to influential boards and commissions and to the Florida courts, thus creating the life blood of a political party, a substantial farm team of candidates for future political contests. As the governor's former speechwriter and communications director put it, Jeb "and his family have created a vigorous infrastructure of fundraising and grass-roots activism that will endure for Republican candidates for many years."

Political Culture and Norms of Government

Governors are remembered for the norms and beliefs about government that guided their behavior in office, that is, for the nature of the political culture that they helped create and operated within. Of particular interest is the extent to which they adopt and adhere to norms of democratic governance. On this dimension, Governor Bush left a legacy characterized by disregard for, if not antagonism to, deliberative government and neglect of the opinion of Floridians about issues he chose as his focus.

The theory of leadership that guided Jeb Bush reflected the views of the governmental reformers who pushed the American states to increase the power of the office of governor and to place it at the center of public policymaking. The theory gave governors responsibility for mobilizing public opinion in order to overcome the inertia inherent in the decentralized political systems of the American states. Following the dictates of this theory, governors are pushed to override the separation of powers doctrine, which was designed to reduce the danger of tyranny from a popular majority. In deciding how hard to push,

Individual governors show preferences, consciously or not, for specific democratic values and leave legacies related to these values.

Adoption of this "strong governor" theory of leadership led Jeb Bush to minimize the primary value in the doctrine of separation of powers. This doctrine was adopted "to maintain liberty not simply by throwing sand into the gears of government but by *perpetuating the principle of deliberative constitutional government*" (Landy and Milkis, 2000: 6; emphasis added). Governor Bush appeared to resent the participation of other branches of government and of other public officials in making state policy and treated the legislature, and especially the judiciary, as impediments to his goals rather than as governing partners. He made no attempt to construct a concensus around his policy proposals, seeking instead to obtain acquiescence for the direction he had created in his own mind. Rather than attempting to foster cooperation with those who disagreed with him, Governor Bush tried to intimidate and defeat his opponents by increasing the political costs of opposition and by creating a situation in which there were winners and losers.

The governor also played down the interests of the public when they went counter to his own. Jeb Bush came to the office of governor with a set of ideas driven by a particular political philosophy and "stayed on message" in an effort to move public opinion to support his policies. Throughout his term, public opinion polls indicated that a majority of Floridians disagreed with major segments of this agenda—for example, school vouchers, tax cuts as a public policy priority, reducing class size in public schools, use of the FCAT, privatization of public services, and his efforts to resolve the Terry Schiavo case. The governor ignored this opinion, responding instead to narrow constituencies that were committed to advancing their own ideologically based policy agendas. Actions such as these left him open to the charge made by one of his Republican colleagues in the legislature that "in his heart of hearts, the governor prefers dictatorship to Democracy" (Cotterell, August 29, 2006). Political theorists suggest that in circumstances such as these "when officeholders persistently disregard the public's policy preferences, popular sovereignty and representative democracy are threatened" (Jacobs and Shapiro, 2000: xvii).

At the end of his term the governor expressed satisfaction with the political culture that he left in Florida (Associated Press, 2006, December 14) but the Republican administration that succeeded him tried to distance itself from it. In the swearing-in ceremonies for the incoming leadership in the Florida House and Senate in 2006, the newly elected Republican senate majority leader said, "we must change the tenor of public discourse and we must offer progress, not politics" and the incoming Republican speaker of the house, himself an acolyte of the governor, admonished new house members to "reject the political culture we have inherited" which is "too much about winning."

Governmental Theory and Policies

The most substantial legacy of the Bush administration lies in the policy agenda and the theory of government that he promoted. This theory and these policies carry the imprint of the governor's personal philosophy and outlook and Jeb left a legacy of activism in their pursuit. He broke from the incremental, moderate approaches that characterized previous governors and reexamined and challenged basic tenets of public policy in Florida. When measured against the most commonly used contemporary standard of gubernatorial performance— passage of legislative initiatives—Bush achieved great policy success. But his victories may have been pyrrhic.

Questions remain as to whether enactment of his policies produced the larger, ultimate outcomes envisioned by the conservative theory that inspired them. For example, the privatization of government services Governor Bush instituted in concert with governmental downsizing was designed to produce a smaller but more productive government. The number of state employees in Florida *was* reduced during the Bush tenure, but information from investigations of the quality of government performance in the state and of problems that emerged in the course of his initiatives suggests that privatized government in Florida is not "better" government. In addition, the governor never articulated a clear conception of how a smaller government was to interact with the multitude of private and nonprofit organizations that he brought into efforts to serve the state's citizens. His goal was simply to reduce governmental regulation and activity, freeing individuals and organizations to pursue their own agenda, whether or not inimical to a general public interest. By doing so, he put the state at a risk that was articulated by the Republican president of the state senate, who said, "The problem you run into with this is, once you dismantle the public apparatus, it's hard to reassemble it. It's gone. The cost to ramp back up and restore our human-resource function, for instance, in our state would just be astronomical" (Cotterell, January 24, 2005).

Other examples of successful reforms that did not produce the ultimate outcomes anticipated by conservative theorists are those in education and in economic development. The governor was able to introduce a form of account- ability into the public school system and he created a series of educational choices to the state's public school system. These reforms did not, however, produce the kind of improvement in academic performance that the governor sought or that he claimed. His economic development policies likewise had minimal effect on the overall economy and did little to change the nature of the state's workforce. The rate of job growth in the state was about what it had been during previous administrations, and the Florida economy remains firmly rooted in the low-paying, low-skill service sector.

Some policy changes did, however, achieve the outcomes hypothesized by Bush's theory of government. The most prominent of these were reductions in the numbers of people receiving economic assistance from the state and tax changes designed to "starve the beast" of government.

The governor's aggressive pursuit of the goals in the federal 1996 Personal Responsibility Act was successful in removing large numbers of low-income Floridians from the state's welfare rolls. This had been a longtime goal of the conservative movement in the United States. However, the accompanying belief that those who left welfare would find employment that would lift them out of poverty did not prove accurate.

The governor's tax policies eliminated completely one of the sources of support for state government, the intangibles tax, and reduced others. Since the governor did not propose an alternative system of taxation, his tax policies had the straightforward effect of reducing the fiscal capacity of state government in Florida and of shifting a greater share of the burden of government onto local units of government and onto Floridians in the lowest income classes. The later outcome of the Bush tax policy had also been a cherished goal of governmental conservatives in the United States.

Despite the achievement of large numbers of Governor Bush's policy goals, the state learned much less than it might have about some of the most important changes in government policy ever enacted in Florida or in the nation. And this may be one of the governor's most substantial legacies. Given Bush's influence over policymaking while governor, it would have been easy for him to have arranged for the kind of research and analysis that would have shed light on some of his conservative hypotheses, especially that providing public services with a smaller, privatized government would be more effective and efficient than doing so with public agencies and that educational vouchers and school choice would improve educational performance. Instead, he fought such efforts. In doing so he left a host of important questions unanswered about how Florida might be more efficiently governed and thereby perpetuated partisan disagreements over issues that might have been avoided. And he left himself open to the charge that he was an ideologue rather than a leader truly interested in finding ways to improve government in the state of Florida.

Governing Institutions

Jeb Bush came to the office of governor bearing antipathy to government in general and, as suggested earlier in this chapter, the underlying theory of his administration can be seen as an attack on the general model of the American political system, which included separation of powers, checks and balances, and consultation and bargaining.

The Florida legislature under Republican leadership responded to Bush's aggressive pursuit of institutional supremacy with passivity and allowed the institution to become subordinate to the governor. When asked, the Florida legislature usually gave the governor the legislation he wanted and rarely challenged his claims about the powers of his office. Thus the default position between the legislature and the governor of Florida moved toward the executive end of the shared powers continuum during the Bush administration.

Contemporary government necessitates executive activism, especially in a political system such as that in Florida characterized by a part-time legislature. The volume of information flowing into government is huge, and even legislative leaders, let alone the rank and file, will usually have access to only a portion of it. Thus it should be expected, even desired, that governors take the lead in identifying policy priorities and in suggesting strategies for their resolution.

Nevertheless, legislators have a critical role to play in the policymaking process, one that the Republicans under the thrall of Jeb Bush often avoided. Their job is to use reasoning and consideration to monitor the policies and actions of other governmental actors and institutions. Failure on the part of the Florida legislature to perform this role and to scrutinize with care the workings of the Bush administration undermined deliberative government in Florida. This failure also generated a hostile tone in public policy debate as opposition leaders resorted to partisan responses to proposals that they had no input into. More important, perhaps, it led to the adoption of flawed public policy. The house Democratic leader from 2002 to 2004 spoke to the later problem when he suggested that "as time goes by, we will probably find a lot of repairs are needed because things...were devoid of debate and public discussion. There were no checks and balances" (Rushing, December 2006).

Finally, public opinion data show that citizen distrust in state government grew during the Bush administration. Since research on this topic shows that trust in American national government and the behavior of the president are related (Citrin, 1974; Citrin and Green, 1986), it is not a stretch to suggest that Governor Bush's relentless criticism of government in general and his efforts to limit the influence of Florida's governmental institutions contributed to a legacy of general distrust in Florida government. Political science research shows that the loss of such trust has at least two important effects: (1) it reduces the chances of building a competent state where citizens feel that they have a more or less equal and potential chance of making a difference in political decision making (Lewicki and Tomlinson, 2003; Sztompka, 1999); and (2) it makes it more difficult for political leaders to succeed (Hetherington, 1998). Thus, lower levels of public support for government undermined both elected officials, including Governor Bush himself, and political institutions in Florida, reducing leeway to govern effectively.

The Future: Is Bush Passé?

In the aftermath of the 2008 presidential election and the demoralizing defeat for the Republican Party, the GOP is engaged in an effort "to figure out what the party stands for, as well as what face to put forward as they struggle to avoid shrinking into a party of Southern white men in an increasingly diverse country" (Nagourney, 2009). Governor Bush has expressed his intention to play a constructive role in this process, "advocating ideas and policies that solve the pressing problems of the day. We must rebuild the Party by focusing on the common purposes and core conservative principles that unite us all" (*TampaBay Buzz*, 2009).

The governor's first idea about what should be done was to form a "shadow government" to engage the Democrats on important issues. The obvious question about this suggestion is, "who will lead the shadow government?" Is it Jeb? If so, what are the assets and liabilities that he brings to the job? In the remainder of this chapter I speak to three questions on this issue: What are Bush's future political intentions and prospects? What are his assets and liabilities in future campaigns? And what would be his strengths and weaknesses as a future leader of the Republican Party and as an officeholder?

Political Intentions: Will He Run for Higher Office?

Governor Bush has always been coy about his future political plans, saying in December 2006 that "I don't know what the future holds for me," and that he is "not ruling in or out" running for president in 2008. He also expressed no interest in the U.S. Senate, deriding it repeatedly as an ineffectual "debating society" and by August 2007, he was claiming that he had "no ambition in politics" (Gallagher, 2007).

While very few Floridians believed this last comment, he did not make an effort to be a candidate for president in 2008 and made no endorsements in the Republican presidential primary in that year. In December 2008, he briefly expressed an interest in the U.S. Senate when the Republican incumbent, Mel Martinez, indicated that he would not be a candidate for reelection in 2010. But two weeks later he took himself out of that race.

Many observers of Florida politics had thought that Bush would bypass the 2008 opportunity in order to return to south Florida and utilize his elevated standing among Republicans to improve his economic fortunes. A former chief of staff suggested that he will "get busy quickly on some private sector, capitalistic opportunity that will just engulf him and I think he'll stay involved in education."

This hint that Bush would utilize his contacts to engage in more "insider" business activities proved to be prescient. Shortly after his term ended, Bush created a consulting firm, Bush and Associates, and "began looking for boards to join." In May 2007, he was appointed to a position on the Tenet Healthcare Corporation Board, the largest publicly traded hospital company in America. Although his compensation for this work was not reported, other members of this board were paid between $97,000 and $129,000 per year. In addition to his regular compensation, Bush also got restricted stock worth $260,000 (Koenig, 2007). Later that year he was also appointed to the private equity advisory board of Lehman Brothers, the ill-fated financial services company, which has strong

Bush family ties (Fineout, 2007). In November 2007 he was appointed to the board of CNL Bancshares, Inc., of Orlando. This appointment raised questions about "political payback" since as governor Bush had approved a tax refund and a road project that benefited the board chairman. The executive director of Florida Common Cause suggested that the governor should have refused this appointment (Van Sickler and Freedberg, 2007), but the chairman's spokeswoman said there was absolutely no quid pro quo involved in the appointment (Jackson, 2007). And in December 2008, he was appointed to the Board of Rayonier, Inc., a forest products company structured as a Real Estate Investment Trust (REIT). His compensation in this position was $40,000, with annual stock options valued at $46,000 (Bender, 2008).

A presidential race in 2012 is possible, although several people who are close to the governor say that he just doesn't like the environment in Washington and would not enjoy working there. Nevertheless, one prominent political commentator (former Republican congressman Joe Scarborough) has proclaimed Bush to be the "future of the Republican Party," and at least one former member of the Bush administration claims that there is a plan already in place for a 2012 presidential race. Gema Hernandez, secretary of elder affairs in the Bush administration who was fired by the governor in 2001, says that the plan currently is limited to the strategic placement of favorable reviews of the governor's performance in media outlets throughout the nation. One example of such a review, in which Bush was described as the "best" governor in the nation, was written by Fred Barnes, a longtime supporter of the governor's brother, for the June 2006 *Weekly Standard.*

Given her strained relationship with the governor, Dr. Hernandez's views must be treated skeptically, but there *are* indications that Governor Bush is keeping his electoral options open. Primary among these signs was the re-creation, in 2005, of the Foundation for Florida's Future, the organization he established in 1995 to keep himself visible after his loss to Lawton Chiles in his first race for governor. In re-opening this organization he appointed to its board of directors three Republican Party "Rangers," the Bush/Cheney Campaign designation for people who raised at least $200,000 for the George W. Bush reelection campaign in 2004. He also hired his former campaign finance director and two other former campaign aides. By June 2006, $1.9 million had been donated to this foundation and about $320,000 of that amount had been spent, nearly $70,000 of which was for a poll, the subject of which Bush would not reveal (Kam, 2006, June 29).

Bush also campaigned for South Carolina governor Mark Sanford in support of Reform SC, the political organization Sanford had created to battle the Republican-controlled South Carolina legislature. Sanford, a Republican himself, had been engaged in an ongoing battle with what he viewed as "big-government" Republicans who had opposed a conservative agenda that featured many elements of the Bush agenda; in particular school vouchers (fitsnews.com, September 5, 2007).

Very few people in Florida politics believe that the actions described above are unrelated to future political plans.

There are also rumors circulating through Florida political circles that Bush may want to be governor again. A former chief of staff says that "if he ever runs for another office, it might be for governor. He loves that job, he loves being chief executive." These rumors quieted markedly since a Republican succeeded him in 2006. Nevertheless, he has expressed concern that his educational legacy, in particular, might be lost if moderate Republicans and Democrats gained power. And in 2009, when the sitting Republican U.S. senator announced that he would not be a candidate for reelection, a rumor circulated that the incumbent Republican governor would abandon his position to run for the Senate and Jeb would run again for governor of Florida.

There will be heavy pressure on him to run for another office from the constituencies that he wooed so assiduously while in office, the religious Right, other social conservatives, and the Florida business community. These groups supported both Jeb and his brother at very high levels and think that he owes them. Nevertheless, the face of the Republican Party in Florida and in the nation is changing and there is some question about the extent to which Bush will fit the profile of a Republican standard bearer in the future. In fact, his own brother, the president, has said that in order for the Republican Party to come back, it must promote a message that "different points of view are included." This is not a position that Jeb has often articulated.

Can He Win?

As was the case when Jeb Bush made his initial foray into electoral politics in Florida, his primary asset as a future presidential candidate is the visibility that comes from his association with the Bush family dynasty. While the Bush "brand" is currently in eclipse due to his brother's low standing with the public and because of "Bush fatigue," the visibility that goes with the Bush name is an asset beyond the reach of any other candidate and guarantees him a prominent place among any group of candidates were he to decide to run.

Governor Bush's support for socially conservative causes and especially the fight over Terri Schiavo has also made him extremely popular within the most conservative segments of the Republican coalition, and he can rely on this important group for enthusiastic support in upcoming elections. Indeed, his support in this wing of the party is allegedly the primary reason that at least two Republican presidential contenders were rumored to have wanted him on their presidential ticket. With the defeat of the Republicans in the presidential election of 2008, many are calling for a return to the conservative values that brought them to power in 1984, and Jeb Bush in a sense defines those values. However, he received no votes in the 2009 National Conservative Political Action Committee straw poll of potential people the organization would like to see as a 2012 presidential candidate.

Jeb Bush is a prodigious fund-raiser. He has access to his family's friends and supporters and to every important individual in the Republican Party's galaxy of money givers. His personal base in Florida, which contributed over 15 percent of all money given by individuals to his brother's 2004 presidential campaign, makes his fund-raising task that much easier.

Governor Bush is not a powerhouse vote getter. He lost his first run for governor, won his second by the second smallest margin of any prior governor in Florida, and ran behind five out of the six statewide candidates who were on that ballot with him. In his third race, he beat a candidate thought by the political literati to have run a poor campaign. In addition, several candidates that he publicly supported for election—there have been relatively few—have been defeated, leaving some question about his coat-tail effect. One of these was the 2006 Republican candidate for the statewide office of chief financial officer, one of only two statewide Republican candidates to lose that year.

The stance Bush took as an ideologue throughout his political career limits his appeal to a broad general election constituency. He also generated special enmity within the African American community. If, as some political observers suggest, there is hunger in the nation for political figures who value problem solving over ideology, then Governor Bush faces substantial problems.

Can He Govern?

Jeb Bush has potentially serious limitations as an effective president. Like his brother the president, Governor Bush is a divisive political figure and as governor he showed no interest in building consensus behind his policies. He is guided by a rigid philosophy of government that he seems unwilling to moderate. His leadership style is confrontational, characterized by proposing solutions that he expects others to agree with. During his term in office, he demonstrated little inclination to compromise and very little interest in developing broad coalitions around contentious issues. Unlike his counterpart Arnold Schwarzenegger, who tried to find the center of politics in California (Weintraub, 2008), Bush mobilized his ideological base and fought off the "heretics."

Compounding the limitations inherent in his leadership style is the fact that he has no experience working with governmental officials who are not in his own party or who do not share his theory of government. Bush's term as Florida governor was marked by an overwhelmingly Republican legislature that was highly united behind his own philosophy of government. Thus he was not forced to compromise or to develop consensus among competing groups. He would need to modify both his governmental theory and his style of leadership to be successful in a more diverse, competitive political arena. There is little evidence that he would be willing to do this.

Summary

Jeb Bush came to the governorship of Florida in what was arguably the most propitious time for an elected official in the state's history. Taking advantage of a good economy and overwhelming political majorities, he adopted a theoretically based philosophy of government, pursued the associated goals aggressively, and successfully implemented a large number of the policies called for by the theory. These policies produced substantial changes in the structure and functions of government in Florida, but it is probably fair to say that what we now see as his accomplishments are about the full story. The governmental theory upon which he based his actions produced no legacy of great improvement in the state and Floridians did not believe that Florida in 2005 when Bush left office was a better place than it had been in 1999 when he took office. The change he brought about is not synonymous with progress and as of this writing, some of it is being reversed. The longest lasting and most substantial legacy of the Bush administration was the elimination of the intangibles tax, the result of which was to tilt advantage to those in the state who were better off at the expense of those who were not.

Bibliography

Ackerman, Sherri. 2007. "Need to Fix DCF 'Urgent,' Its Chief Says." *Tampa Tribune*, July 18. Found at www.tbo.com/news/metro/MGB5N87894F.html. Printed July 18, 2007.

Air Safety Week. 1999. "Older Aircraft Exempted from Lawsuits in Florida Tort Reform Law." May.

Alker, Joan, and Jack Hoadley. 2007. "Assessing Florida's Medicaid Reform." Georgetown University. Georgetown Public Policy Institute.

Andelman, Bob. 1992. "Jeb Bush: Questions, Answers." Originally published in *The Maddux Report* and in *Creative Loafing/Tampa* 1992. Found at http://www.andleman.com/ARTICLES/jebbush-mr.html. Printed August 29, 2005.

Ash, Jim. 2006. "State Food-Stamp Errors Mount." *Tallahassee Democrat*, July 17.

Associated Press. 1993. "Dad's Shadow Stalks Bush Bros." October 30.

Associated Press. 2006. "High School Seniors Scoring Big on AP Tests." Gainesville.com. Printed February 7, 2006.

Associated Press. 2004. "Bush an Asset for Brother's Run." March 7. Found at www.stpetimes.com/2004/03/07/State/Bush_an_asset_for_bro.shtml. Printed January 27, 2005.

Associated Press. 2004. "Officials Knew Felon-Database Problems for Two Months." *Tallahassee Democrat*, August 2.

Associated Press. 2006. "Governor Bashes Town's Eminent Domain Efforts." *Tallahassee Democrat*, June 2.

Associated Press. 2006. "Gov Bush Sums Up His Eight Years in Office." Lakeland, Florida, *Ledger*, December 14.

Associated Press. 2007. "Analysis Finds Florida Schools Have High Dropout Rates." Naplesnews.com/news/2007.oct/30/analysis.

Associated Press. 2009. "Bill Would Limit Funding for Fla's Medicaid Pilot." March 2. www.heraldtribune.com/article/20090302/APN/903021917.

Bardach, Ann Louise. 2002. *Cuba Confidential: Love and Vengeance in Miami and Havana.* New York: Random House.

Bardach, Ann Louise. 2004. "Hoodwinked: Why Is Florida's Voting System So Corrupt?" *Slate*, August 24. Found at www.slate.com/id/2105524/>.

Barnett, Cynthia. 2006. "Biotechnology: Rolling the Dice." *Florida Trend*, September 25.

Barnett. Cynthia. 2007. *Mirage: Florida and the Vanishing Water of the Eastern U.S.* Ann Arbor: University of Michigan Press.

Barone, Michael. 1993. "Snares of a Lost Paradise." *U.S. News and World Report*, October 11.

Barrett, Katherine, and Richard Greene. 2005. "Grading the States: Florida." *Governing.* Found at Governing.com.

Barrilleaux, Charles, and Michael Beckman. 2003. *Political Research Quarterly* 56, no. 4 (December).

Barton, Alan. 2003. "Jeb's Boy: Frank Brogan, Bush's Man in Academia, Must Defuse the FAU Scandals. But Where is He?" *New Times Broward-Palm Beach*, March 27.

Baxter, Eva. 2005. "The Bush Administration: Focusing the Message." Unpublished manuscript, Florida State University, Department of Political Science.

BBC News, Special Report. 1998. "Jeb Bush: Third Way Republican." October 30.

Beck, Paul Allen. 1997. "Partisan De-alignment in the Post-War South." *American Political Science Review* 71: 477–496.

Becker, Jo. 1999. "Senate Tugs at Bush's Purse Strings." *St. Petersburg Times*, November 10.

Becker, Jo. 2000. "Bush Family Turns Out to Campaign in New Hampshire." *St. Petersburg Times*, January 16.

Begos, Kevin. 2006. "Crist Expected to Ease Access to Public Records." *Tampa Tribune*, December 1.

Bell, Maya. 2006. "Gov Bush Ends Drive to Change Law on Patients with Feeding Tubes." Sun-Sentinel.com, April 13.

Bender, Michael. 2008. "$105 in Land Deals for Jeb's New Company." PalmBeachPost.com, December 3, 2008.

Bennett, Brad. 2000. "Poll: Affirmative Action Would Die if Put to a Vote." *Miami Herald*, November 8, 1999.

Benson, J. Edwin. 2007. "The Interplay of Party Leadership and Standing Committees in a Competitive versus a Non-Competitive State Legislative Setting: The Case of Florida." *Florida Political Chronicle* 18: 27–41.

Berke, Richard L. 1994. "Jeb Bush's Florida Foes Team Up against Him." *New York Times*, August 2.

Berlow, Bill. 2005. "Cantero Puts Another Chink in Privatization's Armor." *Tallahassee Democrat*, March 4.

Berlow, Bill. 2006. "Give Bush Credit for Challenging a Complacent Public School System." *Tallahassee Democrat*, January 27.

Berry, William D., Evan J. Rinquist, Richard Fording, and Russell Hanson. 1998. "Measuring Citizen and Government Ideology in the American States, 1960–1993." *American Journal of Political Science* 42, no. 2 (April): 327–348.

Betts, Julian A., Lorien Rice, Andrew Zau, Emily Tang, and Cory Koedel. 2006. *Does School Choice Work? Effects on Student Integration and Achievement*. Berkeley, Calif.: Public Policy Institute of California.

Beyle, Thad. 1999. "The Governors." In *Politics in the American States*, ed. Virginia Gray, Russell Hanson, and Herbert Jacob. Washington, D.C.: CQ Press.

Beyle, Thad. 2004. "The Governors." In *Politics in the American States*, ed. Virginia Gray and Russell Hanson. Washington, D.C.: CQ Press.

Bierman, Noah. 2006. "Packed Colleges Concern Crist." *Miami Herald*, December 11.

Bode, Ken. 2004. "Soft Power." *Boston Sunday Globe*, May 9. Found at www.boston.com/ae/books/articles/2004/05/09/soft_power/.

Bousquet, Steve. 2003."Bullying by Bush Turns Friends into Enemies." *St. Petersburg Times*, July 12.

Bousquet, Steve. 2006. "The Bush Legacy." *St. Petersburg Times*, December 29.

Bousquet, Steve. 2009. "State Inmates are Fed on the Cheap." *Tampabay.com/news/politics/state/*. February 8.

Bousquet, Steve, Joni James, and Jennifer Liberto. 2004. "Governor Accentuates Positive, Rallies GOP." *St. Petersburg Times*, March 3.

Bowman, James S., Marc Gertz, Sally Gertz, and Russell Williams. 2003. "Civil Service Reform in Florida State Government." *Review of Public Personnel Administration* 4 (December): 286–304.

Bowman, James S., Sally Gertz, and Jonathan West. 2006. "Florida's Service First: Radical Reform in the Sunshine State." In *Civil Service Reform in the States*, ed. Lloyd Nigro and J. Edward Kellough. Albany, N.Y.: SUNY Press.

Braun, Henry, Frank Jenkins, and Wendy Grigg. 2006. "A Closer Look at Charter Schools Using Hierarchical Linear Modeling." National Center for Education Statistics. Found at http://nces.edu/gov/Nationsreportcard /pubs/studies/ 2006460.asp. Printed August 23, 2006.

Bridges, Tyler. 2002. "Voters Cool to Bush's A+ Plan, Poll Says." *Miami Herald,* June 14.

Broder, David S. 1994. "Jeb Gives Chiles All He Can Handle." *Washington Post,* October 22.

Brown, Marilyn. 2005. "Schools Getting State Vouchers Must Be Accountable, Bush Says." *Tampa Tribune,* October 18.

Brown University. 2005. "Sixth Annual State and Federal e-Government Study." *Brown University News*. Providence, R.I.

Brownstein, Ronald. 2007. *The Second Civil War*. New York: Penguin Press.

Bruce, Billy. 2006. "Housing Hurting Labor Pool." *Tallahassee Democrat*, September 1.

Brudney, Jeffrey, Ted Herbert, and Deil Wright. 1999. "Reinventing Government in the American States." *Public Administration Review* 59: 19–30.

Bush, Jeb. 2001. "Governor Bush Unveils Service First." Press Release. March 1.

Bush, Jeb. 2003. "Remarks" at the 2003 NRA Annual Meeting. Monday, May 5. Found at http:P//www.nraila.org/news/read/speeches.aspx?ID=30. Printed April 28, 2005.

Bush, Jeb. 2004. *Governor's Priority: Creating a Climate for Job Growth*. Florida's E-Budget, 2004–2005. Found at www.ebudget.state.fl.us/govprioirities/ job_ growth/taxrelief.asp, October 13, 2004.

Bush, Jeb. 2005. "Governor Bush Urges Legislature to Pass Elimination of Joint and Several Liability." Memo to Florida Legislature from Governor Jeb Bush, April 13.

Bush, Jeb. 2006. "Growing the Economy." http://eogtmp.sto.fl.gov/html/ growing_the_economy.html. Printed January 24, 2006.

Bush, Jeb. 2006. *State of the State Address*. March 7.

Bush, Jeb. 2007. "Improvement Requires Willingness to Change." Reason Foundation. Found at www.reason.org/innovators2007/innovators2007_bush.shtml. Printed August 6, 2007.

Bush, Jeb. 2007. Acceptance Speech for Urban Innovator Award, Manhattan Institute.

Calabro, Dominic. 2007. "How Does Florida Compare?" Florida TaxWatch. June.

Callahan, David. 1999. "$1 Billion for Ideas: Conservative Think Tanks in the 1990's." National Committee for Responsive Philanthropy, March.

Camarda, Michael. 2007. "Reform in the States: An Interview with Governor Jeb Bush." Thepolitic.org/content/view/74. Printed February 29, 2008.

Caputo, Marc, and Gary Finewood. 2005. "Deadly Force Bill Passes House." *Tallahassee Democrat,* April 1.

Caputo, Marc, and Breanne Gilpatrick. 2006. "Villalobos Squeaks By." *Miami Hearld,* September 6.

Carter, Dan. 1995. *The Politics of Rage*. Baton Rouge: Louisiana State University Press.

Carter, Jimmy. 2004. "Still Seeking a Fair Florida Vote." Monday, September 27. washingtonpost.com.

Carver, Joan, and Tom Fiedler. 1999. "Florida: A Volatile National Microcosm." In *Southern Politics in the 1990s*, ed. Alexander Lamis. Baton Rouge: Louisana State University Press.

Center on Budget and Policy Priorities. 2008. *Pulling Apart: A State by State Analysis of Income Trends.* Washington, D.C.

Chimerine, Lawrence, and Ross Eisenbrey. 2005. "The Frivolous Case for Tort Law Change." Economic Policy Institute, EPI Issue Brief No. 157, May 17.

Citrin, Jack. 1974. "Comment: The Political Relevance of Trust in Government." *American Political Science Review* 68 (September): 973–988.

Citrin, Jack, and Donald Philip Green. 1986. "Presidential Leadership and the Resurgence of Trust in Government." *British Journal of Political Science* 16 (October): 431–453.

Clark, Lesley. 2005. "Schiavo Inquiry Unpopular with Voters." *Tallahassee Democrat,* July 1.

CNN, ALLPolitics. 1997. "Jeb Bush Jumps Into 1998 Florida Governor's Race." November 12.

CNN.com. 2005. "Jeb BushWins Big in Florida." Found at www.cnn.comlAllpolitics/stories/1998/11/03/electionigovernors/florida. Printed August 31, 2005.

Cockburn, Patrick. 1994. *The Independent* (London), November 5.

Coffey, Daniel. 2005. "Measuring Gubernatorial Ideology: A Content Analysis of State of the State Messages." *State Politics and Policy Quarterly* 5: 88–105.

Conner, Deirdre. 2006. "What about the Kids?" *Naples News*, October 23.

Connley, Cecci, Helen Dewar, and Peter Baker. 1997. "Jeb Bush Seeks Help from Father's D.C. Friends." *Washington Post*, December 3, A12.

Corporation for Economic Development. 2006. "Development Report Cards for the States." Found at http://cfed.org/focus.m'?parentid=34&siteid=1099&id=1102.

Cotterell, Bill. 2001. "State Efficiency Czar Resigns in Protest." *Tallahassee Democrat,* May, 1a–2a.

Cotterell, Bill. 2005. "State Wary of Outsourcing: Accountability Sought in Private Deals." *Tallahassee Democrat*, January 24.

Cotterell, Bill. 2005. "Senator: Contracts Not Right." *Tallahassee Democrat*, January 27.

Cotterell, Bill. 2005. "Under Bush, State Jobs Lose Ground." *Tallahassee Democrat,* February 20.

Cotterell, Bill. 2005. "Bush Disappointed by Inability to Intervene." *Tallahassee Democrat,* March 27.

Cotterell, Bill. 2005. "Governor Told to Watch What He Says." *Tallahassee Democrat,* April 28, 1A.

Cotterell, Bill. 2005. "We Shouldn't be Surprised by Governor's Audacity." *Tallahassee Democrat*, June 27.

Cotterell, Bill. 2005. "Efficiency Bills Get Bush Veto." *Tallahassee Democrat,* June 28.

Cotterell, Bill. 2005. "Bush Calls People First a Success." *Tallahassee Democrat,* August 17.

Cotterell, Bill. 2006. "Legislator Questions Outsourcing." *Tallahassee Democrat,* January 30.

Cotterell, Bill. 2006. "Report: Can't Tell if People First Saves Money." *Tallahassee Democrat*, April 27.

Cotterell, Bill. 2006. "Bush Listens, But He's the Boss." *Tallahassee Democrat*, June 27.

Cotterell, Bill. 2006. "Prisons Chief Questions Merits of Privatization." *Tallahassee Democrat,* August 2.

Cotterell, Bill. 2006. *Tallahassee Democrat*, August 29.

Cotterell, Bill. 2006. "Jeb: State Employees Not Hurt by His Changes." *Tallahassee Democrat,* December 9.

Cotterell, Bill. 2006. "Crist Chooses Experienced Elections Chief." *Tallahassee Democrat*, December 15.

Cotterell, Bill. 2006. "Gov. Bush's Legacy." *Tallahassee Democrat,* December 25.

Cotterell, Bill. 2007. "No Evidence of Information Leaks, Probe Finds Discrepancies in People First Security." *Tallahassee Democrat*, January 19.

Cotterell, Bill. 2007. "Sink Suspends Project Aspire." *Tallahassee Democrat*, May 17.

Cotterell, Bill. 2007. "Revenue Shortfall 'Inevitable.'" Tallahassee.com, August 2. Found at www.Tallahassee.com/apps/pbcs.dll/article. Printed August 2, 2007.

Cotterell, Bill. 2007. "Deal Reached in State Private-Prison Dispute." News-press.com, December 11, 2007. Found at www.news-press.com/apps/pbcs.dll/article?. Printed December 12, 2007.

Cotterell, Bill. 2008. "In Government, Numbers Can Tell Whatever Story You Want." *Tallahassee Democrat,* January 7.

Council on State Governments. 1997. "Survey on Privatization in State Government." Lexington, Kentucky.

Cox, Jeremy. 2007. "Report: Political Climate Threatens to Doom Everglades Restoration." Found at Naplesnews.com/2006/sep/27/report. Printed September 27, 2007.

Crew, Robert E., Jr. 1992. "Florida: Lawton M. Chiles, Jr., Reinventing State Government." In *Governors in Hard Times,* ed. Thad Beyle, 77–106. Washington, D.C.: Congressional Quarterly, Inc.

Crew, Robert E., Jr. 1998. "Gubernatorial Leadership: A Preliminary Model." *Social Science Journal* 35, 1: 15–27.

Crew, Robert E., Jr., Joe Eyerman, Justin Graham, and Nancy McMillan. 2004. "Tracking the Outcomes of Welfare Reform in Florida for Three Groups of People." U.S. Department of Health and Human Services, ASPE. Grant No. 306A.

Crew, Robert E., Jr., and Belinda Creel Davis. 2000. "Florida Welfare Reform: Cash Assistance as the Least Desirable Resource for Poor Families." In *Managing Welfare Reform in Five States,* ed. Sarah F. Liebschutz. Albany, N.Y.: Rockefeller Institute Press.

Crew, Robert E., Jr., and Christopher Lewis. 2007. "Verbal Style, Gubernatorial Strategies and Legislative Success." Paper presented at the annual meeting of the Southern Political Science Association. January 5–7. New Orleans, Louisiana.

Crew, Robert E., Jr., and Gregory Weiher. 1996. "Gubernatorial Popularity in Three States." *Social Science Journal* 33, no. 1: 39–54.

Crew, Robert E., Jr., and Mary Ruggiero Anderson. 2003. "Accountability and Performance in Charter Schools in Florida: A Theory-Based Evaluation." *American Journal of Evaluation* 24, no. 2: 189–212.

Crew, Robert E., Jr., and Scott Lamothe. 2003. "Evaluating the Efficiency of Private Sector Organizations in Helping Welfare Beneficiaries Find Employment." *Evaluation Review* 27, no. 2 (April): 151–164.

Crew, Robert E., Jr., and Scott Lamothe. 2003. "Tracking Individuals Who Left Florida's Welfare Program: A Longitudinal Picture." Florida Department of Children and Families. July.

Crew, Robert E., Jr., David Branham, Gregory Weiher, and Ethan Bernick. 2002. "Political Events in a Model of Gubernatorial Approval." *State Politics and Policy Quarterly* 2, no. 3 (fall): 283–297.

Crowley, Brian E. 2003. "Governor, Courts Often Clash Over 'Separation of Powers.'" *Palm Beach Post,* May 10.

Date, S. V. 2003. "Official: State Altered Voucher School Records." *Palm Beach Post,* July 10.

Date, S. V. 2004. "Squabble over Standards Splits Voucher Advocates." *Palm Beach Post,* January 4.

Date, S. V. 2005. "Despite Denial, Bush's Office Possessed Voucher Proposal." *Palm Beach Post,* November 16.

Date, S. V. 2005. "Tax Credits to Fund Largest Voucher Program Under Study." *Palm Beach Post,* November 16.

Date, S. V. 2005. "State Spending Way Less Than It Predicted to Reduce Class Size." *Palm Beach Post,* January 26.

Date, S. V. 2005. "Gov. Bush Jobs Record Falls Short of Predecessors." *Palm Beach Post,* January 31.

Date, S. V. 2006. *Quiet Passion: A Biography of Senator Bob Graham.* New York: Jeremy P. Tarcher/Penguin.

Date, S. V. 2007. "Appeals Court Throws Out '05 Conviction of Voucher Fraud." Palm Beach Post.com, April 13.

Date, S. V. 2007. "Crist's First 100 Days Depart from Republican Profile, But Enhance His." Palm Beach Post.com, April 20.

Date, S. V. 2007. "Jeb Bush Aide Strives to Get Vouchers in Constitution." *Palm Beach Post,* December 17.

Date, S. V. 2008. "Budget Is Just Right for Anti-Government Crowd." *Tallahassee Democrat,* April 21.

Date, S. V., and Kimberly Miller. 2003. "Voucher Operation Secretive about Grants." *Palm Beach Post,* August 24.

Date, S. V., and Kimberly Miller. 2004. "State Fires Voucher Whistle-Blower." *Palm Beach Post,* March 6.

Dauer, Manning, ed. 1986. *Florida's Politics and Government.* Gainesville: University Presses of Florida. Chs. 7 and 9.

Davis, Chris, and Matthew Doig. 2004. "Bush Urged to 'Pull the Plug' on Voter Purge." *Sarasota Herald-Tribune,* October 16.

Dean, John. 2004. *Worse Than Watergate.* New York: Little, Brown & Co.

Debenport, Ellen. 1994. *St. Petersburg Times*, September 9, City Edition, 1A; AP.

Defede, Jim. 1998. "Jeb Repackaged." *Miami New Times*, October 29.

deHaven Smith, Lance, ed. 2005. *The Battle for Florida.* Gainesville: University Presses of Florida.

Dellatte, Aaron. 2006. "Affordable Housing Has Lawmakers' Attention." *Tallahassee Democrat,* February 8.

Dellatte, Aaron. 2007. "Crist Praised by Legislature." *Tallahassee Democrat,* January 24.

Denslow, David, and Carol Weissert. 2005. *Tough Choices.* Tallahassee: Florida State University, LeRoy Collins Institute.

DeWitt, Dan. 2005. "Growing Pains." *St. Petersburg Times* online, February 27. Printed June 28.

Dill, David, Doug Jones, and Barbara Simons. 2006. "The Diebold Bombshell." OpEdNews.com, July.

Dodenhoff, David. 2007. *Fixing the Milwaukee Public Schools: The Limits of Parent-Driven Reform.* Milwaukee: Wisconsin Public Policy Research Institute.

Dolinski, Catherine. 2006. "Medicaid Reform Shelved for Another Session." December 6. TBO.com. Found at www.printthis.clickability.com/pt/cpt?action. Printed December 7, 2007.

Dorn, Sherman. 2007. *A Comprehensive Assessment of the A-Plus Plan's Impact on Public Education.* Tallahassee, Fla.: Civic Concern.

Douthat, Ross. 2008. "Mark Schmidt on the GOP." *Atlantic Monthly*, May.

Dubose, Lou, and Jan Reid. 2004. *The Hammer: God, Money and the U.S. Congress.* New York: Public Affairs Press.

Dyckman, Martin. 1998. "Perhaps Bush Recalls the Services Tax." *St. Petersburg Times*, March 13.

Dyckman, Martin. 2004 . "Nonrecurring Money Keeps Coming In." *St. Petersburg Times*, February 8.

Economic Council of Palm Beach County, Housing Leadership Council. 2006. 1555 Palm Beach Lakes Blvd., West Palm Beach Florida.

Edsal, Thomas. 2006. *Building Red America.* New York: Basic Books.

Edsal, Thomas, and Mary Edsal. 1991. *Chain Reaction: The Impact of Race, Rights and Taxes on American Politics.* New York: W. W. Norton and Co.

Education Trust. 2006. "Engines of Inequality: Diminishing Equity in the Nation's Premier Public Universities." Washington, D.C.

Education Week. 2003. "Quality Counts."

Education Week. 2006. "Quality Counts."

Ericson, Edward, Jr. 1999. "Campaign Was Built on Solid Foundation." *Capital Eye* 6, no. 1 (January).

Ettlinger, Michael P., et al. 1996. *Who Pays: A Distributional Analysis of the Tax Systems in All 50 States.* The Institute on Taxation and Economic Policy, June.

Federal Deposit Insurance Corporation. 2005. *State Profiles: Florida State Profile—Winter 2005.* Found at www.fdic.gov/bank/analytical/stateprofile/Atlanta/Fl/fl.xml.html. Printed January 30, 2006.

Feldman, Ariel J., Alex Halderman, and Edward W. Felten. 2006. "Security Analysis of the Dielbold AccuVote-TS Voting Machine." Center for Information Technology Policy and Department of Computer Science, Princeton University.

Fenno, Richard. 1996. *Senators on the Campaign Trail.* Norman: University of Oklahoma Press.

Figlio, D. N., and C. Rouse. 2006. "Do Accountability and Voucher Threats Improve Low-Performing Schools?" *Journal of Public Economics* 90 nos. 1–2: 239–255.

Fineout, Gary. 2001. "Higher Education in Turmoil." *Sarasota Herald-Tribune*, February 4.

Fineout, Gary. 2005. "Elections Dispute in Legislature." *Tallahassee Democrat*, April 8.

Fineout, Gary. 2005. "Bush Remains Mum About Potential Political Plans." *Tallahassee Democrat*, June 15.

Fineout, Gary. 2005. "Lasting Legacy of Gov Bush Is on the Bench." *Miami Herald*, October 11.

Fineout, Gary. 2006. "One Florida Still Debated." *Miami Herald*, December 17.

Fineout, Gary. 2007. "Financial Firms Pushing for Private Florida Lottery." MiamiHerald.com.
Found at www.miamiherald.com/458/story/233126.html. Printed September 11, 2007.

Finnegan, William. 2004. "Letter from Miami." *New Yorker*, March 3.

Fischer, Kent. 2002. "Public Schools, Inc." *St. Petersburg Times*, September 15.

Florida Agency for Workforce Development. 2005 and earlier. "Florida Labor Market Trends."

Florida Auditor General. 2001. "Developmental Disabilities Home and Community-Based Waiver Administered by the Department of Children and Families." Report No. 02–038. September.

Florida Department of Community Affairs. 2000. *Community Planning* 9, no. 1 (winter).

Florida Department of Community Affairs. 2001. *A Liveable Feast for Today and Tomorrow.* Florida Growth Management Study Commission. February.

Florida Department of Education. 2005. "History of Statewide Assessment Program." Found at www.firn.edu/doe/sas/hsap/hsap9000.htm. Printed October 24, 2005.

Florida Department of Education. 2006. *Florida's Charter Schools: A Decade of Progress.* November 2006.

Florida Department of Environmental Protection. 2000. "Governor Bush and Department of Environmental Protection Secretary David Struhs Attend Historic Everglades Signing." Press Release, December 11.

Florida Department of Financial Services. 2003. "Audit of the State Technology Office for the Period July, 2003 through September 30, 2001 and Selected Actions Taken Prior to July 1, 2000." June 3.

Florida Department of Management Services. 2007. Letter from Linda South, Secretary. January 18.

Florida Department of Transportation. 2006. "Bush/Jennings Recommended Transportation Budget Benefits Florida's Citizens, Visitors and Business." *News Release.* January 18.

Florida Ethics Commission. 1999. "Full and Public Disclosure of Financial Interests, 1998, Hon. Jeb Bush, Governor." Form 6, June 30.

Florida Governor's Office. 2003. "Statement from Governor Jeb Bush Regarding Everglades Restoration." May 23. Found at Jeb.bush@myflorida.com. Printed May 12, 2005.

Florida Governor's Office of the Chief Inspector General. 2003. "Audit Report: Road Map to Excellence in Contracting." Report No. 2003–03, June.

Florida Insider. 2006. InsiderAdvantage/Majority Opinion Research. *Sunshine Survey.* April 5.

Florida Office of the Auditor General. 2004. *State Technology Office—My Florida Alliance,* Report No. 2005–008, July 22.

Florida Office of the Auditor General. 2005. Auditor General's Report No. 2005–47.

Florida Office of the Auditor General. 2005. Report No. 2005–116.

Florida Office of the Auditor General. 2006. *Department of Management Services: MyFloridaMarketplace.* Report No. 2006–15.

Florida OPPAGA. 2002. "Legislative Options to Control Rising Developmental Disabilities Costs." Report No. 02–09.

Florida OPPAGA. 2002. "Development Disabilities Program Takes Steps to Improve Medicaid Waiver Systems and Control." Report No. 02–18. March.

Florida OPPAGA. 2002. "Legislature Improves Welfare Reform in Florida." Report No. 02–48, September.

Florida OPPAGA. 2005. "Charter School Review Technical Report." Report No. 05–22, April.

Florida OPPAGA. 2005. "Improvements in Independent Living Services Will Better Assist State's Struggling Youth." Report No. 05–61, December.

Florida OPPAGA. 2006. "Additional Improvements Are Needed as DCF Redesigns Its Lead Agency Oversight Systems." Report No. 06–05, January.

Florida OPPAGA. 2006. "The Department of Children and Families Has Taken Steps to Address 2006 Contracting Law." Report No. 06–16, February.

Florida OPPAGA. 2006. "While Improving, People First Still Lacks Functionality, Limitations Increase State Agency Workload and Costs." Report No. 06–39, April.

Florida OPPAGA. 2006. "Child Welfare System Performance Mixed in First Year of Statewide Community-Based Care." Report No. 06–50, June.

Florida School Boards Association, Constitutional Accountability Commission. 2005. *Final Report.* Tallahassee, Fla.

Florida State University. College of Social Sciences. 1999–2005. *Florida Annual Policy Survey.*

Florida TaxWatch. 2002. "Press Release." February 6.

Florida TaxWatch. 2005. "Briefings." April.

Floridians for Alternatives to the Death Penalty. 2002. "Jeb Bush's Death Warrant History: What Does It Say?" September 9. Found at http://www.fadp.org. Printed April 1, 2004.

Floridians for School Choice. 1995. "The Bush-Brogan A+ Plan for Education." Found at Floridians.org/aplusplan.html. Downloaded February 26, 2008.

Floridatoday.com. 2006. "Falling Far Short: Space Commission Offers Plan for Future, but Funding Pitifully Inadequate." January 19.

Follick, Joe. 2005. "Gov Bush Defends his Record of Tax Cuts." *Gainesville Sun,* December 4.

Follick, Joe. 2009. "Jeb Bush's Reforms Could be Reversed." *Sarasota Herald-Tribune,* January 13.

Fording, Richard, Sanford Schram, and Joe Soss. 2006. "The Bottom Line, the Business Model and the Bogey: Performance Management, Sanctions and the Brave New World of Welfare-to-Work in Florida." Paper presented at the Annual Meeting of the American Political Science Association, Philadelphia, Pa.

Forment, Carlos. 1989. "Political Practice and the Rise of an Ethnic Enclave: The Cuban-American Case, 1959–1979." *Theory and Society* 18, no. 1: 47–81.

Frank, Thomas. 2004. *What's the Matter with Kansas?* New York: Metropolitan Books.

FSCC State News Services. 2000. "Jeb Bush's Loaded Survey for Reforming Growth Management in Florida." February 11. Found at http://sustainable.state.fl.us/fdi/fscc/news/state/002/peer-gm.htm. Printed February 22, 2005.

Furillo, Andy. 2003. "California's New Budget Auditor May Target Social Services." *Sacramento Bee,* October 19. Found at http://www.whoseflorida.com/watch-out-california.htm. Printed March 30, 2005.

Gailey, Philip. 1994. "Crime Casts an Ugly Shadow Over Campaign." *St. Petersburg Times,* October 30, 2D.

Gailey, Philip. 2005. "The Fight Isn't Over for Gov Bush." *Tampabay.com*, March 27.

Gais, Thomas, and Lucy Dadayan. 2008. "The New Retrenchment: Social Welfare Spending, 1977–2006." Albany: Nelson Rockefeller Institute of Government, State University of New York.

Gallagher, Noel. 2007. "Jeb Bush Promotes Zeal for Conservative Reform." *Portland Press Herald*, August 17. Found at http://presherald.mainetoday.com/story_pr.php? Printed August 17, 2007.

Gallagher, Peter. 2000. "State Ombudsman is Fired." Found at www.whoseflorida.com/misc_pages/only_one_opinion_allowed.htm. Printed May 12, 2005.

Gladwell, Malcolm. 2008. *Outliers: The Story of Success.* New York: Little, Brown.

Gomez, Alex. "Bush's Proposal to Train Staff Raises Objections." *Palm Beach Post*, January 06.

Goodman, Howard. 2007. "Crist a Breath of Fresh Air for Skeptical Florida Voters." Sun-Sentinel.com, February 1.

Goodnough, Abby. 2005. "Florida Expands Right to Use Deadly Force in Self-Defense." *New York Times*, April 27.

Goodnough, Abby. 2007. "Effort to Save Everglades Falters as Funds Drop." *New York Times*, November 2.

Greenblatt, Alan. 2006. "Jebocracy." Governing.com, December.

Gruskin, Shana. 2003. "State Girls Prison Runs into More Problems." *South Florida Sun-Sentinel*, April 15.

Grunwald, Michael, and Eric Pianin. 2002. "Deals to Block Drilling in Everglades, Gulf." *Washington Post*, May 30, A01.

Grunwald, Michael. 2006. *The Swamp.* New York: Simon and Schuster.

Hargrove, Erwin C. 2009. *The Effective Presidency.* Boulder, Colo.: Paradigm Publishers.

Hauserman, Julie. 1999. "Plan Would Find Judges Compatible with Bush." *St. Petersburg Times*, October 1.

Hegarty, Stephen. 2002. "Cost Estimate Methods Irk Amendment Backers." *St. Petersburg Times*, August 27.

Heintz, James, Jeannette Wicks-Lim, and Robert Pollin. 2005. "Decent Work in America." Amherst: University of Massachusetts, Political Economy Research Institute.

Herbert, Bob. 2005. "Cruel and Unusual." *New York Times*, June 23.

Herbert, Bob. 2005. "Impossible, Ridiculous, Repugnant." *New York Times*, October 6.

Hetherington, Marc J. 1998. "The Political Relevance of Political Trust." *American Political Science Review* 92, no. 4 (December): 791–808.

Hiaasen, Carl. 2006. *Gainesville Sun*, May 16.

Hirth, Diane. 2005. "Bush Warned of Plan's Flaws." *Tallahassee Democrat*, February 7. Found online at www.iamforkids.org/nesdata/view_ind/1276. Printed July 6, 2005.

Hirth, Diane, and Bill Cotterell. 2003. "Senate Experts Dispute 'Myths.'" *Bradenton Herald*, July 15.

Holcombe, Randall G. 2003. "Florida's Intangibles Tax: The Case for Repeal." Policy Report No. 40. Tallahassee, Florida: The James Madison Institute.

Hollis, Mark. 2006. "Legislation Would Give Housing Aid to Public Workers Such As Teachers, Police." SunSentinel.com, April 13. Printed April 13, 2006.

Hollis, Mark. 2006. "Health-care Deal Underperforming, Company Claims." *South Florida Sun-Sentinel,* September 12. Found at www.sun-sentinel.com/news/local/florida/sfl-fprisons.

Homans, Rick. 2006. "Commentary: Florida Kicks Itself for Losing Out on Proposed Spaceport—and Jobs, Revenues It Will Bring." *Albuquerque Tribune*, January 12. Printed January 23, 2006.

Hoover Institution. 2003. *Address* by Governor Jeb Bush of Florida.

Horkan, Jacquelyn. 1999. "Oh What a Relief—For Now." *Florida Business Insight.* Found at http://flabusinessinsight.com/1999issues/july&august99/julylegislative.htm.

Howard, Mark. 2006. "Jeb's Legacy." *Florida Trend*, March 3.

Hu, Winnie. 2006. "Forced to Pick a Major in High School." *New York Times*, August 16. Found at www.nytimes.com/2007/08/16education/16major.html?8dpc. Printed August 16, 2007.

Hunt, April. 2006. "Money Denied As Mentally Ill Crisis Mounted." *Orlando Sentinel,* December 21. Found at www.pdmiami.com?Money_denied_as_mentally_ill_crises_mounted. Printed October 9, 2007.

Hylton, Will S. 2006. "See Jeb Not Run." CQ Features on Men.Style.Com. Printed December 3, 2007.

Institute on Taxation and Economic Policy. 2003. *Florida's Tax System Is Nation's Second Most Regressive.* January 7.

Jackson, Jerry W. 2007. "Orlando-based CNL Rejects Notion That Jeb Bush's Directorship Is 'Political Payback.'" *Orlando Sentinel*, December 6.

Jacobs, Lawrence R., and Robert Y. Shapiro. 2000. *Politicians Don't Pander.* Chicago: University of Chicago Press.

Jacobson, Gary C. 2006. *A Divider, Not a Uniter.* New York: Pearson, Longman.

Jacobson, Gary C. 2006. "The Polls: Polarized Opinion in the States: Partisan Differences in Approval Ratings of Governors, Senators and George W. Bush." *Presidential Studies Quarterly* 36, no. 4: 732–757.

James, Joni. 2004. "Tax Boon in Works for State Business." *St. Petersburg Times,* December 2.

James, Joni. 2005. "Bush Counts His What-Ifs, Both Public and Personal." *St. Petersburg Times,* June 15.

Johnson, Carrie, and Joni James. 2005. "Increased Voucher Scrutiny Fizzles Out." *St. Petersburg Times*, May 9.

Jreisat, Jamil E., and Alvin W. Wolfe. 2002. "Florida's Once-Weak Governorship Has Bulked Up." *Miami Herald,* October 6.

Judd, Alan. 1994. *The Gainesville Sun 1994 Voters Guide.* "Feeney: Right-Wing Specialist for Bush." Found at www.afn.org?~sun/elect/jeb1.htm. Printed March 22, 2004.

Judd, Alan. 1994. *The Gainesville Sun 1994 Voters Guide.* "JEB! Will His Pedigree Carry the Day?" Found at www.afn.org/~sun/elect/jeb1.htm. Printed March 22, 2004.

Kaczor, Bill. 2006. "Jeb on Education: PhD or D minus?" *Tallahassee Democrat,* December 19.

Kaczor, Bill. 2008. "Fla. Court Lifts Voucher, Tax Measures from Ballot." *Tallahassee Democrat*, September 3.

Kahn, Chris. 2005. "Broward School Chief Wants Governor to Reject New State Rule on Co-teaching." *Broward Sun-Sentinel*, August 2.

Kam, Dara. 2000. "Florida Council of 100 Blurs Business, Political Lines." *Florida Today*, December 22.

Kam, Dara. 2005. "Governor, Lawmakers, in Daily Contact on Schiavo, e-mails Show." *Palm Beach Post*, May 24.

Kam, Dara. 2006. "Bill Calls for Limits on State Contracts." *Palm Beach Post Washington Bureau*, March 23. Found at www.palmbeachpost.com/state/content/state/epaper/2006/03/23/a10a. Printed March 23, 2006.

Kam, Dara. 2006. "Governor's Nonprofit Foundation Has Paid Pollster, Former Campaign Finance Chief." *Palm Beach Post*, June 29.

Kam, Dara. 2007. "Privatized Death Row Lawyers May Be Dropped." PalmBeachPost.com, March 29. Found at palmbeachpost.com/state/content/state/epaper.

Kaplan, David A. 2001. *The Accidental President: How 413 Lawyers, 9 Supreme Court Justices and 5,963,110 (Give or Take a Few) Floridians Landed George W. Bush in the White House.* New York: William Morrow.

Kay, Julie. 2004. *Daily Business Review*, January 13.

Kennedy, John. 2005. "Senate Chief Sets Aside $1 Million for Possible Battles With Gov. Bush, House." *South Florida Sun Sentinel*, March 15. Found at www.sun-sentinel.com/news/local/florida. Printed March 15, 2005.

Kennedy, John. 2006. "Bush Saves Tax Cut for Last." *Orlando Sentinel*, July 27.

Kennedy, John. 2006. "Bush Staff Headed to House." *Orlando Sentinel*, October 19.

Kennedy, John. 2006. "Gov Bush Will Leave Enduring Changes." *Orlando Sentinel*, December 31.

Kennedy-Salchow, Shana. 2005. "An Analysis of Florida's Voluntary Pre–K Program." National Center for the Study of Privatization in Education. New York: Teachers College, Columbia University.

Klas, Mary Ellen. 2005. "Deal on Drilling in Works, Bush Says." *Tallahassee Democrat*, July 28.

Klas, Mary Ellen. 2005. "Group Opposed to New Gun Law Targets Tourists." *Miami Herald*, September 23.

Klas, Mary Ellen. 2008. "Cuts Could Halt Courts, Judges Warn." *Miami Herald*, February 20.

Kleindienst, Linda. 2006. "In His Last Year as Governor, Jeb Bush Aims to Ensure His Many Achievements Stand Up to the Test of Time." *South Florida Sun Sentinel*, March 5.

Kleindienst, Linda. 2007. "The Jeb Bush Era Ends in Florida." *South Florida Sun-Sentinel*. January, A04.

Koenig, David. 2007. "Former Florida Gov. Bush Joins Tenet Board." HeraldTribune.com, May 10.

Krauss, Michael I. 2005. "Tort Reform." Washington: D.C.: Cato Institute.

Kuo, David. 2007. *Tempting Faith.* New York: Simon and Schuster.

Landy, Marc, and Sidney M. Milkis. 2000. *Presidential Greatness.* Lawrence: University Press of Kansas.

Lanier, Dale Noble, and Roger Handberg. 2002. "In the Eye of the Hurricane." *Fordham Urban Law Journal* 29 (February): 1045–1046.

Lantigua, John. 2001. "How the GOP Gamed the System in Florida." *Nation*, April 30.

Lauer, Nancy Cook. 2003. "Bush's Power Has New Heights." *Tallahassee Democrat,* January 12.

Lauer, Nancy Cook. 2003. "Governor Bush Wants to Kill Two Watchdog Agencies." *Tallahassee Democrat,* January 29.

Lauer, Nancy Cook. 2005. "Budget Strings May Bind Governor." *Tallahassee Democrat,* May 4.

Lauer, Nancy Cook. 2005. "Educators Offended by State's Award." *Tallahassee Democrat,* July 15.

Leary, Alex. 2006. "Next House Speaker to Hire 18 Staffers from Governor's Team." *St. Petersburg Times,* October 19.

Leary, Alex, and Ron Matus. 2008. "Tax Cut, Voucher Plans Tossed." *St. Petersburg Times,* September 2008.

Lester, Will. 1994. "After Getting Out From Under Shadow of Famous Dad, Jeb Bush Seeks Help." Associated Press, November 1.

Lewicki, R. J., and C. C. Tomlinson. 2003. "Trust and Trust Building." In *Beyond Intractability, Conflict Research Consortium,* ed. G. Burgess and H. Burgess. Boulder: University of Colorado. Accessible at http//www.beyondintractability.org/essay/trust_building/.

Liberto, Jennifer, and Shannon Colavecchio Van-Sickler. 2008. "Pruitt Wants State to Return to Elected Education Chief. Tampabay.com, February 20. Found at www.sptimes.com/2008/02/20/news_pf?State/Pruitt_wants_state_to.shtml.

Lizza, Ryan. 2002. "He Ain't Heavy." *New Republic,* July 29.

Lurie, Irene. 2006. "State Welfare Policy." In *The State of the States,* ed. Carl E. Van Horn. Washington, D.C.: CQ Press.

Lytle, Tamara, and John Kennedy. 2005. "Gov. Bush Reverses On Gulf Drilling." *Orlando Sentinel,* October 5.

Mankiv, N. Gregory, and Matthew Weinzierl. 2004. "Dynamic Scoring: A Back-of-the-Envelope Guide." National Bureau of Economic Research, Working Paper No. 1100.

March, William. 1999. "George W. Bush Raises Big Dollars." *Tampa Tribune,* June 26.

March, William. 2005. "Former GOP Boss Zings Party Leaders." *Tampa Tribune,* March 13.

Mason-Dixon Corporation. 2006. *Poll,* October.

Mason-Dixon Corporation. 2006. *Poll,* November 15.

Matus, Ron. 1999. "DEP Allows Plant Near Ichetucknee." *Gainesville Sun,* November 20.

Matus, Ron. 2005. "Schools Still Rank Near the Bottom." *St. Petersburg Times,* March 6.

Matus, Ron. 2008. "Bush Takes Plan National." *St. Petersburg Times,* January 16.

Matus, Ron. 2009. "Study Finds Vouchers Don't Make Difference." *St. Petersburg Times,* June 29.

Matus, Ron, and Dona Winchester. 2006. "Poll: Majority Oppose Vouchers." *St. Petersburg Times,* March 30.

McClure, Vicki, and Mary Shanklin. 2007. "Risky Choices: Many Charters Prove Poor Options." *Orlando Sentinel,* March 25.

McClure, Vicki, and Mary Shanklin. 2007. "Cashing In on Kids: Even After Pleading No Contest to Grand Theft, School Remains Open." *Orlando Sentinel,* March 27.

McClure, Vicki, and Mary Shanklin. 2007. "Losing Local Say: State Panel Can Supersede Districts on Charters." *Orlando Sentinel,* March 28.

McConnel, Grant. 1967. *The Modern Presidency.* New York: St. Martin's Press.

McGee, Jim, Peter Wallsten, and Jason Grotto. 2002. "Did Cement Deal Pour Money Into GOP?" *Miami Herald,* October 26.

McIntyre, Robert. 2003. *Who Pays? A Distributional Analysis of the Tax Systems in All 50 States.* Washington, D.C.: Institute on Taxation and Economic Policy.

Mead, Sara. 2007. "Information Underload: Florida's Flawed Special-Ed Voucher Program." Washington, D.C.: Education Sector.

Mears, Daniel P. Caterina Roman, Ashley Wolff, and Janeen Buck, 2006. "Faith-Based Efforts to Improve Prisoner Reentry: Assessing the Logic and Evidence." *Journal of Criminal Justice* 34: 351–367.

Meier, Kenneth. 1992. *Politics and Bureaucracy.* Pacific Grove, Calif.: Brooks/Cole Publishing Co.

Meyers, Larry A. 2005. "People First Is a Circus Parade." Letter to the Editor. *Tallahassee Democrat,* September.

Miami Herald. 2004. "House Passes Ban on Listing Gun Owners." April 2.

Miami Herald. 2007. "Crist Seeks Glades Cash." MiamiHerald.com, January 22.

Micklethwait, John, and Adrian Wooldridge. 2004. *The Right Nation.* New York: Penguin Press. 48–52.

Milbank, Dana. 2000. "E-Mails Show Jeb Bush's Office Keenly Interested." *Washington Post,* November 21.

Miller, Carol Marbin. 2005. "Police "Showdown" over Schiavo Averted." *Miami Herald,* March 26.

Miller, Carol Marbin. 2005. "A Bush 'Secret' Exposed." *Miami Herald,* November 18.

Miller, Carol Marbin. 2006. "Florida Children Missing from Foster Care." Found at MiamiHerald.com. June 8. Printed October 31, 2007.

Miller, Carol Marbin. 2007. "Study: Foster Care System in S. Florida is Flawed." MiamiHerald.com. Found at www.Miamiherald.com/news/florida/story/195988.html. Printed August 9, 2007.

Miller, Kent. 2005. "Politicians Ignored Facts in the Terri Schiavo Case." *Tallahassee Democrat,* April 5.

Miller, Kimberly. 2003. "Terror-Tied School Got Scholarship." *Palm Beach Post,* July 17.

Miller, Kimberly. 2004. "State's Education Chief Horne Steps Down." *Palm Beach Post,* August 12.

Miller, Kimberly. 2006. "Despite Ban, Bush Lets Lobbyists Stay on State Universities' Boards." *Palm Beach Post,* January 17.

Minutaglio, Bill. 1999. *First Son.* New York: Time Books.

Morehouse, Sarah McCally. 1977. *State Politics and Policy.* New York: Holt, Rinehart and Winston.

Morgan, Curtis. "EDA: Despite Progress, Pollution Threatens Glades." MiamiHerald.com. Found at www.miamihearld.com/news/miami_dade/story/243791.html. Printed September 20, 2007.

Morgan, Lucy. 1994. "Jeb Bush: A Good Man Who Will Be Back." *St. Petersburg Times,* November 13.

Morgan, Lucy. 2003. "A Climate Where Hard Questions Can't Grow." *St. Petersburg Times,* January 11.

Morgan, Lucy. 2003. "Bush Signs Glades Bill—For Now." *St. Petersburg Times,* May 21.

Morley, Jefferson. 1991. "The Bush Legacy: Cocaine Profits." *Miami New Times,* February 27.

Mormino, Gary R. 2005. *Land of Sunshine, State of Dreams.* Gainesville: University Press of Florida.

Morris, Dick. 1999. *The New Prince.* Los Angeles: Renaissance Books.

Moss, Bill. 1994. "Chiles, Bush Pull No Punches." *St. Petersburg Times,* November 2, 1A.

Nagourney, Adam. 2009. "At Key Moment, Diverse G.O.P. Leadership Choice." *New York Times,* January 11.

Nation. 2001. "Florida's Disappeared Voters." February 5.

National Center for Education Statistics. 2005. *The Nation's Report Card: Florida.*

National Institute for Early Education Research. 2006. *The State of Preschool: 2007 Preschool Yearbook.* New York: Teachers College, Columbia University.

National Public Radio. 2005. George Fletcher on "Talk of the Nation." May 2.

National Research Council. 2006. "Progress Toward Restoring the Everglades: First Biennial Review." September.

National Review. 1998. "Gentle Jeb: Jeb Bush Runs a New Kind of Campaign in His Race for Governor of Florida." October 26.

National Science Foundation. 2006. *Science and Engineering Indicators 2006.* Arlington, Va.: Division of Science Resources Statistics.

Neal, Terry, and David Broder. 1999. "Affirmative Action Tears at Florida GOP." *Washington Post,* May 15.

Neustadt, Richard. 1960. *Presidential Power.* New York: Free Press.

New York Times. 1994. "The 1994 Campaign: Florida Governor and Jeb Bush Debate, Exchanging Taunts and Claims of Distorting the Truth." October 19. Found at http://query.nytimes.com/gst/fullpage.html?res=9CO7EOD6103CF93AA25753C1A 962958260.

Nickens, Tim. 1998. "Commentary: Jeb Bush's Business is the Public's Now." *St. Petersburg Times,* June 2.

Nickens, Tim. 1999. "Presidential Hopefuls Raking in Florida Funds." *St. Petersburg Times,* April 24.

Nickens, Tim. 2000. "Jeb Bush in Back Seat for This Race." *St. Petersburg Times,* September 22.

Nickens, Tim. 2001. "It's Hard to Peg Jeb Bush." *St. Petersburg Times,* March 4.

Nissen, Bruce. 2005. *State of Working Florida.* Miami: Florida International University, Florida International University Center for Labor Research and Studies.

Nolin, Robert, Linda Kleindienst, and Brittany Wallman. 2005. "Gov. Bush Accepts Blame for Slow Relief Response Days After Wilma." Sun sentinel.com, October 27. Found at www.sun-sentinel.com/news/local/southflorida/sfl-wilma,0,1180061. story?coll. Printed January 17, 2006.

Nye, Joseph. 1990. *Bound to Lead: The Changing Nature of American Power.* New York: Basic Books.

Office of Governor Jeb Bush. 2001. Address to DCIP summit in Orlando, August 28.

Orlando Sentinel. 2006. "Bush: Give Money Back to Floridians." February 12 Opinion page.

Ormond, Barbara. 2004. "State Responses to Budget Crises in 2004: Florida." Urban Institute, February 1. Found at http://www.urban.org/url.cfm?ID=410950.

Padgett, Tim. 2004. "Why Jeb Won Big." *Time*, Online edition, June 21.

Padgett, Tim. 2006. "First Brother: Is There a Second Act for Jeb Bush?" *Time*, Online edition, June 15.

Padilla, Maria T. 1998. "Jeb Bush Has Edge with Hispanics." *Puerto Rico Herald*, *Orlando Sentinel*, October 4.

Palast, Greg. 2001. "Florida's 'Disappeared Voters': Disfranchised by the GOP." *Nation*, February 5.

Palast, Greg. 2003. *The Best Democracy Money Can Buy*. Middlesex, England: Plume.

Palm Beach Post. 2005. "No Grants Left Behind," Editorial, February 8.

Pappas, Alceste T. 2007. "Florida's Higher Education System." Stamford, Conn.: Pappas Consulting Group.

Pavetti, LaDonna, Michelle Derr, Gretchen Kirby, Robert Wood, and Melissa Clark. 2004. "The Use of TANF Work-Oriented Sanctions in Illinois, New Jersey and South Carolina." Washington, D.C.: Mathematica Policy Research, Inc..

Peck, Robert, Richard Marshall, and Kenneth D. Kranz. 2000. "Tort Reform 1999: A Building without a Foundation." *Florida State University Law Review* 27 (winter): 349–564.

Peterson, Paul. 1995. *The Price of Federalism*. Washington, D.C.: Brookings Institute.

Peterson, Paul. 2006. *Reforming Education in Florida*. Palo Alto, Calif.: Hoover Institution.

Pew Charitable Trust. 2006. *Government Performance Project*. "Florida State Government Performance, 2005."

Phillips, Kevin. 2004. *American Dynasty*. New York: Viking.

Pinzur, Matthew. 2006. "Jeb's Last Semester." *Miami Herald*, August 6.

Pittman, Craig. 2005. "Judge Faults State for Failing to Clean Up Everglades." *St. Petersburg Times*, June 3.

Pizzo, Stephen. 1992. "Bush Family Value$." *Mother Jones*, September 1.

Portes, Alexander, and Alex Stepick. 1993. *City on the Edge: The Transformation of Miami*. Berkeley and Los Angeles: University of California Press.

President's Council of Economic Advisors. 2003. *The 2003 Economic Report to the President*.

"Privatization Follies, Florida Politics." 2005. January 27. Found at flapolitics.blogspot.com/2005/01/privatization-follies_27.html. Printed February 2, 2005.

Quinnipiac University Polling Institute. 2004. "Quinnipiac Poll." December 7.

Quinnipiac University Polling Institute. 2005. "Quinnipiac Poll," November 23; February 24; November 16.

Quinnipiac University Polling Institute. 2006. "Quinnipiac Poll," May 24; February 22; December 20; February 26.

Ramos, Victor Manuel. 2005. "New Hispanic Judge is Rarity in Central Florida." *Orlando Sentinel*, October 19.

Reder, Dottie. 2004. "Raiding the State's Trust Funds Hurts Florida's Cities." *Tallahassee Democrat*, March 25.

Rehfuss, John. 1989. *Contracting Out in Government*. San Francisco: Josey-Bass. Ch. 6.

Reinhard, Beth. 2006. "Bush's Legacy as Governor: A Republican Revolution." *Miami Herald*, December 17.

Rich, Andrew. 2004. *Think Tanks, Public Policy and the Politics of Expertise.* London: Cambridge University Press.

Richards, Clay F. 2005. Quinnipiac University Polling Institute, *Poll.* November 23.

Ritchie, Bruce. 2006. "Bush Spent Billions on Environment." *Tallahassee Democrat,* December 31.

Robinson. Peter. 2007. Uncommon Knowledge. Interview with Jeb Bush. www.hoover.org/multimedia/uk/10945026.html. Broadcast November 1, 2007.

Roig-Franzia, Manuel. 2004. "Jeb Bush's Influence in Fla. Inspires Awe, Rage." *Washington Post*, October 30, A08.

Rosenbaum, David E. 1994. "The 1994 Campaign: Florida; The Political Scion vs. the Veteran Politician." *NewYork Times,* October 23.

Rosenthal, Alan. 1986. "The State of the Florida Legislature." *Florida State University Law Review* 14, no. 2: 399–431.

Rousseas, Stephen. 1982. *The Political Economy of Reaganomics.* New York:. M. E. Sharpe.

Rowe, Sean. 1998. "Trinchi Warfare." *Broward-Palm Beach New Times*, October 8.

Roy, Judy R. 2005. "AARP Reacts to Bush Medicaid Proposal (Jeb Bush)." Found at http://www.nfbnet.org/pepermail/4alabama/2005–January/001622.html. Printed May 18, 2005.

Royse, David. 2006. "Senate Passes Bill to Change How Lawsuit Damages Are Divided." *Sarasota Herald-Tribune,* March 30.

Rushing, J. Taylor. 2006. "DCF Chief to Leave in January." *Florida Times Union,* December 2. Found at www.jacksonville.com/tu~online/stories/120206/met_6587356.shtml. Printed October 9, 2007.

Rushing, J. Taylor. 2006. "Governor Declares his Legacy is 1 of Activism." *Jacksonville Times Union.* Jacksonville.com, December 30.

Rushing, J. Taylor. 2007. "New CFO Saw Stormy Early Days." *Florida Times Union,* February 14.

Russell, Bertrand A. 1992. *The Basic Writings of Bertrand Russell.* London: Routledge.

Sabato, Larry. 1983. *Goodbye to Good-time Charlie.* Washington, D.C.: CQ Press.

Saloma, John S., III. 1984. *Ominous Politics: The New Conservative Labyrinth.* New York: Hill and Wang.

Sandham, Jessica. 1998. "Moderation the Theme in Gubernatorial Races." *Education Week* 18, November 11.

Sass, Tim. 2006. "Charter Schools and Student Achievement in Florida." *Education Finance and Policy* 1, no. 1 (winter): 91–122.

Saunders, Jim, and Deborah Circelli. "State's Disabled Citizens Facing Care Crises." 2007. *Daytona Beach News Journal.* Newsjournalonline.com, September 5. Printed September 5, 2007.

Scher, Richard. 1994. "The Governor and the Cabinet." In *The Florida Public Policy Management System,* ed. Richard Chackerian. Tallahassee, Fla.: Reubin O'D Askew School of Public Administration and Policy.

Schweizer, Peter, and Rochelle Schweizer. 2004. *The Bushes: Portrait of a Dynasty.* New York: Doubleday.

Scott, Rocky. 2006. "Housing is a Key to State's Future." *Tallahassee Democrat,* January 26.

Scott, Rocky. 2006. "Education Tops State To-Do List." *Tallahassee Democrat,* February 8.

Segal, Geoffrey F. 2005. "The Florida Model: Competing to Raise Efficiency, Lower Costs." Reason Foundation, January 16.

Segal, Geoffrey. 2003. "Florida Reforming Its Privatization Efforts." Reason Institute, 2003.

Shanklin, Mary. 2005. "Transfers Don't Equal Success, Data Suggest." *Orlando Sentinel,* July 31.

Shanklin, Mary, and Vicki McClure. 2007. "Deals and Debts: Nearly Half of Florida's Charters Had Operating Deficits." *Orlando Sentinel,* March 26.

Shanklin, Mary, and Vicki McClure. 2007. "Florida Senate Proposes Reforms for State's Charter Schools." *Orlando Sentinel,* December 4.

Sharp, Debra. 1994. *USA Today,* November 9, SA.

Shayon, Kristyn. 2005. "Florida Leadership Mobilizes for Major Legal Reform Campaign." *American Justice Partnership,* March 15. Found at www.legalreformminthenews.com/stateprofiles/F/FL_Main.html. Printed May 31, 2005.

Sherrill, Robert. 1987. "Can Miami Save Itself?" *New York Times,* July 19, sec. 6, 18.

Sigelman, Lee, and C. Nelson Domietius. 1988. "Governors as Chief Administrators: The Linkage between Formal Powers and Informal Influence." *American Politics Quarterly* 16 (April): 157–170.

Simmons, Jeff. 2005. "Insurance Coverage Issues Arise." *Independent Florida Alligator,* March 18.

Simons, Arthur. 1968. *Claude Kirk: A Man and His Words.* Tallahassee, Fla.: Executive Press.

Skene, Neil. 2006. "Calmest Guy in the Room." *Florida Trend,* May, 126–128.

Skene, Neil. 2007. "Calling Growth Management a Mess, New DCA Secretary Tom Pelham Wants a Rewrite." *Florida Trend,* August 1.

Skrowronek, Stephen. 1997. *The Politics That Presidents Make.* Cambridge, Mass.: Harvard University Press.

Skowronek, Stephen. 2006. "Presidential Leadership in Political Time." In *The Presidency in the Political System,* ed. Michael Nelson, 8th ed. Washington, D.C.: CQ Press.

Slivinski, Stephen. 2006. "Fiscal Policy Report Card on America's Governors: 2006." The Cato Institute. *Policy Analysis* 581 (October 24).

Smith, Adam. 2002. "Ex-Partner of Jeb Bush Hid Assets Abroad, U.S. Says." *St. Petersburg Times,* April 6.

Smith, Adam. 2002. "Money Pours in to Benefit Gov Bush." *St. Petersburg Times,* April 21.

Smith, Adam. 2005. "Bush's Allies Promote Legacy." *St. Petersburg Times,* August 19.

Smith, Adam. 2007. "Crist Leaves Little Doubt Bush Reign Has Ended." Tampabay.com, March 29.

Smith, Daniel. 2004. Testimony before the Florida House Select Committee on Constitutional Amendments. February 13.

Sokoloff, Brian. 2006. "Bush's Legacy on Environment is Successes, Missed Opportunities." Gainesville.com, December 14.

Sommer, David, and Elaine Silverstrini. 2005. "Legal Defeats Mount for Schiavo's Parents." *Tampa Tribune,* March 25.

Sommer, David, and Elaine Silverstrini. 2005. "Legal Defeats Mount for Schiavo's Parents." *Tampa Tribune,* March.

St. John, Paige. 2003. "Malpractice Rift Could be Trouble for Republicans." *Ganett News Service,* August 1. Found at www.floridacapitalnews.com/legislature2003/stories/080103rift.htm.

St. John, Paige. 2003. "Senate Hearing Clarifies Malpractice Facts." *Gannett News Service,* July 15.

St. John, Paige. 2003. "Bush Combs For Money in Trust Funds, Fees." *Florida Today,* January 23. Found at http://www.floridacapitalnews.com/legislature2003/stories/o123trustfunds.htm. Printed March 30, 2005.

St. John, Paige, and Valerie Boey. 2003. "Legislators, Bush Strike Deal on Cap." *Gannett News Service,* August 8. Found at www.floridacapitalnews.com/legislature2003/stories/080malpractice.htm. Printed May 23, 2005.

St. Petersburg Times. 1999. "A Test for Bush." January 10.

St. Petersburg Times. 2000. "Jeb Bush: Cut 25% of State Workers." July 11.

St. Petersburg Times. 2001. "Power and Patronage." May 13.

St. Petersburg Times. 2001. "Jeb's Voodoo Economics." August 25.

St. Petersburg Times. 2002. "Florida Governor Jeb Bush Says He Will Reject Senate President McKay's Tax Reform Plan." February 6.

St. Petersburg Times. 2004. "Bills Ban Gun Range Lawsuits, Gun Owner Lists." May 14. Found at http://sptimes.com/2004/05/14/bills_ban_ gun-range_1.shtml. Printed March 27, 2005.

Stacy, Mitch. 2006. "Housing Crises Hits Florida." *Tallahassee Democrat,* September 16.

State of Florida, Agency for Health Care Administration. Office of the Inspector General. 2007. *Program Review of the Medicaid Reform Pilot Project.*

State of Florida, Council on Efficient Government. 2007. *2007 Annual Report.*

State of Florida, Department of Children and Families. Office of the Inspector General. 2007. "IG Investigation 2007–0061." July 16. Tallahassee, Florida.

State of Florida, Department of Management Services. 1999. *Annual Workforce Report,* 1999. Tallahassee, Florida.

State of Florida, State Board of Administration, Division of Bond Finance. 2005. "2005 Debt Affordability Report." Tallahassee, Florida.

Stockfisch, Jerome R. 2007. "Jeb's Legacy." *Tampa Tribune* January 1.

Stoddard, Missy. 2006. "UF Researchers' Study Challenges 10-20-Life Rule." *South Florida Sun Sentinel,* January 22.

Stuart, Guy. 2004. "Databases, Felons and Voting: Errors and Bias in the Florida Felons Exclusion List in the 2000 Presidential Elections." *Political Science Quarterly* 119, no. 3: 453–476.

Swasy, Alecia, and Robert Trigaux. 1998. "Commerce Job Led to Overseas Ventures." *St. Petersburg Times,* September 20.

Sztompka, P. 1999. *Trust: A Sociological Theory.* Cambridge: Cambridge University Press.

Tait, Robert. 2000. "Jeb Under Fire for Low-Key Approach." *The Scotsman,* September 27.

Tallahassee Democrat. 2005. "Hanging Tough." May 5.

Tallahassee Democrat. 2005. February 18.

Tallahassee Democrat. 2004. July 11.

Tallahassee Democrat. "State of the State: A Few Items the Governor Left Out." March 3.

Tallahassee Democrat. 2004. "Leaner and Meaner." June.

TampaBay Buzz. 2009. www.tampabay.com/buzz/2009/01/jebs-not-runnin.html.

Tapper, Jake. 2001. *Down and Dirty: The Plot to Steal the Presidency.* New York: Little, Brown.

Tax Foundation. 2008. *State and Local Tax Burdens: All States, One Year, 1977.* August.

Tisch, Chris, and Joni James. 2005. "Schiavo Timeline Troubles Governor." *St. Petersburg Times,* June 17.

Travis, Scott. 2006. "Most New Community College Students Lack Basic Skills, Studies Find." *South Florida Sun Sentinel,* October 15.

Trigaux, Robert. 2000. "Influence and Bailouts a Business Tradition in Bush Family." *St. Petersburg Times,* October 29. Found at www.sptimes.com/news/102900/ business/influence_and_bailout.shtml. Printed May 31, 2006.

Troxler, Howard. 1995. "Jeb Bush Starts Conservative Push." *St. Petersburg Times,* July 24.

Troxler, Howard. 2003. "Public Money, Private School and No Answer for Tinkerbell." *St. Petersburg Times,* August 6.

Turnbull, Agustus B., and John Phelps. 1994. "The Florida Legislature as Policy Manager." In *The Florida Public Policy Management System,* ed. Richard Chackerian, 107–131. Tallahassee: Florida Center for Public Management.

Ulferts, Alisa. 2005. "Bill Would Paint Target on Backs of Intruders." *St. Petersburg Times,* February 10.

Ulferts, Alisa. 2005. "Bush Medicaid Plan is Stalled in Legislature." *St. Petersburg Times,* April 16.

Ulferts, Alisa. 2005. "Bush's Pick to Run Health Agency Gets Senate Snub." *St. Petersburg Times,* April 26.

Ulferts, Alisa, and Steve Bousquet. 2002. "Judge Named to High Court." *St. Petersburg Times,* December 31.

Unger, Craig. 2004. *House of Bush, House of Saud.* New York: Scribner.

U.S. Commission on Civil Rights. 2001. "Executive Summary." *Voting Irregularities in Florida During the 2000 Presidential Election.* June.

U.S. Department of Commerce, Bureau of Economic Analysis. 2005. *Survey of Current Business.* Found at www.bea.doc.gov/bea/regional/spi. Printed January 25, 2006.

U.S. Department of Justice, Bureau of Justice Statistics. 2000. "Tort Trials and Verdicts in Large Counties." August.

Vann, Kim McCoy. 2005. "School's Admissions Standard at Issue." *Tallahassee Democrat,* May 13.

Van Osdol, Paul. 1998. WJXT Radio, Target 4 Investigation, Broadcast March 4.

Van Sickler, Michael, and Sydney Freedberg. 2007. "Bush Post Raises Eyebrows." *St. Petersburg Times,* December 5.

Vidmar, Neil, Paul Lee, Kara MacKillop, Kieran McCarthy, and Gerald McGwin. 2005. "Uncovering the 'Invisible' Profile of Medical Malpractice Litigation: Insights from Florida." *DePaul Law Review* 54 (winter): 315.

Viglucci, Ames, and Alfonso Chardy. 2002. "Bush and Business: Fast Success, Brushes with Mystery." *Miami Herald,* October 5.

Viscusi, W. Kip, and Michael J. Moore. 1993. "Product Liability, Research and Development and Innovation." *Journal of Political Economy* 101, no. 1 (February): 161–184.

Waddell, Lynn. 2000. "Florida's Electoral Fruit Ripe for Plucking." *Christian Science Monitor,* October 4.

Wald, Kenneth D., and Richard Scher. 2003. "Necessary Annoyance? The Christian Right and the Development of Republican Party Politics in Florida." In *The Christian Right in American Politics,* ed. John C. Green, Mark J. Rozell and Clyde Wilcox. Washington, D.C.: Georgetown University Press.

Waller, Nikki. 2006. "State legal-aid agency is broke." *Miami Herald*, November 15.

Wall Street Journal. 2009. "A Charter Setback in Florida." www.online.wsj.com/article/SB123128805154659199.htm/. February 10.

Washington Post Florida Statewide Election Poll. 2004. ICPSR Study No. 4144. October.

Weintraub, Daniel. 2008. *Party of One: Arnold Schwarzenegger and the Rise of the Independent Voter.* Sausalito, Calif.: Poli Point Press.

Weissert, Carol, and William Weissert. 2008. "Florida's Health Care Policy: Making Do on the Cheap." In *Government and Politics in Florida*, ed. J. Edwin Benton, 357–382. 3rd ed. Gainesville: University Press of Florida.

Werhane, Peter. 1999. "Justice and Trust." *Journal of Business Ethics* 21: 238–249.

Wilkie, Curtis. 2000. "Jeb Bush Stays in Shadows As Brother Vies for Florida.*" Boston Globe*, October 14.

Williams, Mike. 1994. "Mudslinging Campaign Tarnishes Chiles' Easy Going Image." *Atlanta Journal and Constitution*, November 13.

Williams, Russell L., and James S. Bowman. 2007. "Civil Service Reform, At-Will Employment and George Santayana: Are We Condemned to Repeat the Past?" *Public Personnel Management* 22 (March).

Wong, Kenneth. 1989. "Policy Making in the American States: Typology, Process and Institutions." *Policy Studies Review* 8: 527–548.

Yardley, William. 2002. "Jeb Bush began ascent in Dade." *Miami Herald*, September 29. Found at www.miami.com/mld/miami/4178599.htm?template=contentModules/printstory.jsp. Printed March 24, 2004.

Zernike, Kate. 2006. "Kerry Pressing Swift Boat Case Long After Loss." *New York Times,* May 8.

Appendix 1
State Agencies Classified by Policy Area

<u>Regulatory</u>
    Business Regulation
    Environmental Protection
    Public Service Commission
    Management Services
    Department of Revenue

<u>Redistributive</u>
    Children and Families
    Elder Affairs
    Health and Rehabilitation Services
    Health Care Administration
    Community Affairs
    Juvenile Justice
    Workforce Innovation
    Labor and Employment Security
    Veterans' Affairs

<u>Distributive</u>
    Transportation
    Corrections
    Law Enforcement
    Fish/Wildlife Conservation Commission
    Highway Safety & Motor Vehicle Department
    Parole and Probation Commission
    Military Affairs

Appendix 2
Comparative Budget Data

Bush	1999	2006	Difference	% increase	% average annual increase
Regulatory	5537141	7509731	1972590	35.62	5.09
Redistributive	16482190	18459624	1977434	12.00	1.71
Distributive	7116773	10286798	3170025	44.54	6.36
Education	14890741	21195083	6304342	42.34	6.05
Total Budget	50545428	64230306	13684878	27.07	3.87
Chiles	1991	1998			
Regulatory	2903124	5447991	2544867	87.66	12.52
Redistributive	12196631	15619931	3423300	28.07	4.01
Distributive	5540875	6404946	864071	15.59	2.23
Education	11268541	14251561	2983020	26.47	3.78
Total Budget	36688810	47967872	11279062	30.74	4.39

Values are in 2000 dollars.

Appendix 3
Annual Florida Budgetary Spending

Year	Regulatory	Redistributive	Distributive	Education	Total
1968	164248	1486431	2000953	4743185	9392481
1969	85965	1729280	1996961	4754375	9621382
1970	91301	1957304	2147559	4938679	10270341
1971	95505	2560105	2556918	5071063	11605513
1972	107835	3111960	2146815	5566005	12857370
1973	135615	3385772	2900270	6382905	14721120
1974	206078	3344067	2567263	6788792	15024370
1975	188369	3628937	2497354	6463972	15045197
1976	214916	3852334	2285418	6676142	15231290
1977	222282	4118797	2385034	6513719	15900285
1978	160169	4112772	2521716	6642891	15320378
1979	1401701	4081259	2978171	6983155	17323387
1980	1391834	3891792	2465689	6756444	16621577
1981	1302690	4575340	2264714	6816401	16964290
1982	1169923	4669133	2626294	7138586	17689640
1983	1354830	5214672	3090041	7680922	19455753
1984	2108039	5634795	3077283	8139845	21241778
1985	2002765	6065365	3350088	8274710	22121329
1986	2087198	6886874	3761126	8501132	25612753
1987	2309090	7508470	3910379	9184741	26163698
1988	2588400	8171970	2407179	10217354	26897897
1989	2657301	9090746	4027171	12342890	31977779
1990	2953277	11079210	5524875	12440924	36324981
1991	2903124	12196631	5540875	11268541	36688810
1992	3114971	14484778	5423270	11972555	38769431
1993	4031271	17309356	5193978	12251109	44040967
1994	4505845	18278428	5824765	12705204	44996570
1995	4594814	17472013	5733849	12541675	44111668
1996	4693510	16309864	5694690	13069491	43647371
1997	4924863	15362832	6007543	14308697	46280120
1998	5447991	15619931	6404946	14251561	47967872
1999	5537141	16482190	7116773	14890741	50545428
2000	5560046	15963728	6665157	15552334	47872670
2001	6533473	16417504	8022940	15507254	50737789
2002	6934310	18079021	7594259	15207913	52285813
2003	6579318	18498481	8434322	16157281	54156663
2004	6967560	20105325	8646765	16465416	57058807
2005	7055594	19618408	9177350	18144763	60080823
2006	7509731	18459624	10286798	21195083	64230306

Values are in 2000 dollars.

The data in the tables are from the following sources: Florida's Final Budget Report and Ten Year Summary of Appropriations Data: 1990–1991 through 1999–2000; The Budget of the State of Florida; and The Annual Appropriations Summary.

Index